Dein Englischbuch enthält folgende Teile:

Unit 1 bis 5	Die fünf Kapitel des Buches
Unit 6	Ein zusätzliches Kapitel
Diff-Bank	Weitere Aufgaben – unterschiedlich schwer
Wordbank	Zusätzliche Wörter zu bestimmten Themen
Text file TF	Interessante Texte, passend zu den Units
Skills file SF	Beschreibung wichtiger Lern- und Arbeitstechniken
Language file LF	Zusammenfassung wichtiger Sprachregeln
Vocabulary	Wörterverzeichnis zum Lernen der neuen Wörter
Dictionary	Alphabetisches Wörterverzeichnis zum Nachschlagen (*English-German* und *German-English*)

Die Units bestehen aus diesen Teilen:

Lead-in	Einstieg in die neue Unit
Theme 1 / Theme 2	Neue Themen mit vielen Aktivitäten und Übungen
Focus on language	Texte und Aufgaben zum Entdecken von Regeln und Üben wichtiger Strukturen
Story	Eine Geschichte zum Lesen
Skills training	Hören – Lesen – Sprechen – Schreiben – Sprachmittlung – Viewing
STOP! CHECK! GO!	Üben, Vertiefen, Lernfortschritt feststellen

In den Units findest du diese Symbole:

	Partnerarbeit / Gruppenarbeit
	nur auf CD / auf CD und im Schülerbuch
	Filme auf der DVD
○	leichtere Übungen
●	schwierigere Übungen
○ //●	Bei dieser Aufgabe gibt es eine leichte Variante in der Unit und eine schwierigere in der Diff-Bank.
More help p. 125	Hilfen zu einer Aufgabe in der Diff-Bank
More practice 1 p. 123	Weitere Übungen in der Diff-Bank

INHALT

Nice to meet you!

Unit 1 · Welcome to our school

Unit 2 · At home with Ellie

Unit 3 · My Plymouth

INHALT

Unit 4 · Berry's world

Unit 5 · All about Adam

*Unit 6 · School is out – for summer

Anhang

L *Listening*
R *Reading*
S *Speaking*
W *Writing*
M *Mediation*
V *Viewing*
I *Intercultural competence*
ST *Study skill*
* Fakultativ

Die Angebote des Schülerbuches sind nicht obligatorisch abzuarbeiten. Die Auswahl der Übungen und Übungsteile richtet sich nach den Schwerpunkten des schulinternen Curriculums.

Nice to meet you!

► Folie 2 ► IAT 0.1 ► KV 1 ► DFF N1 ► DFF N7 ► INKL 0.1 ► INKL 0.2

1 Meet Cyril[2]

a) Listen. (1.02)

b) Repeat. (1.03)

c) Listen and answer Cyril's questions. (1.04)

2 Meet your class

Walk around: Talk to different partners.

Hi, I'm ... What's your name?

I'm ten / eleven / twelve / ... What about you?

I'm from ... What about you?

1 ['plɪməθ] 2 ['sɪrɪl]

► Workbook 1, p. 2

► Folie 1 ► DFF N2 ► KV 1

3 GAME **I can see ...**

a) What can you see? Find five things in the picture.

b) Play the game.

4 **Cyril's song**

1.05

Listen to Cyril's song and sing the chorus.

Box: Voc., p.180

CYRIL'S SONG

I'm Cyril the crab
°And I °like the °sea.
I °love °water
°All around me.

°Chorus:
I °run and I °hide,
I °dive in the °sand.
°Don't pick me up
°Or °I'll pinch your °hand.

My favourite colours

1 Colours

Box: Voc., p. 181

a) Make colour cards.

green red yellow brown
black blue purple grey
white pink orange

1.07

b) Listen to Ellie.
What colours can you hear?

c) Listen again. Ellie says:
- I like ...
- I don't like ...
- My favourite colour is ...

2 Your favourite colour

a) Walk around:
Talk to different partners.

– Hi, Anna. What's your favourite colour?
– Blue!

b) Write the answers on the board.

Name	Favourite colour
Anna	blue
Ilja	...

c) Talk about favourite colours in your class.

– Three students like blue.
– Two students like red.

Box: Voc., p. 181

► Workbook 2, p. 3

▸ KV 3 ▸ DFF N4 ▸ Folie 4 ▸ INKL 0.5

My favourite sports and hobbies

1

2

3

dancing • football • playing games • reading books • riding • skateboarding • swimming • watching TV

4

6
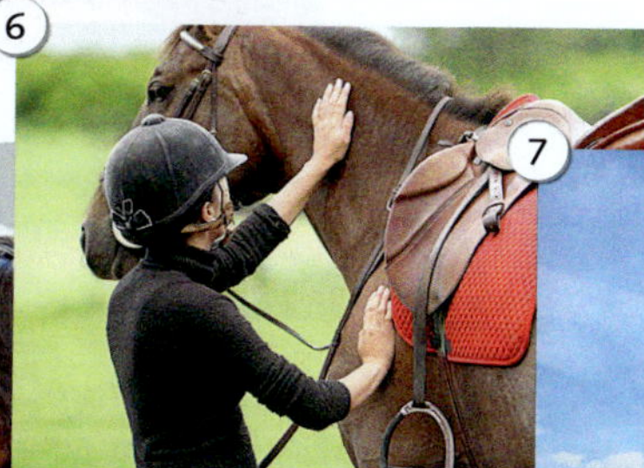

8

5

7

1 What are the sports and hobbies?

Find the names of the eight sports and hobbies: *1 football, 2 ..., ...*

Box: Voc., p. 181

2 What about you?

a) Find the names of your favourite sports and hobbies. ▸ Wordbank 1, p. 173

b) Talk to different partners.

I like ... What about you?

I like ... too.

I don't like ...

My favourite hobby is ...

My favourite sport is ...

3 A sports and hobbies poster

Make a big class poster. Write labels.

1 [ɒz'mænəvɪtʃ]

My favourite animals

Box: Voc., p. 182

1 Can you remember?

a) Look at the animals for one minute. Then close your book. How many animals can you and your partner remember?

b) Pets or wild animals? Make a table. Add more animals.

Pets	Wild animals
pony	...

2 GAME Animal pairs

Make your own animal cards or ask your teacher for animal cards. Then play the *Animal pairs* game.

1 ['dɒnəvən] 2 ['pəʊni]

▸ Workbook 5, p. 4

► Folie 6 ► INKL 0.7

My favourite thing

1 Luca's favourite thing

1.08 a) Listen to Luca. Put the sentences (A–G) in the right order: *C, ...*

I'm Luca Boateng[3].
A It's blue and black.
B I can go to the park on it.
C My favourite thing is my bike.
D It's great and it's fun!
E And it's small.
F It's old.
G I like my bike.

1.09 b) Now listen and repeat.

2 Your favourite thing

a) What's your favourite thing?

► Wordbank 2, p. 174

b) Write about your favourite thing.

My favourite thing is my ...
It's old / new / ...
It's red / green / black / ...
It's big / small / ...
I can go to ... / play / ... on it.
It's great / cool / nice / fun / ...
I like my ...

c) Talk to the class about your favourite thing.

My favourite thing is ...
It's ...
I can ...
I like ...

► Workbook 6–7, p. 5

3 ['bwɑːteŋ]

The last day of the holidays

Box: Voc., p. 183

1 A story

a) Look at the pictures on this page. Who can you see?

1.10 b) Listen to part one of the story. Put the pictures (A–F) in the right order.

A

B

C

D

E

F

1.11 **c)** Listen to part two of the story. Put the pictures (A–E) in the right order.

A

B

C

D

E

2 Chant[1]

Listen and repeat.

Holidays are great,
Holidays are fun!
°No more work °or °school °for me,
°Just °sitting in the °sun.

The holidays °are over,
The holidays °are done.
No more sitting on the °beach,
No more °summer fun!

1 [tʃɑːnt]

Unit 1 Welcome to our school

▸ *KV 7* ▸ *IAT 1.1*

1 **School sounds** (1.14)

Listen. What can you hear? Point at the right pictures.

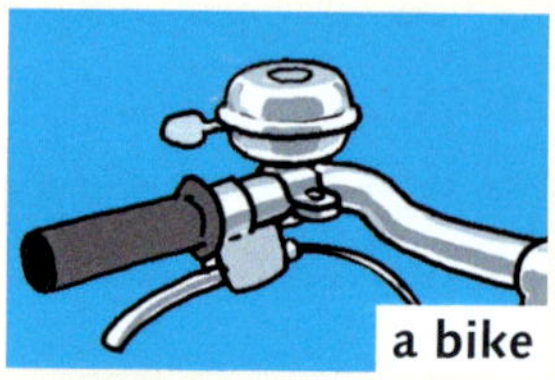
a bike

boys and girls

a teacher

a bird

a car

a mobile phone

a dog

a football

► *INKL 1.1*

2 The first morning

1.15 **a)** Listen. Put the pictures (A–D) in the right order.

1.16 **b)** Listen to the people and repeat.

c) Pick a card. Practise with a partner. Find a new partner, pick a new card and practise.

1

A: Hello, I'm ...
What's your name?
B: Hi, I'm ...
A: Nice to meet you, ...
B: Nice to meet you too.

2

A: Hi, ...
B: Hi, ... How are you?
A: I'm fine, thanks.
How are you?
B: I'm OK, thanks.

3

A: Goodbye, ...
B: Bye, ...
A: Have a good day.
B: You too. See you later.
A: OK, see you.

► *Workbook 1–2, p. 7*

Me and my class

1 Good morning, class 7Y

1.17

a) Who's in class 7Y? Who's the English teacher?

Good morning, class 7Y.
I'm Ms[1] Lee – your English teacher.
And who are you?

Box: Voc., p. 184

Hi, I'm Berry.
I'm eleven.
I'm not from Plymouth[2].
I'm from Woolwell, a village near Plymouth.
I have no brothers and sisters.
I have a pony[3] – Harry.
He's twelve.
My hobby is riding.

I'm Ellie. I'm twelve.
I have two brothers and one sister.
We're from Plymouth.
My hobby is tae kwon do[4].
My best friends are Ruby and Charlie. They're at this school.
They aren't in class 7Y. They're in class 7X. Oh, and I have two cats.

Box: Voc., p. 184

Hi, I'm Luca.
I'm from Plymouth too.
I'm not twelve, I'm ten.
I have one brother – Jack. He's fourteen and he's at this school.
And I have one sister – Grace.
She's six. She isn't at this school.
We have no pets. My hobby is riding my BMX[5].

Box: Voc., p. 184

Box: Voc., p. 184

b) Copy and complete the table.

Name	Age	From	Brothers	Sisters	Hobbies	Pets
Berry						
Luca						
Ellie						

1.18

c) Listen to Adam.
Which is the right picture?

1

2

d) Listen again.
Complete the table for Adam.

1 [mɪz, məz] 2 ['plɪməθ] 3 ['pəʊni] 4 [taɪ kwɒn 'dəʊ] 5 [biː em 'eks]

▸ Workbook 3, p. 8

2 NOW YOU

a) Copy the table and make notes about you.

Name:	Brothers:
Age:	Sisters:
From:	Pet:
School:	Best friends:
Class:	Hobby/Sport:
Class teacher:	Favourite colour:

b) Use your notes. Talk to your group.

○ Start like this:

I'm ... (name)
I'm ... (age)
I'm from ...
I'm at ... school.
I'm in class ...
My class teacher is ...

● Say more:

I have one brother. He's ...
I have one sister. She's ...
I have no pets / a pet / ...
My best friends are ...
My favourite hobby / sport is ...
My favourite colour is ...

c) ● Who's like you?

– Anna is eleven. I'm eleven too.
– Hendrik has one sister. I have one sister too.

Box: Voc., p. 184

3 About me and my class

Box: Voc., p. 185

Write a short text about you for your class.
You can put your text in your DOSSIER[6].

Das Dossier ist eine Mappe, in der du deine wichtigen und schönen Arbeiten sammeln kannst. Es gehört zum Portfolio.

Me and my class

○

I'm Vanessa.
I'm eleven.
I'm at Erich-Kästner-School.
I'm in class 5a.
My class teacher is Mrs Schmidt.

●

Hello, I'm Tim. I'm from Düsseldorf in Germany.
I'm at Erich-Kästner-School.
My favourite teacher is Mr Jahn. He's great!

I have two sisters and one dog.

My best friends are Samir and Patrick. They're cool.

My favourite sport is football and my favourite colours are red and white.

The first day at school

1 A tour of the school

1.19

a) Class 7Y is on a tour of the school with Ms Lee.
Listen and point at the pictures in the right order.

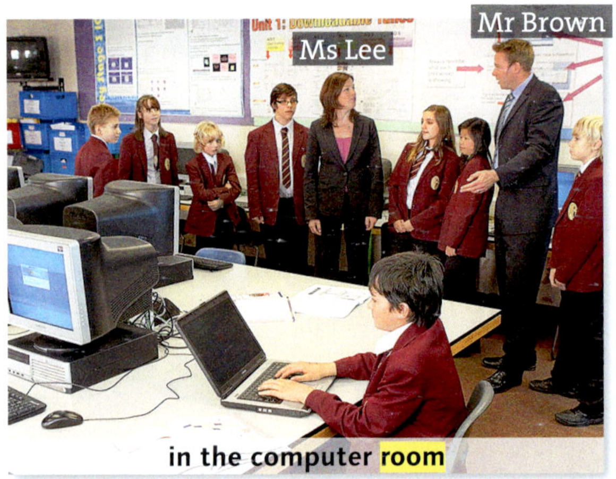

in the computer room

in the canteen

in the art room

in the science lab

in the sports hall

b) Listen again. Match the speech bubbles 1–5 with the rooms.

1 in the sports hall, 2 ..., 3 ...

1 We aren't in a PE lesson[1] now.

2 Welcome to Eggy!

3 Where's Ellie? She isn't here.

Box: Voc., p. 185

4 I'm your ICT[2] teacher.

5 I'm not lost. I'm here.

1 [piː ˈiː] 2 [aɪ siː ˈtiː]

► KV 8 ► Folie 8 ► INKL 1.5

2 School rap

1.20
1.21

a) Listen to the rap. Then sing it.

b) What lessons in the rap do you know?

Chorus °All my teachers °say,
°Work °hard °every day!

Every day I go to class,
I have English, I have maths,
I have French, I have German,
I °do lots and °lots of °learnin'.

Chorus All my teachers say, ...

Science, French and ICT,
Art, history and PE,
Drama and technology,
Music and geography.

Chorus All my teachers say, ...

3 The new timetable

Eggbuckland Community College[1]

Class 7Y timetable

Box: Voc., p. 185

Lesson	Time	Monday	Tuesday	Wednesday	Thursday	Friday
	8.40 – 9.00	ASSEMBLY / °REGISTRATION				
1	9.00 – 10.00	English	music	technology	geography	PE
2	10.00 – 11.00	maths	English	history	French	PE
	11.00 – 11.25	BREAK				
3	11.25 – 12.25	art	history	English	science	geography
4	12.25 – 1.25	art	science	maths	science	English
	1.25 – 2.05	LUNCH				
5	2.05 – 3.05	French	drama	science	ICT	technology

a) Look at the Eggy timetable.
What's right? What's wrong?

1 Class 7Y has lunch at school every day.
2 Class 7Y has six lessons every day.
3 Lesson one on Monday is French.
4 Lesson two on Tuesday is music.
5 Lesson three on Wednesday is English.
6 Lesson four on Thursday is science.

1.22

b) Listen to Ellie and Adam.
What's right? What's wrong? More practice 1 p. 121

► Workbook 6–7, pp. 9–10

1 [eg'bʌklənd kə'mju:nəti kɒlɪdʒ]

▸ KV 9 ▸ INKL 1.6 ▸ INKL 1.7

1 The unit quiz

How many questions can you answer?
You can work with a partner. Write your answers.
Check your answers on page 147.

1. It's in England. It's a city. It starts with 'P'. What is it?
2. We're two girls in class 7Y. We aren't sisters. Who are we?
3. He's a student at Eggy. He's ten. Who is he?
4. They're brothers. They aren't Adam and Zack[1]. Who are they?
5. He isn't a student. He's a pony. Who is he?
6. I'm at Eggy too. I'm not a student, I'm an English teacher. Who am I?
7. She isn't from Plymouth. She's from Woolwell. Who is she?
8. They're four new students in class 7Y. Who are they?
9. She's a girl. She's six. She isn't at Eggy. Who is she?
10. I'm a girl. I'm not eleven – I'm twelve. Who am I?
11. It's a lesson. It isn't in a classroom. It's in the sports hall. What is it?
12. You're a student. You aren't at Eggy. What's your name?

2 'm 's 're = Yes

a) Complete the sentences.

1 I... at Eggy too. (Card 6)
2 You... a student. (12)
3 He... ten. (3)
4 She... from Woolwell. (7)
5 It... in England. (1)
6 We... two girls in Class 7Y. (2)
7 They... brothers. (4)

b) Make the rule with: *'m • 's • 're*

FOCUS Yes
I + ...
he / she / it + ...
we / you / they + ...

3 'm not isn't aren't = No

a) Complete the sentences.

1 I... eleven – I'm twelve. (Card 10)
2 You ... at Eggy. (12)
3 He ... a student. (5)
4 She ... from Plymouth. (7)
5 It ... in a classroom. (11)
6 We ... sisters. (2)
7 They ... Adam and Zack. (4)

b) Make the rule with: *'m not • isn't • aren't*

FOCUS No
I + ...
he / she / it + ...
we / you / they + ...

▸ *Language file 2, pp. 166–167*

1 [zæk]

▸ Workbook 8, p. 11

▸ Folie 9

4 At Eggy

p. 121

Put in: *He • She • It • They*

1 Eggy is my new school. ...'s big.
2 Ellie is a new student at Eggy. ...'s cool.
3 Mr Brown is at Eggy too. ...'s our ICT teacher.
4 Mrs Ford isn't our English teacher. ...'s our art teacher.
5 Adam and Berry aren't in the classroom. ...'re in the sports hall.
6 Look at our new books. ...'re nice.

More practice 2 p. 121

▸ *Language file 1, p. 166*

5 Pets and friends

a) Put in: *'m • 's • 're*

Box: Voc., p. 186

Hi, I... (1) Berry. Remember Harry? He... (2) my pony. Connie and William are our ponies too. They... (3) fun. Connie is old. She... (4) seventeen. William is five. He... (5) small. Harry is twelve. He... (6) big. He... (7) my favourite pony. But we... (8) all friends.

b) Write about your friend or pet.

More help p. 122

Bei Tieren, zu denen man eine persönliche Beziehung hat (z.B. Haustiere), sagt man *he* oder *she*, also merke:
dog → it
Charlie → he

6 People and places in Plymouth

a) Write about the people and places in Plymouth – as many sentences as you can.

Plymouth Eggy Cyril Sandy Mr Brown Ellie and Berry Luca and Adam Ms Lee and Mr Brown	isn't aren't	students. a seagull. teachers. in Germany. girls. a crab. a maths teacher. in London.

b) Write more sentences: *Plymouth isn't in Germany. It's in England.*

More help p. 122

7 Make a quiz for the class

a) Write quiz cards – as many as you can.

More help p. 122

It's a lesson. It isn't English. It's lesson one on Friday. What is it?	She's in our class. She isn't from Halle. She's from Berlin. Who is she?	They're best friends. They're in our class. They aren't girls. Who are they?

Maths.
Paul and Leo.
Sandra.

b) Read a card for the class. Who/What is it?

▸ *Workbook 9–13, pp. 11–12*

1 Before you read

What can you see?

I can see a green ... / black ...

blazer • pullover[1] • shirt • shoes • skirt • socks • sweatshirt • tie • tights • trousers

Box: Voc., p. 187

The uniform[2] is important!

1.23

It's assembly at Eggy.

Miss Borowski[3] Good morning, boys and girls. I'm Miss Borowski, the school principal[4]. I hope you're happy at this school. Please remember – the uniform is important!

Ellie Oh no! My tie!

Assembly is over.

Miss B Hello. What's your name?

Ellie Hello, Miss Borowski. I'm Ellie Cole.

Miss B Where's your tie, Ellie?

Ellie Sorry. It's at home.

Miss B That isn't good, Ellie. Remember – the uniform is important!

Box: Voc., p. 187

In the English lesson ...

Luca Where's your tie, Ellie?

Ellie It's at home.

Luca The uniform is important!

Ellie I know, I know.

In the science lesson ...

Berry Where's your tie, Ellie?

Ellie It's at home.

Berry Oh, but the uniform is ...

Ellie ... important! I know, I know.

1 ['pʊləʊvə] 2 ['juːnɪfɔːm] 3 [bə'rɒvski] 4 ['prɪnsəpl]

5

In the art lesson ...

Ellie — Look, Adam – no tie. It's at home.
Adam — That's bad, Ellie.
Ellie — I know, I know. The uniform is important!
Luca — Hey, I have an idea.
Berry — What's your idea, Luca?
Luca — We need paper, scissors[5], colours, ...

Box: Voc., p. 187

6

In the canteen ...

Berry — I like your tie, Ellie.
Adam — Yes, it's a cool tie.
Luca — Nice colours.
Ellie — Thanks, guys.
Miss B — A very nice tie, Ellie.
Ellie — Thanks, Miss Borowski.
Miss B — But it isn't the school tie.
All — The uniform is important!
Miss B — Yes, that's right.

2 People in the story

1 Who has no tie?
2 Who has a good idea?
3 Who has a cool tie?
4 Who says, "Where's your tie?"?
5 Who says, "The uniform is important!"?

More practice 3 p. 123

3 Uniforms: What do you think?

1 I think uniforms are a good / bad idea.
2 I like / don't like the Eggy uniform.
3 Our school has no uniform. That's good / bad.
4 I think ties are / aren't cool.
5 I like / don't like Ellie's tie.

4 Eggy uniform words

Finish the lists in your exercise book.

Uniforms

for boys and girls	for girls
pullover	...

5 THEATRE[6] TIME

a) Make groups of six students: Ellie, Luca, Adam, Berry, Miss Borowski and a narrator. Read the scenes.

b) Act the scenes for the class. What's the best group?

More practice 4 p. 123

► Workbook 14–16, p. 13

5 ['sɪzəz] 6 ['θɪətə]

▸ DFF 1.7 ▸ Folie 11

1 A brochure[1)]

Before you read: What's Martins? (A) a book? (B) a school? (C) a shop?

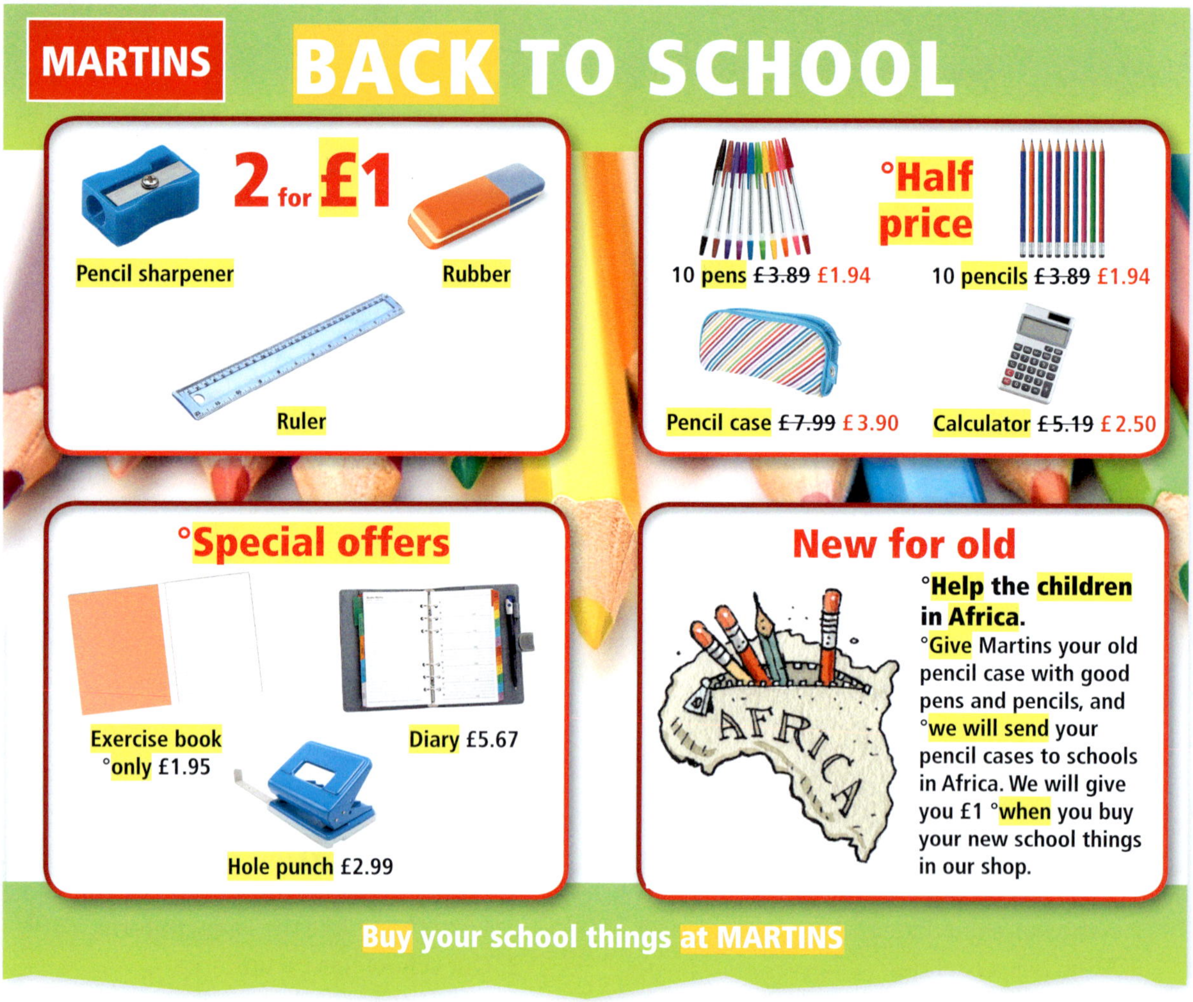

2 School things at Martins

Look at the brochure.

What can you buy for …

1 maths lessons? → *a pencil, …*
2 half price?
3 £1?

3 Your school things

a) Make a list of the things in your pencil case: *a ruler, …*

b) You can buy some things at Martins. You have £10. Write a shopping list.

4 MEDIATION Help children in Africa

Wie kannst du Mädchen und Jungen aus Afrika mit der Aktion *New for old* helfen? Wähle (A), (B) oder (C).

(A) Schicke dein Federmäppchen an eine Schule in Afrika.
(B) Kaufe bei Martins so viele neue Dinge wie möglich.
(C) Martins schickt dein altes Federmäppchen an eine Schule in Afrika.

1 ['brəʊʃə]

▸ Text file 2, pp. 150–151

▸ KV 13 ▸ DFF 1.8 ▸ INKL 1.9 ▸ INKL 1.10

1 Make networks

a) Copy the network.
Complete it with words from the box.

Friday • Monday • school days • Thursday • Tuesday • weekend

Besonders gut behält man Vokabeln, wenn man sie aufschreibt, zum Beispiel in einem *network* (Aufgabe 1) oder auf kleinen Kärtchen (Aufgabe 2).

b) Now copy this school network. Find words for every group – as many as you can.
Then compare networks with your partner. More help p. 124

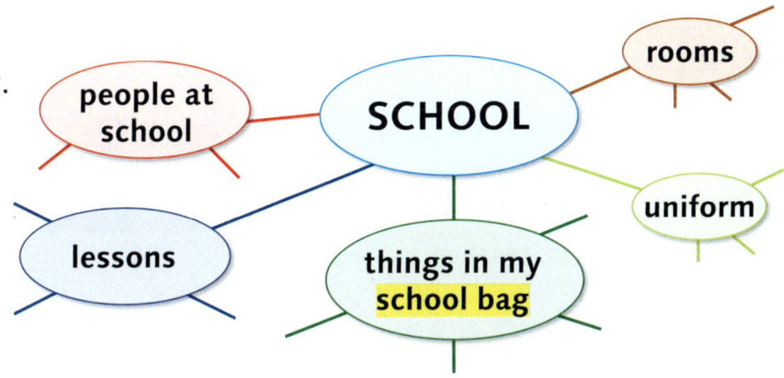

2 Make word and phrase cards

a) Pick words and phrases from the green box and make cards.

Nice to meet you.
Have a good day.
How are you?
Fine, thanks.
See you later.
Good morning.
Hello.
I'm in class 5.
Sorry.
Welcome to our school.
Thanks.
I'm from Germany.
We're best friends.
What's your name?
That's right.
I have an idea.
I know.
It's at home.

b) Write the German phrase on the back of the card.

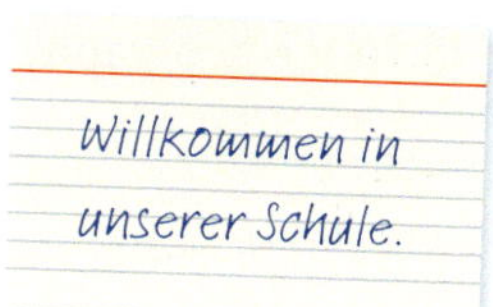

c) Put the cards in a box.

d) Swap cards with your partner. Ask your partner to check you. Then check your partner.

What's 'Willkommen in unserer Schule' in English?

Welcome to our school.

Right.

Lerne Vokabeln regelmäßig – lieber jeden Tag 5–10 Minuten als einmal die Woche zwei Stunden.
Mehr Tipps zum Wörterlernen findest du im *Skills file*.

▸ *Skills file 1, pp. 160–161*

1 Talking to friends at school

1.24

a) First listen. Then put Berry's answers (A–E) in the right order.

1 Hi, Berry. How are you?

2 I'm fine too, thanks. Can I borrow a pen, please?

3 Thanks. What's the next lesson? Box: Voc., p. 189

4 It's science. And who's your favourite teacher?

5 I like Luca.

A I like Luca too.

B Hi, Ellie. I'm fine, thanks. What about you?

C Mr Brown. He's nice. And who's your favourite boy in our class?

D Sure, here you are.

E It's PE. I like PE. What's your favourite lesson?

b) Listen again and check. Then write the dialogue.

c) Practise the dialogue with a partner. Then swap partners.

2 NOW YOU // ● p. 124

Write the dialogue with a partner. Then practise with your partner.

Your names

A: Hi, ... How ... you?
B: Hello, ... I'm OK. What about ...?
A: ... fine, thanks. Can I borrow a ...?
B: Sure, here ...
A: Thanks. ...'s the next lesson?
B: It's ...
A: Oh, good. I like ...

hole punch • pen • pencil • rubber • ruler • ...

English • science • maths • German • history • geography • ...

3 Interviews

a) Copy the table and answer the four questions for you.

	ME	NAME: ...	NAME: ...	NAME: ...
1 Who's your favourite teacher?				
2 Who's your best friend in our class?				
3 What's your favourite hobby?				
4 What's your favourite animal?				

Who's ...? = Wer ist ...?
What's ...? = Was ist ...?

b) Walk around: Ask different partners. Write the names and the answers in the table.

c) Tell the class:

My favourite ... Tina's best ... Karim's favourite ...

▸ Workbook 19–23, pp. 15–16

▸ KV 15 ▸ KV 16 ▸ IAT 1.2

1 The kids from Harbour Road[1]:

Meet the kids!

a) Watch the film. Where are the kids first? And then?

First they're in ... And then[2] they're in ...

assembly

the canteen

Harbour Road

a maths lesson

the sports hall

b) Who says what? Match the sentences (1–5) with the kids.

Anna says ...
Paul says ...
Sarah says ...

1 It's assembly now.

2 The uniform is important!

3 Maths is my favourite lesson.

4 I like lunch.

5 I love sport.

Then watch again and check.

c) What do you think about the kids? Tell your partner.

Example: Anna is nice / fun / great / cool / ... Sarah is ... I like Sarah. Paul is ....

2 People and places: Eggbuckland Community College

a) Watch the film. What do you think? Talk to a partner.

– I think the school is big / new / nice / terrible[3] / ...
– I think the film is cool / great / OK / boring[4] /...
– I like / don't like the music.

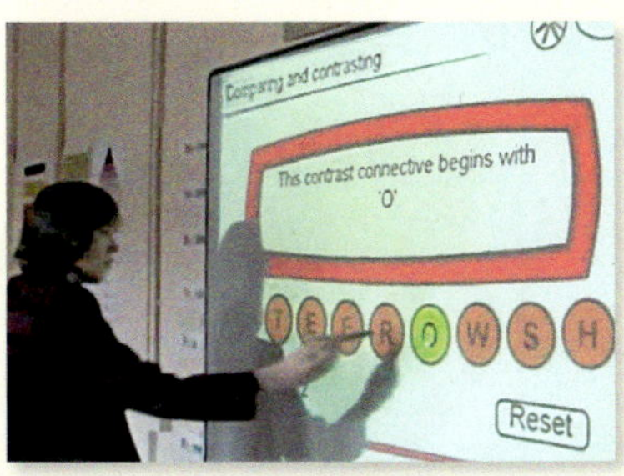

b) Watch the film again. Then work in groups. Write a list of things, people, places, lessons, sports that you see in the film – as many as you can. Which group has the best list?

[1] Harbour Road [hɑːbə 'rəʊd] *Hafenstraße* [2] then [ðen] *dann, danach* [3] terrible ['terəbl] *schrecklich*
[4] boring ['bɔːrɪŋ] *langweilig*

°STOP! °CHECK! GO!

▸ KV 18 ▸ DFF 1.1 ▸ DFF 1.2 ▸ INKL 1.12

Ein Lösungsblatt für die Aufgaben 1 bis 9 kannst du von deiner Lehrerin / deinem Lehrer erhalten.
Den Hörtext (S. 32) findest du auch auf der Audio-CD im Workbook.

1 WORDS School things

°Example: *1 blazer, 2 ..., 3 ...*

2 WORDS °More school things

a) What's the wrong word?

1 pen, pencil, shirt, rubber → *shirt*
2 maths, Monday, French, science → ...
3 lunch, °badminton, football, tae kwon do[1]
4 science lab, school, classroom, art room
5 assembly, break, lesson, calculator
6 brother, student, teacher, principal

b) Look at a) again. Find more words for 1–6. Example: *1 ruler, ...*

c) Finish the sentences.

1 My favourite school day is ...
2 My favourite lesson is ...
3 I have ... in my school bag.

3 READING Remember Cyril[2]?

a) Read the text. Put the pictures (A–D) in the right order.

Hi, I'm Cyril. I'm from Kingsand beach. It's nice. It's near Plymouth. Benny and Babe are my friends. They're from Kingsand too. We're crabs! Oh, look. This is Sandy. She isn't a crab. She's a seagull. Oh no! Mr Johnson is here. He isn't nice. °He likes crabs!

b) Right or wrong?

1 Cyril isn't from London.
2 Kingsand is near Plymouth.
3 Benny and Babe are students.
4 They're crabs.
5 Sandy is a crab too.
6 Mr Johnson is OK.
7 Mr Johnson and Cyril aren't friends.

1 [taɪ kwɒn 'dəʊ] 2 ['sɪrɪl]

▸ KV 18 ▸ DFF 1.3 ▸ INKL 1.12

4 LANGUAGE Remember Sandy?

Put in: *'m • 's • 're • is • are*

5 LANGUAGE Remember Ellie? p. 124

Ellie is with her dad. She has some pictures on her mobile. What's the right word?

1 Look, this is / am my new school.
2 It's / 're very big.
3 The students in my class is / are OK.
4 The teachers is / are OK too.
5 This are / is my new friend, Berry.
6 She's / 're great.
7 My friends Ruby and Charlie am / are at my school too.
8 But they aren't / isn't in my class.
9 This is / are my new uniform.
10 It aren't / isn't very nice.

6 LANGUAGE That's wrong, Sandy!

Sandy is wrong. Cyril is right. Finish Cyril's sentences.

1 Plymouth is in Germany.
2 Eggy is in London.
3 Cyril, you're a seagull.
4 I'm a crab.
5 Berry and Ellie are teachers.
6 Ms Lee and Mr Brown are students.
7 We're students at Eggy.

1 Plymouth isn't in Germany. – It's in ...
2 Eggy isn't ... – It's in ...
3 I'm ... – I'm ...
4 You ... – You're ...
5 They ... – They're ...
6 They ... – They're ...
7 We ... – ... animals.

STOP! CHECK! GO!

▸ KV 18 ▸ DFF 1.4 ▸ DFF 1.5 ▸ INKL 1.12

7 °LISTENING Adam and Luca

1.25

a) Listen. What things are Adam and Luca talking about? Write 1–10.

1 

2 

3 

4 

5 

6 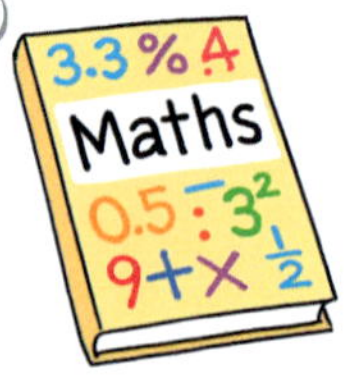

7 

8 

9 

10 

b) Match Adam's and Luca's questions and answers. Then listen and check.

1 How are you?
2 I like the Kaiser Chiefs. What about you?
3 What's your hobby?
4 Who's your favourite teacher?
5 What's the next lesson?
6 Can I borrow your calculator, please?

A I like football.
B Sorry, it's at home.
C French.
D I'm fine, thanks.
E They're OK.
F Ms Lee. She's great.

8 WORDS Talking to friends

Complete the mini-dialogues.

1 Hi. How are …? – I'm fine, thanks.
2 Welcome … our school. – Thanks.
3 I'm in … 7B. – Me too.
4 See … later. – OK, see you.
5 I like … sweatshirt. – Oh, thanks.
6 I'm Emma. – … to meet you, Emma.
7 What's the next …? – It's maths.
8 Have a … day. – You too.

9 °WRITING A °dialogue[1] with a new student

Write a dialogue. What can Berry say? What can Tamara say?

Berry
- Hi – I – Berry
  What – name?

Tamara
- Tamara
  I – from London
  What – you?

Berry
- I – from Woolwell
  I – class 7Y
  What – you?

Tamara
- class 7D
  favourite lesson?

Berry
- I – science
  … you?

Tamara
- history

Berry
- See – later – Tamara

Tamara
- OK – you

More help p. 125

1 ['daɪəlɒg]

10 °SPEAKING A timetable

a) Partner B: Look at page 118.

Partner A: Copy this timetable into your exercise book. Some lessons are missing. Ask partner B. Complete the timetable. And answer partner B's questions.

Lesson	Monday	Tuesday	Wednesday	Thursday	Friday
1	English	....	technology	geography	....
2	....	English	history	....	PE
3	science	history	....	music	....
4	....	....	maths	....	German
5	German	German	maths	science	technology

b) Write your timetable in English.

▸ Wordbank 3, p. 174

Check your answers with your partner's timetable.

11 My °learner log

Write your learner log. You can put it in your DOSSIER.

Im *learner log* schreibst du auf, was du gelernt hast, was du jetzt gut kannst und was noch nicht so gut geht.
Führe dein *learner log* regelmäßig.
Wichtig: Versuche immer ehrlich zu antworten!

My learner log

I THINK ENGLISH IS:
– OK.

MY FAVOURITE °CHARACTER[2]:
– Berry

MY FAVOURITE PHRASES:
– That's cool!
– See you later.
– Have a good day!
– How are you?

MY FAVOURITE WORDS:
– timetable
– lunch
– Eggy
– pony

DIFFICULT WORDS:
– scissors
– trousers
– remember
– science

I REMEMBER:
Lessons: French, German, English, history, ...
School things: pens, pencils, books, ...
Uniform words: pullover, shirt, shoes, ...
Animals: dog, cat, snake, ...
Colours: red, black, green, ...

°I'M GOOD AT:
– Listening, reading

I'M NOT GOOD AT:
– Speaking, writing

°I'M OK AT:
– Words, language

2 ['kærəktə]

Unit 2

At home with Ellie

▸ IAT 2.1 ▸ KV 19

1

2

Box: Voc., p. 189

5

6

1 Homes

a) Talk to a partner about the eight photos on pages 34–35.

– What can you see? – What do you like?	– In photo 1/… I can see a – I like/don't like the	big small …	house/flat/ kitchen/bedroom/ garden/living room

1.26 **b)** Listen. Ellie is with Berry. What photos (1–8) show Ellie's house? Write the numbers.

c) Listen again. What's right? What's wrong?

1 Ellie's mum has a house.
2 The house is in Greatfield Street.
3 Ellie lives in Hill Road.
4 Ellie lives with her dad.
5 Ellie's bedroom is small.
6 Ellie is happy with her bedroom.

► KV 19 ► DFF 2.2 ► INKL 2.1

4

3

7

8

1.27 **2 A new flat**

a) Listen to Ellie and her dad. Point at the right photos (1–8).

b) Listen again. Find words in the box for the pictures (A–C):

A

B

C

a hall • a °balcony[1)] • a toilet • a bathroom • a garage[2)]

3 ACTIVITY My dream house

a) Draw your dream house. Make room labels. More help p. 125

b) Walk around: Talk to different partners about your picture.

My dream house is big. It has three bedrooms, two bathrooms and a garden. The garden is …

It's nice / big / cool.

► Workbook 1–3, p. 21

1 ['bælkəni] 2 ['gærɑːʒ]

► IAT 2.1 ► Folie 12

Ellie's family

1 Meet the family

1.28

a) Look at the pictures: Who's Ellie's mum? Who's Ellie's dad? Guess and point. Then read and check.

Ellie — Hi, Mum, this is Berry.
Mum — Hi, Berry. Nice to meet you. I'm Jackie.
Berry — Hello.
Ellie — Is Zoe[1] upstairs?
Mum — Yes, she is. And Conor[2] is in the living room.
Ellie — Oh no! He's always in the living room. There's no space for Berry and me!
Mum — Oh, here's Conor. This is Berry, Ellie's new friend.
Conor — Hi, Berry. Are you at Eggbuckland?
Berry — Yes, I am. What about you?
Conor — I'm at Plymouth High School.
Mum — And here's Zoe, Ellie's big sister.
Zoe — Hi, welcome to the °madhouse!
Mum — Conor, can the girls go into the living room? Is that OK?
Conor — Oh, OK.

Berry and Ellie are in the living room.
Berry — Your family is fun. They're all nice.
Ellie — They're OK.
Berry — What about your stepdad? Box: Voc., p.190 Is he nice?
Ellie — He's OK. But I miss my real dad. Box: Voc., p.190 He lives with his new partner and his baby boy. Look, I have a photo on my mobile.
Berry — The baby is cute. You're lucky. You have a baby brother, a sister and a big brother.
Ellie — You're lucky. You live with your mum and your dad. That's cool.

b) Finish the sentences.

1 Berry is ...
2 Jackie is ...
3 Conor is ...
4 Ellie's dad has ...
5 Ellie lives with ...
6 Berry lives with ...

... her mum and stepdad. • ... at Ellie's house. • ... a new family. • ... Ellie's mum. • ... her mum and dad. • ... Ellie's big brother.

1 ['zəʊi] 2 ['kɒnə]

► KV 20 ► Folie 12 ► DFF 2.1 ► INKL 2.2

2 Ellie's family tree

a) ◯ Choose the right words for Ellie. //● p. 126

1 My mum and dad are / aren't together.
2 I live with my mum / dad.
3 This is Pete. He's my stepdad / real dad.
4 Pete has two / three children.
5 Zoe is my stepmother / stepsister.
6 Conor is my baby brother / stepbrother.
7 My dad has a new partner. Her name is Alisha / Jackie.
8 This is Finn, my baby brother / big brother.

b) Put the family words into three lists.

♀	♂	♀ ♂
mum	dad	cousin
...	...	...

aunt[4] • baby • brother • children • cousin[5] • dad • father • grandfather • grandmother • grandparents • mother • mum • parents • partner • sister • stepbrother • uncle

Box: Voc., p. 190

3 ACTIVITY Your family tree

a) Draw your family tree or your dream family tree. You can put it in your DOSSIER. ► Wordbank 4, p. 175

b) Talk to a partner about your family tree.

I have a big / small family.
I have ... brothers / cousins / aunts / uncles / ...
I live with my ...
My mum's / dad's name is ...
My grandparents live in ...
...

c) ● Write sentences about your family – as many as you can.

► Workbook 4, p. 22

3 [əˈlɪʃə] 4 [ɑːnt] 5 [ˈkʌzn]

Problems at home

1 What's your problem?

1.29 a) Read and find out: Is Zoe happy?
– Yes, she is. / No, she isn't.

Ellie shares a bedroom with her stepsister, Zoe.

Zoe — Ellie, look at the room!
Ellie — What's your problem? It's OK!
Zoe — OK? What about the pullover? Is it yours?
Ellie — Yes, it is.
Zoe — And the shoes? Are they yours too?
Ellie — Yes, they are. What's your problem?
Zoe — The room is messy! That's my problem!
Ellie — Is it your room? No, it isn't. It's my room too!

1.30 b) Now Ellie is in the kitchen. Is she happy?
– Yes, she is. / No, she isn't.

Mum — Are you OK, Ellie?
Ellie — No, I'm not. Zoe is bossy, Mum.
Mum — Oh, Ellie!
Ellie — And there's no space in our room. I can't do my homework. Box: Voc., p. 190
Mum — What about the kitchen?
Ellie — It's too busy!
Mum — What about the living room?
Ellie — It's too noisy!
Mum — Oh, Ellie!

2 Ellie's problems

Look at the dialogues in 1 again. Pick A, B or C.

	A	B	C
1 It's ...	A Ellie's room.	B Zoe's room.	C Ellie and Zoe's room.
2 The room is ...	A OK.	B messy.	C big.
3 Ellie has no ...	A space.	B bedroom.	C shoes.
4 The kitchen is too ...	A busy.	B new.	C small.
5 The living room is too ...	A big.	B pink.	C noisy.

3 Zoe is bossy!

a) Write Zoe's questions and Ellie's answers.

tie | books | T-shirts
football | shoes | pullover

b) Act the dialogue.

4 Ellie's dream room

1.31

a) Ellie is talking to her friends. Listen. What's her dream room – 1 or 2?

b) Listen again. What's in Ellie's dream room? Write the numbers.

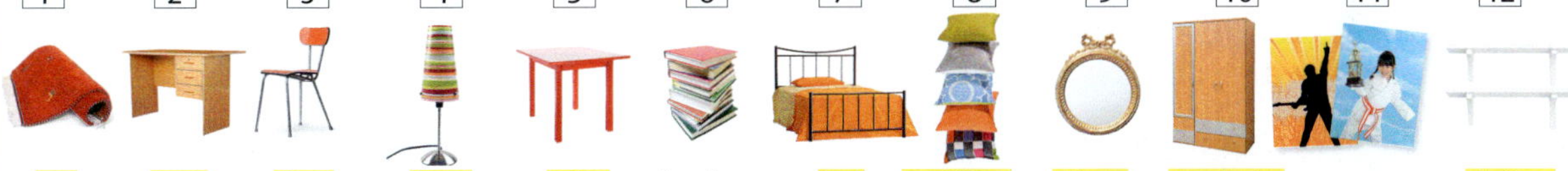

1	2	3	4	5	6	7	8	9	10	11	12
a **rug**	a **desk**	a **chair**	a **lamp**	a **table**	books	a **bed**	**cushions**	a **mirror**	a **wardrobe**	posters	**shelves**

c) Things in Ellie's dream room:
Make two lists.

There's ...	There are ...
a rug	shelves
...	...

More practice 1 p. 126

► Language file 4, p. 168

5 What's **different**?

Partner B: Go to page 118.

Partner A: Look at room A. Talk about your room to your partner. Partner B starts.
Find four different things or more. Make notes about the different things.

Partner B There's a bed in room B.
Partner A There's a bed in room A too.
Partner B OK. There are three cushions in room B.
Partner A There are no cushions in room A. That's different!

Room A	Room B
no cushions	3 cushions
...	...

▸ Folie 14

1.32

1 Are you OK?

Right or wrong? Read and check.

1 Ellie's dad is happy in the new flat.
2 Ellie is happy in her mum's house.

Dad — Hi, Ellie. This is a nice surprise.
Ellie — Hi, Dad. Is Finn OK?
Dad — Yes, he is. He's fine.
Ellie — And Alisha? Is she OK?
Dad — Yes, she is. She's fine too, but she's tired.
Ellie — And the new flat? Is it OK?
Dad — Yes, it is. It's really nice.
Ellie — Are you and Alisha happy in the flat?
Dad — Yes, we are. We love it ... Ellie, are you OK?

Ellie

Steve

Ellie — Yes, I am. I'm fine.
Dad — Are you sure? Are you really OK?
Ellie — ... No, I'm not. I'm not happy.
Dad — Oh! What's the problem? Is your stepdad too strict?
Ellie — No, he isn't. Pete is OK.
Dad — And what about Zoe and Conor? Are they mean to you?
Ellie — No, they aren't. They're OK. But I share a room with Zoe and she's really bossy. And Conor is really noisy. There's no space for me. Dad, I'm not happy in this house.
Dad — Oh, Ellie. Listen. I have an idea.

Box: Voc., p. 191

2 Questions and answers

a) Complete the answers. Then find the sentences in 1 and check.

1 Is Finn OK? – Yes, he ...
2 And the new flat? Is it OK? – Yes, ...
3 Are you and Alisha happy in the flat? – Yes, we ...
4 Ellie, are you OK? – Yes, I ...
5 Are you really OK? – No, ...
6 Is your stepdad too strict? – No, ...
7 Are Zoe and Conor mean to you? – No, ...

Im Englischen antwortet man auf eine Frage oft nicht nur mit *Yes* oder *No*, sondern mit Kurzantworten. Das ist höflicher.

b) Questions

Complete the examples with:

Am • Is • Are

FOCUS

... I OK?
... he / she / it OK?
... you / we / they OK?

c) Answers

Complete the examples with:

am • is • are • 'm not • isn't • aren't

FOCUS

Yes, I ... – No, I ...
Yes, he / she / it ... – No, he / she / it ...
Yes, you / we / they ... – No, you / we / they ...

▸ Language file 3, p. 167

3 NOW YOU

p.127

a) Write the answers for you.

1 Are you noisy? – Yes, I am. / No, I'm not.
2 Are your friends fun?
– Yes, they are. / No, they aren't.
3 Is your grandmother from Germany?
– Yes, she is. / No, she isn't.
4 Is your dad strict? – Yes, he is. / No, he isn't.
5 Is your mum bossy?
– Yes, she is. / No, she isn't.
6 Is your room messy? – Yes, it is. / No, it isn't.

b) Ask your partner the same questions.

4 Who am I?

Play this game with a partner. You're one of the people in the house. Can your partner guess who you are?

Are you a girl / boy?
Are you upstairs / downstairs?
Are you in the kitchen / ...?
Are you big / small?
Are you Ben / Liz / ...?

Yes, I am.

No, I'm not.

5 Quiz questions

Answer the questions.

1 Is Finn cute? – Yes, he ... / No, he ...
2 Is Berry Ellie's friend? – ...
3 Is Ellie's house big? – ...
4 Are Zoe and Conor mean? – ...
5 Are Pete and Jackie together? – ...
6 Is Alisha Ellie's sister?
7 Is Jackie Ellie's mum?
8 Is Steve Ellie's real dad?
9 Is Berry's family big?
10 Are you and your family from Plymouth?

More practice 2 p.127

6 An interview: What do you think?

a) Copy the table and answer the questions.

b) Walk around: Ask as many partners as you can.

c) Pick one interesting answer. Tell the class.

Meike says she isn't bossy!

Jan says school is fun!

	Me	Partner 1	Partner 2	...
1 Is English easy?	✓			
2 Is school fun?	✗			
3 Is the principal strict?				
4 Are your teachers nice?				
5 Are you bossy?				

▸ Workbook 9–11, p. 25

▸ KV 23 ▸ Folie 15 ▸ INKL 2.6 ▸ INKL 2.8

1 Before you read Ellie's diary

Choose a picture (1–7). Answer the questions about your picture. Then tell the class.

1 Where is Ellie? (at her mum's house / at her dad's flat / in the kitchen / in the ...)
2 Is Ellie happy?

Example:
In picture 1 Ellie is at her mum's house.
She's in the kitchen. She's happy.

The best of both worlds

1.33

MONDAY
Dear Diary
Great news! I can live with dad,
Alisha and the baby, Finn.
Tuesday is the big day!
Zoe is happy. But mum isn't happy.

TUESDAY
Dear Diary
I'm in my new home. I'm in my new bedroom.
I have a desk and a lamp and a red rug.
I can do my homework here.
No bossy Zoe. This is my dream room.
It's pink, but it's great!

WEDNESDAY
Dear Diary
Finn is very cute. And Alisha is really nice.
Dad and Alisha are at the cinema now.
Finn is with me.
No Conor! Now I can watch all my
favourite TV programmes.

Box: Voc., p. 192

THURSDAY
Dear Diary
Dad is at work. Alisha is tired.
She's in the bedroom.
Finn is with me. He isn't very happy.
I hope dad is home soon!

FRIDAY
Dear Diary
Dad and Alisha are at a restaurant.
It's Alisha's birthday. Finn is with me – again!
And he isn't very happy – again!
Be quiet, Finn!

Box: Voc., p. 192

6

7

SATURDAY
Dear Diary
Dad and Alisha are in town.
And Finn? Yes, he's with me – again!
Dad has no time for me. He's °in love!
I miss mum. And I miss Conor and Pete
and my cats and I miss Zoe! I'm lonely.
Oh, a text. Is it from mum?

SUNDAY
Dear Diary
I have a new idea!
From Monday to Friday I'm with mum.
On Saturday and Sunday I'm with dad.
The best of both worlds! I'm happy again.

2 Ellie's week

Read the text. Match the headings with the days (Monday–Sunday) in Ellie's diary:
Example: Monday: Good news for Ellie   Tuesday: ...

Lots of TV now   A new idea   Good news for Ellie   Alisha's birthday
Day one in a new home   Dad at work   Ellie misses her mum

3 //○ Is Ellie happy? //● p. 127

Pick the right endings. Write the sentences.

1 On Monday Ellie is happy because ...	she can watch her favourite TV programmes.
2 On Tuesday Ellie is happy because ...	she's lonely.
3 On Wednesday Ellie is happy because ...	Finn isn't happy.
4 On Thursday Ellie isn't happy because ...	she has a new idea.
5 On Friday Ellie isn't happy because ...	she can live with her dad.
6 On Saturday Ellie isn't happy because ...	dad and Alisha are at a restaurant.
7 On Sunday Ellie is happy again because ...	she has a nice room.

4 ● A week later

Write Ellie's diary for this picture.

Dear Diary
happy again / mum's house / in – bedroom – Zoe /
cats – happy / mum – happy / Zoe – happy too /
Conor – here / Finn – ~~here~~ / OK

More help p. 127

More practice 3 p. 128

1 Cyril's house

Look at Cyril's mind map and finish the text in your exercise book.

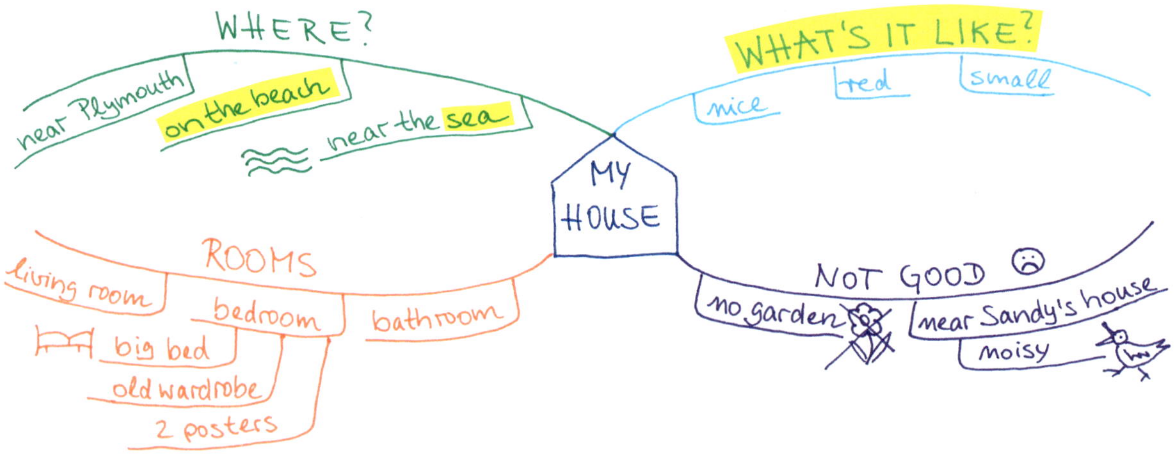

My house

Hi. This is my ... It's near Plymouth. It's on the ..., near the ...
It's nice. It's ... and it's ...
There are three rooms in my house. There's a ..., a ... and a ...
My favourite room is my bedroom. There's a big ... and an old ... in my bedroom. There are two ... too.
What isn't good about my house? – There's ... garden and it's near Sandy's ...
She's very noisy!

2 NOW YOU

a) Make a mind map for your house or flat, or for your dream house. Use ideas from Cyril's mind map. ▸ *Wordbank 5, p. 175*

b) Write about your dream house or flat with the words from your mind map. Cyril's text can help you. You can put your text in your DOSSIER. More help p. 128

Mind maps
Bevor du einen Text schreibst, ist es immer gut, deine Ideen zu sammeln und zu ordnen. Eine *mind map* kann dir dabei helfen.

▸ *Skills file 2, p. 162*

► IAT 2.2 ► KV 24 ► DFF 2.8 ► Folie 16

1 Classroom phrases

a) Match the phrases (A–L) with the pictures (1–12) in the game.

Example: 'What's that in English?' goes with picture 7.

A What's that in English?	E Quiet, please!	I Listen, please!
B It's your turn.	F Can I go to the toilet, please?	J What page is it, please?
C Work with a partner.	G What's for homework?	K Please look at the board.
D Close the door, please.	H Can you say that again, please?	L Sorry, I forgot my homework.

1.34

b) Listen. When you hear the classroom phrases from 1a, point at the pictures in the game.

More practice 4 p. 128

2 GAME The °banana skin game

Play this game in groups of three or four.

WAS? 1 Würfel und 3 oder 4 Spielsteine.
WIE? Landest du auf einem Nummernfeld, nenne die *classroom phrase*. War sie korrekt, bleibe auf dem Feld. Hast du einen Fehler gemacht, gehe zwei Felder zurück. Dann ist der/die Nächste an der Reihe.

1 The alphabet chant

Box: Voc., p. 193

1.35 1.36 Listen to Cyril and repeat.

AB – CDE We're a happy family.
FG – HIJ °Come and °visit °us °today.
KL – MNO Plymouth is the place to go.
PQ – RST Lots of fun for you and me.
UVW – XYZ Now we're tired and °off to bed!

2 Addresses and phone numbers

More practice 5 p. 129

1.37 **a)** Listen. What are the right answers?

1 Ellie talks to her friends about ...
A her mum's house. B her dad's flat. C her new room.

2 What's the right address?
A 11 Great Field Road. B 10 Gratefeld Street. C 11 Greatfield Street.

3 Two numbers are wrong in Ellie's phone number.
What's her phone number?

01752 803 3647

Bei Telefonnummern sagt man *oh* oder *zero* für die 0.

1.38 **b)** Listen and repeat the questions.

1.39 **c)** Listen and write Berry's address. More help p. 129

3 What's your address?

a) How can you say your address and phone number in English? Think about it.

b) Double circle:
Talk to different partners.
Find out their address or their phone number.

What's your address?
What's your phone number?

Im Englischen gibt es kein **ä**, **ö**, **ü** und **ß**.
Du kannst sie ersetzen durch:
ä → ae **ö → oe**
ü → ue **ß → ss**

▸ Workbook 20–23, pp. 29–30

► *KV 25 A/B*

1 The kids from Harbour Road: Homework time

a) Watch the film. Then put the photos (A – F) in the right order.

First we see ... Then we see ...

A

B

C

D

E

F
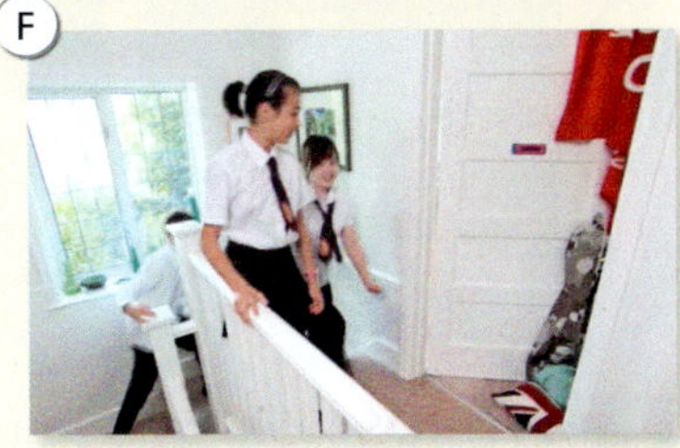

b) Before you watch again: What's the right answer? Then watch and check.

1 The three friends are at Sarah's / Anna's house.
2 They have lots of / no homework.
3 They talk about shopping / football.
4 Then they go upstairs into Sarah's / Tom's room.
5 Tom is Sarah's big brother / cousin.
6 Tom is / isn't happy because Sarah, Paul and Anna are in his room.
7 Anna and Paul say Tom is mean / OK.
8 Later Tom and Sarah are / aren't friends again.

2 People and places: A tour of my room

a) Before you watch: What are your five favourite things in your room? Write a list. Then tell a partner.

b) Now watch Joe's film. Name his favourite things – as many as you can. Make a list. Compare your list with a partner.

c) Watch the film again. Pick the right words:

1 Joe's favourite lesson is English / history.
2 Joe's pet is a dog / cat.
3 Joe's tie / guitar isn't his favourite thing.
4 Joe has a baby brother / sister.
5 Joe is good at music / sport.
6 Joe's most favourite thing is his computer / football.

d) Copy and complete this diagram:

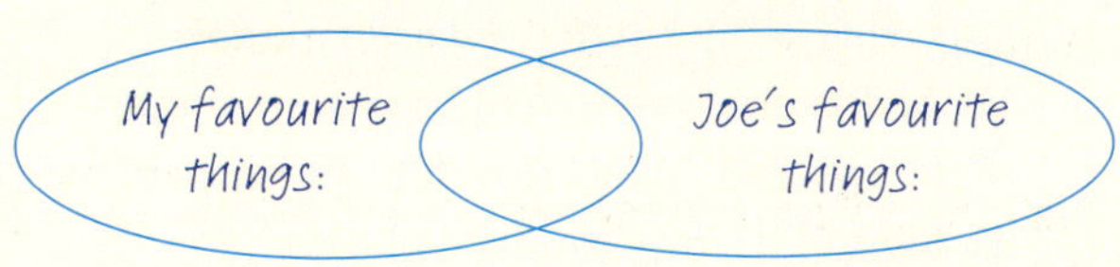

STOP! CHECK! GO!

▸ DFF 2.1 ▸ DFF 2.2 ▸ DFF 2.3 ▸ KV 26 ▸ INKL 2.12 A/B

Ein Lösungsblatt für die Aufgaben 1 bis 6 kannst du von deiner Lehrerin / deinem Lehrer erhalten. Die Hörtexte (S. 49) findest du auch auf der Audio-CD im Workbook.

1 WORDS Can you remember Ellie's family?

a) Find the right family word and write the sentences.

b) Do you know five more family words?

2 WORDS Sandy's house

a) Match the labels (A–H) with the places (1–8) in the picture.

A kitchen
B hall
C living room
D bedroom
E bathroom
F toilet
G garden
H garage

b) It's all wrong. But what's right? Correct the mistakes.

Hi! Welcome to my **madhouse** *house*.
The **~~hall~~** is yellow. And the **bathroom** is pink. This is my kitchen – it's very **~~small~~**.
My **bedroom** is red – cool! Look at my living room – it's **red**. Great! Now look at my garden.
It's **~~big~~**, but it's my favourite place.

c) House quiz: Name the rooms.

1 It's a very small, white room!
2 I make lunch here.
3 My bed and wardrobe are here.
4 My bike is here.
5 I watch TV here.

3 REVISION Sandy's family

Complete the text for Sandy. Use: *'m • 's • is • are • 're*

My family ... (1) big. This ... (2) my father. Dad ... (3) very strict, but he ... (4) fun too. This ... (5) my mum. She... (6) cool, but she... (7) strict too.

My brothers and sisters ... (8) OK. But they... (9) very messy. We... (10) all very noisy. I... (11) happy because I... (12) in my new house. It... (13) great!

4 Questions for Sandy

p.129

Cyril has questions for Sandy. Choose the right answers.

1 Hey, Sandy. Are you happy?
2 Is your family small?
3 Are your parents strict?
4 Is your mum cool?
5 Are your brothers and sisters mean?
6 Are you and your family noisy?
7 Is your new house messy?

Yes, they are.
Yes, I am.
No, it isn't.
Yes, it is.
Yes, she is.
Yes, we are.
No, they aren't.

5 LISTENING Numbers and addresses

1.40 **a)** Numbers: The mobile numbers are wrong. Listen. Write the right numbers.

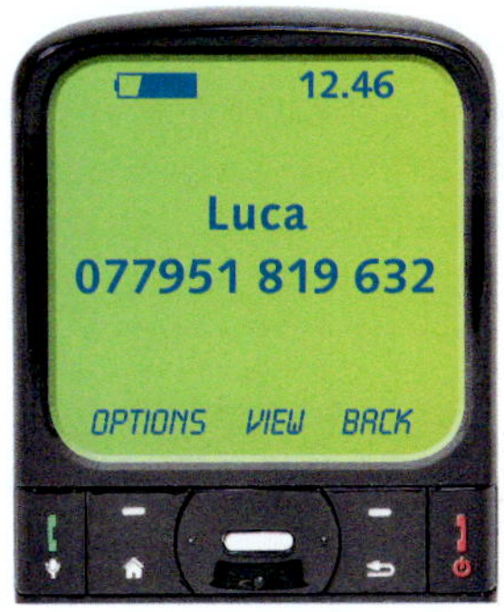

1.41 **b)** Addresses: Listen. Which address (1, 2 or 3) is Luca's address?

1. 9 Windsor Road[1] Plymouth PL3 1TE
2. 9 Windsor Street[2] Plymouth PL3 2ET
3. 19 Winsbury Road[3] Plymouth PL6 7NN

1.42 **c)** Listen. Write Adam's address.

1 [wɪnzə 'rəʊd] 2 ['wɪnzə striːt] 3 [wɪnzbəri 'rəʊd]

6 WRITING An email to a new °e-pal[1]

Hi! I'm Tom, your new e-pal.
I live in England, but I'm from America. My family is small.
My parents aren't together. I live with my mum and my sister.
Our house is in Plymouth. Plymouth is nice. It's a big city in England.
My room is OK. I have a computer. I play games with my friends.
My school is in Plymouth too. It's very big. I have lots of friends.
They're very cool. My teachers are OK too. I have lots of questions for you.

a) ○ Read Tom's email.
Then write Tom's questions.

1 ... you from England?
2 ... your family small?
3 ... your house in a city?
4 ... your room nice?
5 ... your school big?
6 ... your friends cool?
7 ... your teachers OK?

b) Write your answers to Tom's questions.

Tom's questions	*My answers*
1 Are you from England?	*No, I'm not.*
2 Is ...	

c) ● Write Tom an email about yourself.

7 SPEAKING Good shops

PARTNER B: Go to page 119.

a) PARTNER A:
Imagine you're in Plymouth.
You want to find a good mobile shop.
Ask partner B these questions.
Write: – the name of the shop
– the address
– the phone number.

b) Partner B doesn't know this sports shop. Answer partner B's questions.

1 ['i:pæl] 2 ['sɔ:ltæʃ]

8 READING A new hobby

a) Read the story.

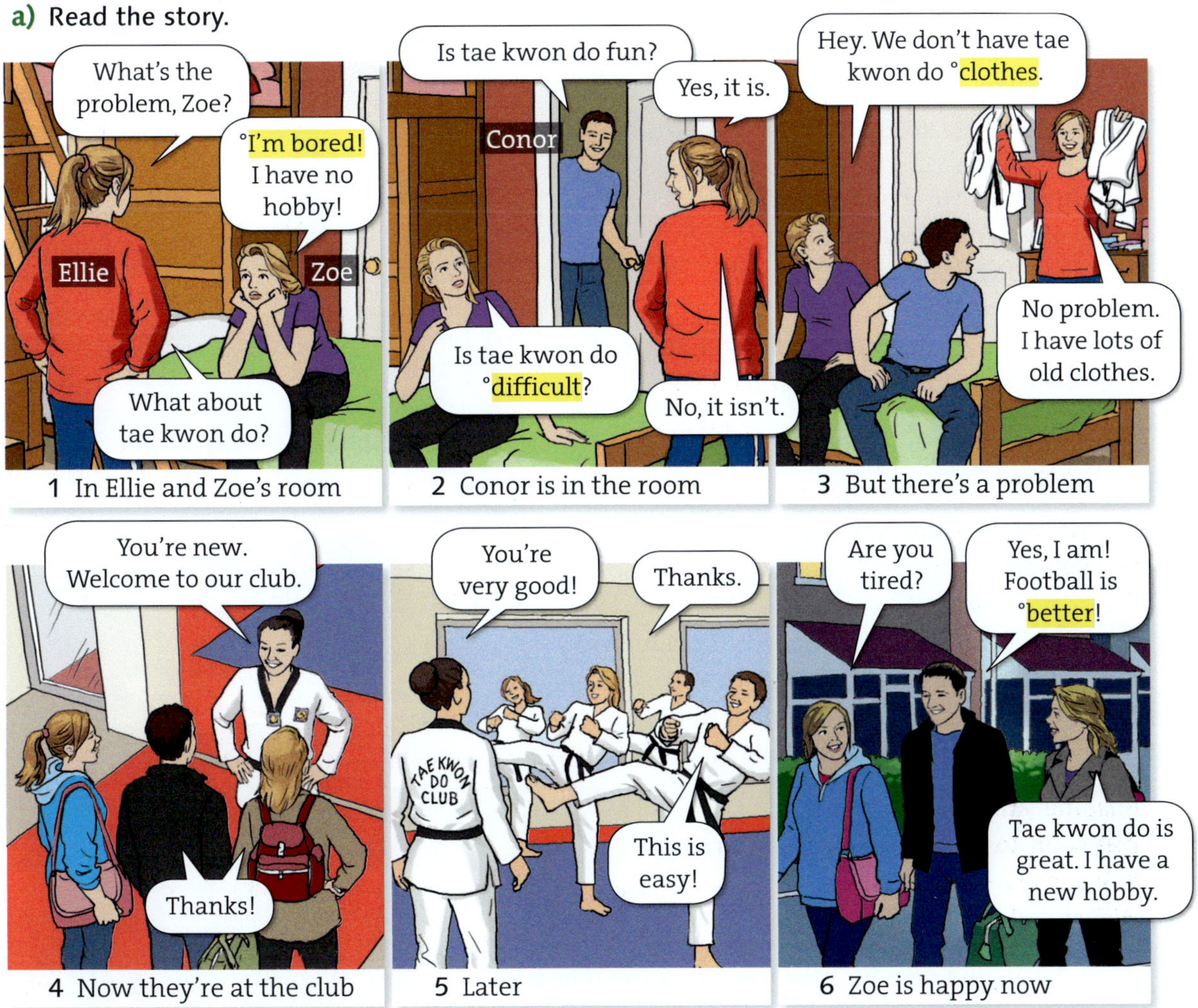

1 In Ellie and Zoe's room
2 Conor is in the room
3 But there's a problem
4 Now they're at the club
5 Later
6 Zoe is happy now

b) Answer the questions about the story.

1 Who's bored?
2 Who has an idea?
3 Who has no tae kwon do clothes?
4 Who's new at the club?
5 Who thinks tae kwon do is easy?
6 Who's tired?
7 Who has a new hobby?

9 My learner log

Write your learner log for Unit 2.
Put it in your DOSSIER.

My learner log

My favourite °pages in Unit 2 are: ...
My favourite text in Unit 2 is: ...
My favourite phrases in Unit 2 are: ...
Difficult words in Unit 2 are: ...

My °progress in English is: GREAT! / OK / NOT VERY GOOD

My Plymouth

► KV 27 A/B ► IAT 3.1 ► INKL 3.1 ► INKL 3.2 ► DFF 3.1 ► Folie 17

1 This is my town

a) Before you listen to Luca, match the sentences (A–F) with the photos (1–6).

A My favourite shop is a mobile shop.
B I often go to the cinema with my friends.
C I ride my BMX bike in the park. Box: Voc., p. 193
D We live in Windsor Street[1].
E We go to a swimming pool in the summer.
F My dad works at a fire station.

1

2.02

b) Listen and check.

c) Listen again and pick the right notes.

Family name:	Boateng[2] / Windsor
House number:	1/9
Name of mobile shop:	Phones 4U / Mobiles 4U
Name of park:	Plymouth Park / Central Park
Name of fire station:	Greenbank / Charles
Name of swimming pool:	Big Pool / Tinside Lido[3]
Name of cinema:	Reel Cinema / Plymouth Cinema

d) Check your notes with a partner.

4

2 Your town

a) Make a mind map for your town or a town near you.

► Wordbank 6, p. 176

6

b) Compare your mind map with a partner. Can you find more ideas for your mind map?

c) Talk to your class about your town. Use your mind map.

1 ['wɪnzə striːt] 2 [bwaːteŋ] 3 [tɪnsaid 'laidəʊ]

► Workbook 1–2, p. 37

2

3

5

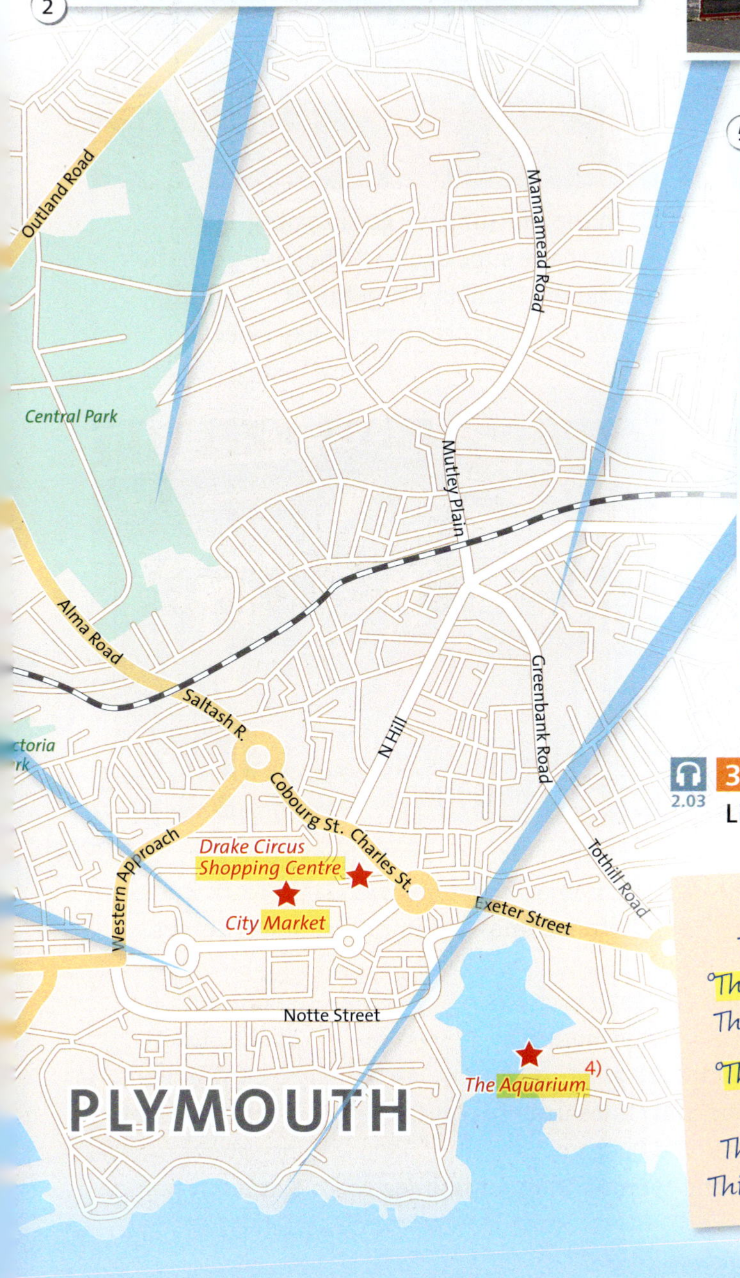

2.03 **3 SONG This is my city**

Listen to the song and sing along.

This is my city

This is my town, this is my city.
°Through my °eyes it °looks °so °pretty.
This is my town, this is my city now.

°These are my people, this is my song.
°Dirty streets, where I °belong.
This is my town, this is my city now.
This is my city now.

Timothy Victor

4 [ə'kweəriəm]

Weekends in Plymouth

2.04

1 Saturdays are great

a) Before you read, look at the pictures: Where is Luca?

In picture ... Luca is at the cinema / at the market / in the park / at home / ...

A

Saturdays are great. I have no school. Mum always works on Saturdays. But dad always stays at home. I make a big breakfast for everybody. °Yummy!

B

In the morning we go shopping. First we go to the supermarket. Then we go to the market. Dad buys vegetables[1] – boring! We can buy nice things – like sweets.

C

In the afternoon dad and Grace usually[2] play games at home. Jack and I go to Central Park. We ride our BMX bikes there.

D

In the evening I sometimes go to the cinema. I meet my friends there. Jack often comes too. But Grace never comes.

Box: Voc., p. 194
Box: Voc., p. 194

b) Match the sentence parts.

1 On Saturdays Luca has no school.
2 Luca always makes ...

1 On Saturdays Luca has ...	shopping.
2 Luca always makes ...	to the cinema.
3 Then they all go ...	to Central Park.
4 Dad and Grace usually play ...	a big breakfast.
5 Jack and Luca go ...	no school.
6 In the evening they sometimes go ...	games at home.

1 ['vedʒtəblz] 2 ['juːʒuəli]

▸ Text file 4, p. 155

▸ Folie 18 ▸ INKL 3.3 ▸ KV 28 ▸ DFF 3.4 ▸ DFF 3.6

2 NOW YOU

a) Make a table about your Saturdays. Use ideas from the box. p. 130

I always	I sometimes	I never
go shopping	...	...

buy sweets • go shopping • go to the park • have a big breakfast • have lunch at a restaurant • meet friends • play football • play games • play music • ride my bike • stay at home • watch TV • ...

b) Tell the class. Throw a ball to the next student.

I always go shopping on Saturdays. What about you?

3 Shopping for a birthday present

2.05

a) Does Luca like shopping with his dad? Read and find out.

It's Luca's birthday soon. He's in a sports shop with his dad. They want to buy Luca's birthday present today.

Dad — Look, Luca. What about the black trainers?
Luca — Oh no, Dad! I don't like black trainers. What about the red trainers? They're cool. Box: Voc., p. 195
Dad — Red? Oh no! And they're too expensive – £99!
Luca — What about a hoodie then? I love the green hoodie!
Dad — It's OK. But what about the brown hoodie? It's nice.
Luca — A brown hoodie? Oh, Dad! I hate brown. It's boring. Shopping with you is terrible!

b) Finish the sentences.

A

B
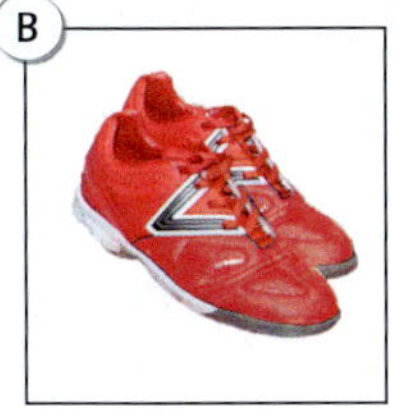
C

D

1 Dad likes the ... trainers and the ... hoodie.
2 Luca likes the ... and the ...
3 Luca hates the ...

4 I love the hoodie!

a) What do you love? What do you hate? Talk to different partners – as many as you can.

I love the hoodie! What about you?

b) Tell the class.
– Everybody loves / hates the ...
– Lots of boys love ...
– Lots of girls hate the ...

▸ Workbook 3–5, pp. 38–39

Birthdays

1 Birthday ideas

2.06

a) Listen. Which picture (1–4) is Luca's birthday, Ellie's birthday, Adam's birthday or Berry's birthday? Example: Picture ... is Luca's birthday.

1

2

3

4

b) Match the activities with the pictures (1–4).

A I usually go to a nice place with my family – like the aquarium.
B We always stay at home on my birthday.
C I usually have a party with my friends.
D I sometimes go to the beach with my parents.

Box: Voc., p. 195

c) Listen again. Match the names with the birthdays.

Luca
Ellie
Berry
Adam

Box: Voc., p. 195

A 9th September
B 14th February[1]
C 1st August[2]
D 25th December

2 You and your birthday

a) What about your birthday? Write sentences.

On my birthday I	always usually sometimes never	go swimming. stay at home. get presents. go shopping. visit my aunt. have a party. go to a restaurant. go to the cinema. ...

b) Double circle: Talk to different partners about your birthday.

On my birthday I always / sometimes ... What about you?

Me too.

I usually ...

1 ['februəri] 2 ['ɔːgəst]

▸ Workbook 6, p. 39

► Folie 19 ► KV 29 ► KV 30 ► INKL 3.5 ► DFF 3.3

3 Months[3] and dates

a) Write the months in the right order in your exercise book.

b) Listen. What months do you hear? (2.07)

c) Listen again. What dates do you hear, A or B?

1 A 15th January B 30th January
2 A 1st May B 5th May
3 A 2nd December B 22nd December
4 A 7th October B 11th October
5 A 16th July – 3rd September
B 17th July – 23rd September

d) Listen and repeat the dates. (2.08)

Box: Voc., p. 195

4 When's your birthday?

a) Write your birthday. How do you say it?
My birthday is on ...

You write:	You say:
1st March	the first of March
2nd July	the second of July
3rd September	the third of September
4th November	the fourth of November
5th December	the fifth of December

Box: Voc., p. 195

► More dates, p. 229

b) Birthday game: Throw the ball. Ask the question.

5 Talking about birthdays

a) Copy the table. Complete the 'Me' column for you.

Questions	Me	1 o'clock Tina	2 o'clock ...	3 o'clock ...
When's your birthday?	6th March	...	...	
When's your best friend's birthday?	10th July	...		
When's your mum's / dad's birthday?	mum 29th April			
When's your brother's / sister's birthday?	...			

b) Appointments: Make appointments for 1, 2 and 3 o'clock with three students. Write the names in the table.

c) Go to your appointments. Your teacher will tell you when it is 1, 2 or 3 o'clock. Talk to your partners. Ask two questions, or more. Write the birthdays on your table. More practice 1 p. 130

► Workbook 7–8, p. 40

3 [mʌnθs] 4 [dʒu'laɪ] 5 ['eɪprəl]

▸ KV 31 ▸ Folie 20 ▸ INKL 3.6

1 Luca's day

Match the sentences (A–I) with the pictures (1–9). Example: *1D, 2 …*

A I get up early. I make breakfast for Grace.

B I usually have lunch at school.

C Lazy Jack! He gets up late. He never has breakfast!

D Dad often works at night. He comes home in the morning. Box: Voc., p. 196

E After dinner we watch TV. Mum sometimes watches TV with us. Dad goes to work.

F Mum often comes home late. We always have dinner together and we talk about the day.

G In the afternoon dad stays in bed. We do our homework.

H Jack and I go to school together. We usually go by bus. But I sometimes walk. Jack never walks. Lazy Jack!

I In the evening dad usually makes dinner.

2 The simple present

a) There are lots of verbs in Luca's text, for example *get* and *gets*. Make two lists:

Verb ohne s	*Verb mit s*
I get up early.	*He gets up late.*

b) Pick the right answers and make the rules.

FOCUS

Mit dem *simple present* sprichst du darüber, …	*I, you, we, they* → mit oder ohne 's' am Verb?
A was jeden Tag, oft, manchmal oder nie passiert.	*he, she, it* → mit oder ohne 's' am Verb?
B was schon passiert ist.	

▸ *Language file 6, p. 169*

► *Folie 21*

3 Dad's day

Complete the sentences about Luca's dad.

1 Luca's dad ... (get up) late in the afternoon.
2 Then he usually ... (make) dinner.
3 In the evening he often ... (go) to work. He ... (work) at a fire station.
4 He usually ... (go) to work by car, but he sometimes ... (ride) his bike.
5 Sometimes it's quiet at the fire station and Luca's dad ... (watch) TV.
6 But usually it's busy and he ... (have) no time.
7 In the morning he ... (go) home.
8 He sometimes ... (have) breakfast with the kids.
9 Then he ... (go) to bed.

Vorsicht bei diesen Verben:
watch – watches
go – goes
have – has

4 Who is he?

2.09

Listen to the poem. Then repeat it. Who is 'he'?

He lives on the beach.
He walks on the °sand.
He swims in the sea.
He °pinches my hand.

He °chats and he °sings.
He °sits in the °sun.
He watches the °fishermen.
Then he °jumps up and °runs!

5 Cyril and Sandy's day

p. 130

Write about Cyril and Sandy. Pick the right form of the verbs.

1 In the morning I ... up early.

2 Sandy is lazy. She ... up late.

3 I usually ... breakfast on the beach.

4 I often ... my friends.

5 We ... swimming together.

6 Sandy often ... to Plymouth with her friends.

More practice 2 p. 131

6 NOW YOU

a) Make notes about your day. You can use a mind map.

More help p. 131

b) Use your notes and write a text about your day. You can put it in your DOSSIER[1].

More help p. 131

1 ['dɒsieɪ]

1 Before you read

Look at the photos. Is Luca's birthday fun?
Talk to a partner.

– I think Luca's birthday is / isn't fun.
– Look at photo ... He's happy / unhappy.

Happy birthday, Luca!

2.10

1 It's Thursday. Luca's birthday is on Saturday. He wants to do something different for his birthday. But what? He has no ideas.

2 It's Saturday morning. Luca is excited. It's his birthday. He likes his presents.

3 Mum is at work. Grace and dad are at the shops. Luca and Jack are on their bikes.

Box: Voc., p. 196

1 [plɪməθ pə'vɪliənz] 2 ['kɒnsət] 3 [həʊ]

► DFF 3.7 ► DFF 3.8

4 Jack and Luca go to the Hoe. Jack meets his friends. They have great BMX bikes and they go down the hill fast.

5 Jack goes down the hill first. He's OK. Now it's Luca's turn.

6 Luca goes down the hill. But he falls.

7 Luca and Jack are back from the hospital. Luca has a sore leg. His mum is not happy!

2 Right or wrong?

1 Luca wants a party.
2 Luca likes mum's idea.
3 Luca and Jack go shopping with dad on Saturday.
4 Jack meets his friends at the Hoe.
5 Luca goes down the hill first.
6 Luca falls.
7 Luca stays in the hospital.
8 Luca is happy at home.

3 Luca's birthday

Write the story.

On Thursday Luca has no ideas for ...
But his mum has a great ...
On Saturday morning Luca gets ...
Later the boys meet Jack's friends at ...
Jack goes down ...
Then Luca goes ..., but ...
Jack and Luca go ...
Luca has ...

More help p. 132

4 The end of the story

2.11

a) Listen to the end of the story. Who comes to Luca's house? Is Luca happy in the end?

b) Listen again. What presents does Luca get from his friends?

► Workbook 14–16, p. 43

1 Luca's garage[1] sale

▸ Language file 5, p. 168

More help p. 132

a) Luca needs money for a new bike. Look at the picture. What's in Luca's garage sale? Make two lists:

There's …	There are …
a bike	2 footballs
a …	3 …

2.12 **b)** Look at your lists. Listen and tick (✓) in your list what you hear.

c) Listen again. How much are the things in the garage sale? //● p. 133

1 The calculator is …
2 The mobile is …
3 The crab is …
4 The posters are …
5 The computer is …
6 The school bag is …
7 The blazer is …
8 The footballs are …

£5 £20 £9.50 £10 £4 £1 £5.50 50p

You write:	You say:
£1.50	One pound fifty
50 p	Fifty p

2 British money

a) Write labels for a sale: A: £1.50, B: …

A: One pound fifty
B: Ninety-nine p
C: Seventeen pounds
D: Four pounds twenty-five
E: Five pounds thirty

b) What do you say? Practise with a partner.

1 £3.99
2 20p
3 £8.50
4 £11.25
5 £24.90
6 £15

More practice 3 p. 133
2.13

1 [gæraːʒ]

▸ Workbook 17–18, p. 44

▸ KV 32 ▸ DFF 3.2 ▸ DFF 3.9 ▸ Folie 22 ▸ INKL 3.10

2.14

1 In a bike shop

Can Luca buy his dream bike? Read and find out.

Luca — Mum, it's the Montana. It's my dream bike.
Mum — It **looks** nice. Is it expensive? Box: Voc., p. 197
Luca — **Excuse me**, please. How much is this bike?
Man — It's £ 279.
Luca — That's too expensive. How much is the 5 Star?
Man — It's £ 159. It's a **special offer**.
Mum — That's OK. It looks nice too.
Luca — Yeah, and it's **good value**[2]. Jack has **the same** bike. Can I buy it, Mum?
Mum — It's your money.
Luca — Can I **try** it?
Man — Sure.
Luca — ... Wow, it's really great. **I'll take it**.
Man — Good. **That's** £ 159, please.

2 A new **helmet**

a) Copy and complete the dialogue. Look at 1 for help.

Luca — This helmet looks ... (1). I like it. Excuse me, ... (2). How ... (3) is the red helmet?
Man — ... (4) £ 24.99.
Luca — That's too ... (5)! ... (6) much is the white helmet?
Man — It's a ... (7) offer. It's £ 16.99.
Luca — That's OK. I'll ... (8) it. More help p. 133

2.15 **b)** Listen to the dialogue and check.

3 ROLE-PLAY

A garage sale

Partner B: Go to page 119.
Partner A: You're at a garage sale in Plymouth. You have £ 15. Buy some things.

Excuse me, please.
How much is the ...?
That's too expensive / OK!
I'll take it.
Here you are.

Swap roles.

▸ Workbook 19–20, p. 45

2 ['vælju:]

▸ INKL 3.11 ▸ DFF 3.5

1 Plymouth adverts[1)]

Match the sentences with the adverts: A, B or C. Sometimes there are two answers.

1 You can go there in February. – *Adverts A, C.*
2 You like music.
3 You like fish and the sea.
4 It's summer in Plymouth.
5 You can go there in July.
6 You can go there in March.
7 You don't need money.
8 You can watch a film here.

A

B

C

2 Guessing new words

What are these words in German?

1 on stage (advert A), fireworks (advert B)
2 theatre (advert A), festival (advert B)
3 opening times (advert C), adults (advert C)

So kannst du manche neue Wörter verstehen:
1. Schau auf die Bilder.
2. Gibt es ein ähnliches Wort im Deutschen?
3. Schau auf die Wörter vor oder nach dem Wort.

More help p. 133 More practice 4 p. 134

▸ Skills file 3, p. 163

1 ['ædvɜːts]

▸ Workbook 21, p. 46

1 The kids from Harbour Road: Sarah isn't happy!

a) Watch part 1 of the film. Why isn't Sarah with Anna and Paul at the shops?

1 Because Paul and Anna don't like Sarah.
2 Because Sarah hates shopping.
3 Because they want to buy Sarah a present.

b) Watch part 2 of the film. Then match the photos (1–4) with the sentences (A–D).

1
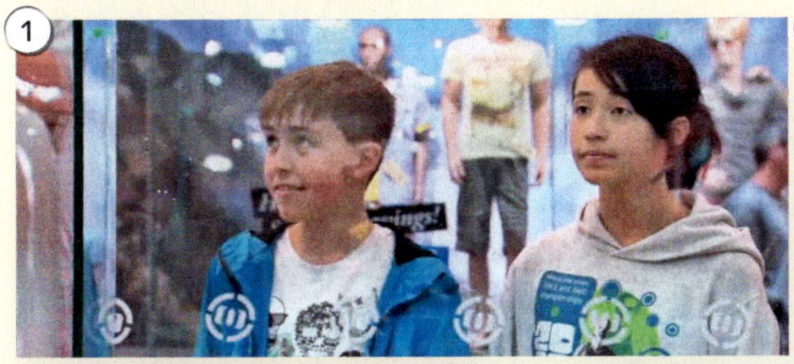
2

3

4

A It's £5.99.
B I'll take this hat[1], please.
C This is Sarah's favourite shop.
D What about this one[2]?

c) Watch part 3. Describe Sarah's feelings.
First she's ... Then she's ... Then ... In the end she's ...

angry[3] • happy • surprised[4] • unhappy

2 People and places: Plymouth, England

a) Watch the film about Plymouth. Which places can you see in the film?

The Reel Cinema

The Hoe[5)]

The Lido[6)]

The aquarium

The shopping centre

The market

b) What do you think about Plymouth? What place do you want to visit?

Plymouth looks big / nice / great / boring / ...

I want to visit / see the ... What about you?

[1] hat [hæt] *Hut* [2] this one *der/die/das da* [3] angry ['æŋgri] *wütend* [4] surprised [sə'praɪzd] *überrascht*

5 [həʊ] 6 ['laɪdəʊ]

STOP! CHECK! GO!

▸ INKL 3.12 ▸ KV 34 ▸ DFF 3.1 ▸ DFF 3.2 ▸ DFF 3.3

Ein Lösungsblatt für die Aufgaben 1 bis 5 kannst du von deiner Lehrerin / deinem Lehrer erhalten.
Die Hörtexte (S. 66) findest du auch auf der Audio-CD im Workbook.

1 WORDS In a town

a) ○ What are the places? Write the names in your exercise book.

b) Finish the sentences.

1 You can watch a film in a ...
2 You can buy vegetables in a ... or a ...
3 You can buy trainers in a ...

c) ● Make sentences.

1 ... in a park. → *You can play games in a park.*
2 ... in a restaurant. → *You can ...*
3 ... in a shopping centre.
4 ... in a swimming pool.
5 ... in a mobile phone shop.
6 ... in a bike shop.

More help p. 134

2 LISTENING In a sports shop

2.16

Listen to Ellie. She's in a sports shop. Pick the right answer – A, B or C.

	A	B	C
1 Ellie wants ...	a T-shirt.	a hoodie.	a sweatshirt.
2 The hoodie is ...	£ 14.99.	£ 40.19.	£ 40.99.
3 The T-shirts are ...	good value.	expensive.	a special offer.
4 The red trainers are ...	£ 58.	£ 85.	£ 18.50.
5 The white trainers are ...	expensive.	boring.	good value.
6 Ellie buys ...	a T-shirt.	trainers.	a hoodie.

3 WORDS Days, months and dates

a) ○ Write correct questions.

1 month / what / it / is ?
2 your / when's / birthday ?
3 date / it / what / is / today ?
4 best friend's / when's / your / birthday ?
5 day / what / today / is / it ?

b) What do you write?

1 3. 1. – *3rd January*
2 9. 3. – ...
3 12. 5. – ...
4 18. 7. – ...
5 20. 10. – ...
6 25. 12. – ...

2.17 **c)** ● Listen. Write the six dates.

4 REVISION Stupid Cyril!

a) Cyril has lots of questions for Sandy. Write the questions with *Is* or *Are*.

1 ... Eggbuckland school busy?
Is Eggbuckland school busy?
2 ... the students at school ?
3 ... Luca on his bike ?
4 ... the town quiet?
5 ... Grace and Mr Boateng at the market?
6 ... Mrs Boateng at work?

b) Write Sandy's answers.

1 No, ...
No, it isn't.
2 No, ...
3 Yes, ...
4 Yes, ...
5 No, ...
6 No, ... It's Sunday, Cyril! You stupid crab!

5 LANGUAGE Cyril's birthdays

a) Complete the text with the words in the box.

get up • go • have • love • meet • play • talk

On Cyril's birthdays Cyril and Sandy usually ... (1) early. They ... (2) to the beach. They ... (3) about the day.

Cyril — It's my birthday today. I always ... (4) a party. I ... (5) all my friends.

Sandy — Great! I ... (6) your parties. We always ... (7) lots of games.

b) Complete this text. Use the *simple present*.

come • go • help • make • plan • stay • work

Sandy always ... (1) to the market. She usually ... (2) home with lots of nice things: vegetables and pizza. Cyril always ... (3) at home. He ... (4) in the kitchen. He ... (5) a big birthday lunch for his friends. Cyril always ... (6) lots of good games. Sandy ... (7) Cyril with the games too.

c) Complete the sentences about Cyril's parties with the verbs in brackets. Use the simple present.

1 All Cyril's friends ... (come) to the party.
2 Cyril always ... (get) lots of presents.
3 Sandy ... (meet) Cyril's friends.
4 They usually ... (play) games.
5 They often ... (go) swimming in the sea.
6 Cyril ... (have) a great day.

6 SPEAKING At the weekend

a) What about your weekends? Copy the table. Fill in the table for you.
Write: always, usually, often, sometimes, never.

At the weekend	Me	Partner 1	Partner 2
I ... go shopping.	often	...	...
I ... play football.	...		
I ... watch TV			
I ... go to the cinema.			
I ... meet friends.			
I ...			

b) Appointments: Talk to two partners and fill in the table.

I **sometimes** go shopping at the weekend. What about you?

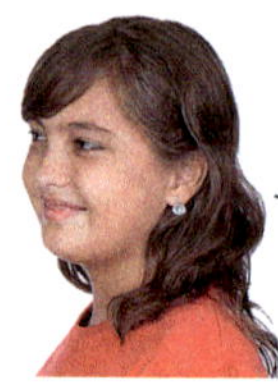

I **usually** go shopping at the weekend. And I ...

c) Use your table. Tell the class about one of your partners. Don't say the name. Can the class guess?

This girl **usually** goes shopping at the weekend.
She **never** plays football.
She **sometimes** watches TV.
...

Is it Lisa?

Is it Abida?

7 WRITING My favourite day

Write about your favourite day.

My favourite day is
- Friday.
- Saturday.
- ...

I get up
- early.
- late.
- ...

Then I have breakfast
- in the kitchen.
- with ...
- ...

After breakfast I
- play ...
- meet friends ...
- go to ...
- ...

I have lunch
- at home with ...
- in town with ...
- ...

In the afternoon I
- go shopping.
- ride my bike ...
- ...

In the evening I
- visit ...
- watch ...
- ...

I love	Friday Saturday ...	because	– I go to school. – I stay at home. – I do something different. – I meet my friends. – ...

Use **always** · **usually** · **often** · **sometimes** · **never**:
– I often get up late.
– Then I always have breakfast ...
– I never go shopping.

► DFF 3.5 ► INKL 3.12

8 READING Casper[1] the cat

a) ○ Look at the text. Is it from a book, a comic or a newspaper? What do you think?

THE PLYMOUTH NEWS — Saturday, 16th January 2010

A cat story from Plymouth

Casper is a cat. He's twelve. He lives in Plymouth with Susan Finden.

Every morning Casper leaves the house at the same time. He walks to the bus stop and he waits there for the number 3 bus. When it comes, Casper gets on the bus. He sits on a seat and looks out of the window. The bus goes to the centre. Then it goes to the harbour. Casper watches everything. He watches the people, the cars, the buses, the houses. The bus travels 11 miles. When the bus comes to Casper's house again, the bus driver opens the doors and Casper gets out.

Everybody on the bus knows Casper. Everybody loves Casper. And Casper loves the number 3 bus. But he never buys a ticket.

b) Read the text. Finish the sentences and tell Casper's story.

Casper is a ... (1). He's from ... (2). Every day he travels on the number 3 ... (3). He watches ... (4). Everybody loves ... (5). Casper never ... (6).

c) ● Find these words in the text.
Guess what they mean in German.

1 leaves (line 3)
2 bus stop (l. 4)
3 waits (l. 4)
4 sits (l. 5)
5 window (l. 6)
6 travels (l. 8)
7 bus driver (l. 9)
8 gets out (l. 9)

More help p. 134

Was hat dir geholfen, unbekannte Wörter zu verstehen?
– Das Bild zum Text?
– Ein ähnliches deutsches Wort?
– Andere Wörter im Text?

9 My learner log

Copy and complete your learner log.

You can put it in your DOSSIER.

My learner log

I can ...	Examples	😀	😐	☹
– say the names of places in a town:	cinema ...	...	...	
– say what I do at the weekend:	I often go shopping.	...	...	
– say what I do every day:		...	...	...
– say what I like and don't like:		...	...	...
– say the numbers 1–100:		...	...	...
– say the months:		...	...	...
– say today's date:		...	...	...
– say what I do on my birthday:		...	...	...
– buy things in a shop:		...	...	...

My progress in English is: GREAT! / OK / NOT VERY GOOD

► Workbook pp. 48–50

1 ['kæspə]

Unit 4

Berry's world

▸ KV 4A ▸ IAT 4.1 ▸ INKL 4.1

1 On Merryweather Farm
How many different animals can you find in the brochure[1]?
Check with a partner.

Welcome to Merryweather Farm

Lots of visitors come to Merryweather Farm.

Watch the ducks on the pond!

Children can ride the ponies in the fields.

You can meet the animals in Pets Corner.

1 ['brəʊʃə]

You can go into the **barn** and **stroke** the **donkeys**.

Everybody loves the °**trampolines**[2] and the °**zip wire**.

There are lots of nice things in the shop.

2 Welcome to the farm

2.18

a) Which animals are on Berry's farm? Listen. Write the numbers or point at the pictures (1–12).

b) Listen again. Pick the right answer.

1 Berry is ... A in the field. B in the shop. C in the barn.

2 The tickets are ... A £15.50. B £60.00. C £59.50.

3 They don't have ... A cows. B sheep. C pigs.

4 The kids don't like ... A pets. B rats. C cats.

5 The toilets are near the ... A shop. B field. C barn.

More practice 1 p.135

3 NOW YOU

a) Think: You're at Merryweather Farm. Where do you want to go? Pick two places.

b) Pair: Talk to a partner. Agree on two places.

- I want to go to the zip wire / ...
- I like donkeys / ...
- I don't like ...
- ... are boring / great / nice.
- OK. Let's go to ... and ...

c) Share: Tell the class.

▸ Workbook 1–2, p. 51

2 ['træmpəli:n]

Life on the farm

1 From Monday to Friday

2.19

Box: Voc., p. 198

Berry doesn't have an alarm clock. She has Sam. Sam is Berry's dog. Every morning Sam wakes Berry at 6 o'clock. He lives in the house with the family. The other animals don't live in the house. They live outside on the farm.

Berry goes outside before breakfast. She feeds her pony, Harry.

After breakfast Berry gets ready for school. She doesn't go to school by bus. She goes by car with her dad.
Berry stays at school all day. She usually comes home before 4 o'clock. Then she eats something and does her homework.

At about 5.30 she goes outside again. Sam comes too. First she looks after Harry. Then she helps with the other animals. She sometimes does sport in the evening. She doesn't watch TV. She doesn't have time!

Read the text. Then finish the sentences.

1 Every morning ... (mum / the alarm clock / the dog) wakes Berry.
2 Before breakfast she ... (watches TV / does nothing / feeds Harry).
3 She goes to school by ... (car / bike / bus) .
4 She comes home ... (at 4 o'clock / before 4 o'clock / after 4 o'clock).
5 In the evening she sometimes ... (does nothing / watches TV / does sport).

2 NOW YOU

a) Write sentences.

1 Every morning my ... wakes me.
2 Before breakfast I ...
3 I go to school by ... / I walk to school with ...
4 I come home at / before / after ... o'clock.
5 In the evening I ...

More help p. 135

b) Tell a partner about your day.

▸ Workbook 3–5, p. 52

3 At the weekend

a) Look at the board. Then put the photos (A–F) in the right order.

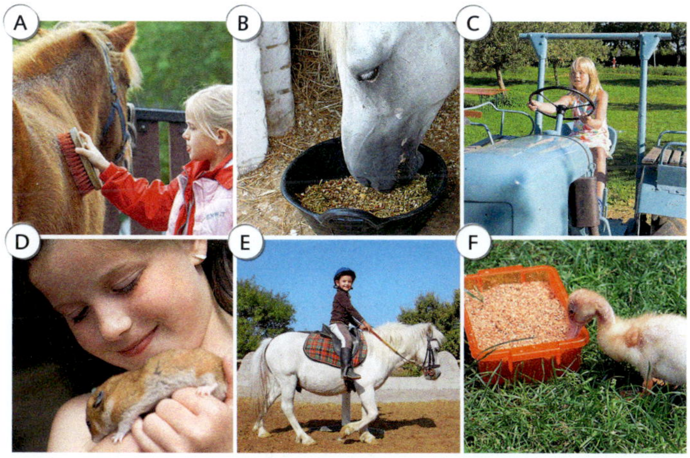

2.20 **b)** Listen to the four dialogues.
What activities (A–F) do the visitors want to do?
Dialogue[2)] 1 is photo …, …

c) Listen again. What's the right time?
Dialogue 1: 10.40 / 10.45
Dialogue 2: 10.55 / 11.15
Dialogue 3: 12.00 / 12.45
Dialogue 4: 4.30 / 4.45

4 The time

2.21 **a)** Listen and repeat.

1.00 10.00 12.05 4.05 5.10 9.15 7.20

8.25 3.30 12.30 11.35 2.45 6.50 1.55

You write:	You say:
2.00	two o'clock
2.05	two oh five
2.15	two fifteen
2.30	two thirty
2.45	two forty-five

2.22 **b)** Say one of the times in a). Your partner points at it.

c) Listen and write the times.

Sometimes people say:
– °quarter past two (2.15)
– °half past two (2.30)
– °quarter to three (2.45)

More practice 2 p. 135

Name	Time
Paul	6.15
…	…

5 What's the time, please?

a) Draw a digital clock and write a time on it.

b) Talk to a partner like this:
A: What's the time please? B: It's … Box: Voc., p. 199
A: Thanks. B: You're welcome.
Write your partner's name and time.
Then swap clocks.

c) Walk around: Find a new partner. Write your new partner's time.
Then swap clocks again. Talk to as many partners as you can.

▸ Workbook 6–8, p. 53

1 ['gru:mɪŋ] 2 ['daɪəlɒg]

▸ KV 37 ▸ INKL 4.5

Feelings

2.23

1 A class discussion

a) Ms Lee, the English teacher, has two questions for the students in her class.

Partner A: Copy table A. Listen and write the names: Adam, Luca, Berry or Ellie.

Partner B: Copy table B. Listen and write the names: Adam, Luca, Berry or Ellie.

A

I feel great when ...	
... I do sport.	Luca, ...
... I'm with my animals.	
... I'm with my friends.	
... I listen to music.	
... I don't have homework.	

B

I feel fed up when ...	
... my sister is bossy.	Ellie
... my mobile doesn't work.	
... my friends don't text me.	
... people don't talk to me.	
... I have lots of homework.	

b) Swap[1] tables with your partner. Listen again and check your partner's answers.

2 NOW YOU

a) When do you feel great? When do you feel fed up? Make notes like this:

More help p. 135

I feel great ...	I feel fed up ...
when I play football.	when my dad is bossy.
when I ...	...
...	

b) Talk to your partner.
Ask and answer the questions:

When do you feel great?

When ...

When do you feel fed up?

When ...

c) Write two sentences on a piece of paper. Then put it on the wall.

I feel really great when ...	I feel really fed up when ...

d) Reading circle: Walk round and read other people's sentences. You can write your name and a comment:
Me too! or *Not me!*

1 [swɒp]

▸ KV 37 ▸ DFF 4.7 ▸ Folie 24 ▸ INKL 4.6

3 Berry's homework

2.24

a) Read Berry's homework.
Put the photos in the right order.

Feelings *by Berry Donovan*

I feel great when I'm with the animals at home. I really love animals.

I sometimes feel a bit fed up because I'm the only student at school in a wheelchair. I'm always different.

But I feel great when I'm with my friends. With my friends I'm not 'the girl in the wheelchair'. I'm a normal teenager!

I feel great when I do sport. My favourite sport is wheelchair basketball. When I'm in my wheelchair I can go really fast. And I feel really great when my team wins.

I feel really fed up when people don't talk to me. They do that because I'm in a wheelchair. They ask my mum: 'Does she want a drink?' They don't ask ME: 'Do YOU want a drink?' At school people ask my friends: 'Does she understand?' But I can speak for myself. My legs don't work well. But my mouth works fine.

A

B

C

D

E

b) Read the text again. Find sentences in the text for the photos.
Example: Photo A – I feel great when I'm with my friends.

c) Copy and complete Berry's notes.

I feel great	I feel fed up
when I'm with ...	because I'm ...
when ...	when ...

d) Write a short text about your feelings. Use your notes from exercise 2 on page 74. Write more than one sentence for each feeling. You can put your text in your DOSSIER[2].

More help p. 136

▸ Workbook 9–10, p. 54

2 ['dɒsier]

1 A pet or a wild animal?

2.25

Berry has lots of pets. But do Ellie, Luca or Adam have pets? Can you remember? Read and check.

Luca Do you have a cat or a dog, Adam?
Adam No, we don't have a pet.
Luca What about you, Ellie? Do you have a pet?
Ellie Yes, I do. I have two cats at mum's house.
Luca What about your dad? Does he have a pet?
Ellie No. Dad and Alisha don't have a pet. They don't have time.
Berry And what about you, Luca?
Luca No, we don't have a pet. Dad is the problem. He doesn't like dogs.
Adam And what about your mum? Does she like animals?
Luca She likes dogs, but she doesn't like cats. But I want a pet!
Ellie I have an idea. What about a °chipmunk[1)]?
Luca A chipmunk? Does it look like a monkey?

A chipmunk

Ellie No, it doesn't look like a monkey – you °idiot[2)].
Berry We have chipmunks on the farm. They're small and furry[3)]. They're really cute.
Ellie Do they like cats?
Berry No, they don't like other animals. And they hate cats!
Luca I want a chipmunk.
Berry I don't know. A chipmunk is a wild animal. It isn't really a good pet for a house.
Luca Oh!

2 The simple present – negative sentences

a) Put in *doesn't* or *don't*.

1 We ... have a pet. (line 2)
2 They ... have time. (l. 10)
3 He ... like dogs. (l. 13)
4 She ... like cats. (l. 16–17)
5 It ... look like a monkey. (l. 22)
6 I ... know. (l. 31)

b) Complete the rules with *doesn't* or *don't*.

FOCUS No

I, you, we, they	+	...	+ verb
he, she, it	+	...	+ verb

▸ Language file 7, p. 169

3 NOW YOU

Write sentences about you.

1 I have / don't have a pet.
2 My mum /dad likes / doesn't like animals.
3 We have / don't have a big garden.
4 I like / don't like cats / dogs / chipmunks / ...
5 My best friend has / doesn't have a pet.
6 He / She wants / doesn't want a dog / cat / ...

1 ['tʃɪpmʌŋk] 2 ['ɪdiət] 3 ['fɜːri]

4 That's wrong!

a) Complete the sentences. Use *doesn't* or *don't*. // p. 136

1 Berry lives in the city. – That's wrong! She doesn't live in ...
2 Berry's parents have a pet shop. – That's wrong! They don't ...
3 Berry rides a donkey. – That's wrong! She ...
4 Berry has a cat. – That's wrong! She ...
5 Berry's mum and dad have cows on the farm. – That's wrong! They ...
6 Sam the dog lives in the field. – That's wrong! He ...
7 Berry goes to school in Woolwell. – That's wrong! She ...
8 Luca and Adam have dogs. – That's wrong! They ...
9 Ellie has two ponies. – That's wrong! She ...
10 Chipmunks like cats. – That's wrong! They ...

b) Work with a partner. Write five wrong sentences about Ellie, Luca and Adam. Swap your sentences with other students. Can you correct all the sentences?

5 My interesting pets // p. 136

Complete the text. Put in *don't* or *doesn't*.

1 I live in a small flat and we ... have a garden.
2 My mum likes small pets. She ... want a big pet.
3 I ... have a 'normal' pet, like a dog. I have three °degus.
4 A degu ... come from England. It comes from Chile.
5 A degu needs a friend. It ... like to be lonely. Box: Voc., p. 200
6 Degus need lots of space. They ... like small cages.
7 And degus ... like other animals. They hate dogs and cats.
8 I often play with Pip, my favourite degu. But we ... go outside.

Me and my degu[4]

6 The simple present – questions

a) Put *do* or *does* in the questions.
You can look at text 1 on p. 76 again.

1 ... you have a pet? (line 4)
2 ... he have a pet? (l. 8)
3 ... she like animals? (l. 15)
4 ... it look like a monkey? (l. 20)
5 ... they like cats? (l. 27)

b) Complete the rules with *do* or *does*.

FOCUS ?

... + I, you, we, they + verb ?
... + he, she, it + verb ?

▸ *Language file 8, p. 170*

7 NOW YOU

a) Complete the questions with *do* or *does*.

1 What about you? ... you like animals?
2 What about your parents? ... they like animals?
3 And your best friend? ... he / she have a pet?
4 And your teacher? ... he / she have a pet?

2.26 **b)** Listen. Answer the questions about you.

Yes, I do.

No, I don't.

4 ['deɪguː, 'deguː]

8 A good pet?

2.27

Are rats good pets? Read and find out.

Luca — What pets do you have, Berry?
Berry — I have a dog – Sam. And we have hamsters, rabbits, chipmunks and rats.
Luca — Rats? Are they good pets?
Berry — Yes. I love our rats.
Ellie — Why do you love rats? Box: Voc., p. 200
Berry — Because they're friendly. They play. They sit on my shoulder. They're very cute.
Luca — Where do they live?
Berry — They live in a cage in Pets Corner.
Adam — What do they eat?
Berry — Lots of things like fruit and nuts and ...
Ellie — When do they sleep?
Berry — At night. I have an idea. Come to the farm and see our pets.

9 Question words

a) Find five questions in the dialogue with question words: what, when, where, why.

b) Match the English and the German question words.

FOCUS

English:	German:	
What?	Was? Welche?	Warum?
When?		
Where?	Wo? Wohin?	Wann?
Why?		

▸ Language file 9, p. 170

10 What pet do you have?

Find the right question words for the interview.

1 ... pet do you have?
2 ... do you like rabbits?
3 ... does your rabbit live?
4 ... does your rabbit eat?
5 ... do you feed your rabbit?
6 ... other pets do you have?

– I have a rabbit. His name is Bunny.
– Because they're fun and friendly.
– He lives in a big cage in my room.
– He eats lots of things. He loves vegetables.
– In the morning and in the evening.
– A snake, a monkey, a fish, a duck, a ...

The orange words can help you.

11 Talking about pets

a) Make a dialogue with a partner.

▸ Wordbank 7, p. 177

A: Do you have a pet?

B: Yes, I do.
A: What pet do you have?
B: I have a ...
A: Where does your pet live?
B: It lives inside / outside / ...

B: No, I don't.
A: Do you want a pet?

B: Yes, I do.
A: What pet do you want?
B: I want a ...

B: No, I don't.
A: Why not?
B: Because ...

More practice 3 p. 137

b) Write about your favourite pet or a friend's pet. You can put your text in your DOSSIER. More help p. 137

▸ Workbook 14–16, p. 56

12 Who is it?

a) Match the answers (A–F) with the questions (1–6). Who is it?

1 When do you get up?
2 What do you like?
3 Where do you go to school?
4 When do you come home?
5 What do you do after school?
6 Where do you live?

A Eggy.
B Before 4 o'clock.
C I like my animals.
D Very early - at 6 o'clock.
E In Woolwell.
F My homework.

b) Make the questions for the answers. Who is it?

1 Where / you / live / do / ? – In Plymouth.
2 What / like / do / you / ? – My bike!
3 Where / to school / do / you / go / ? – In Plymouth too.
4 When / to the cinema / you / go / do / ? – At the weekend.
5 What / do / on Saturdays / you / do / ? – I ride my bike.
6 Where / bike / do / ride / you / your / ? – In Central Park.

c) Now make questions for these answers. Who is it?

1 On the beach in Kingsand.
2 I don't go to school!
3 On Saturdays I play with Sandy.
4 I like swimming and games.
5 I don't go to the cinema!
6 I get up late, at 10 o'clock.

13 Find a person who ...

a) You want to find interesting people in your class. Pick three things in this box – or more.

Find a person who ...
– has an interesting pet.
– has an interesting hobby.
– gets up very early.
– goes to a nice place in the holidays.
– likes an English football team.
– likes homework.

b) What questions can you ask? More help p. 137

Do you have a pet?

What pet do you have?

Do you go to a nice place in the holidays?

Where ...?

c) Walk around: Talk to different people. Ask your questions. Take notes.

d) Write about the interesting people in your class.

Dana has an interesting pet – a snake!
Jakob gets up very early – at about 6 o'clock.
Hanna loves homework. She loves maths!
Kenan ...

▸ KV 39 ▸ INKL 4.10 A/B

1 Before you read

Look at the pictures. Who is it – Adam, Berry, Ellie or Luca?

1 Ellie and ... are on the bus.
2 ... doesn't have his sweets.
3 ... has a problem with a chipmunk.
4 ... doesn't like cows.
5 Luca and ... are in the barn.
6 ... isn't nervous.

Adventures[1] in the country

2.28

Scene 1 Berry wants to invite her friends to the farm. This is her email.

> Hi guys
>
> Do you want to see our chipmunks? Do you want to come to the farm for a sleepover[2]? What about next Saturday? There's a bus at 3 o'clock. Bring your sleeping bags.
> Berry

Scene 2 It's 3 o'clock on Saturday. Luca, Ellie and Adam are excited. They all have their sleeping bags. Ellie has a bag with fruit. Adam has a bag with sandwiches.
"OK. Let's go!" Ellie says.
"Yeah, let's go to the country!" Adam says.
"Yeah, for lots of adventures!" Luca says.

Scene 3 It's 3.45. The three friends are in Woolwell. They are excited. But Luca is unhappy.
"Oh no!" Luca says. "I don't have my sweets."
"Don't worry, Luca," his friends say.
"We have lots of nice things." Box: Voc., p. 201

Scene 4 It's 4.30. The friends do a tour of the farm. They visit the donkeys, ponies and sheep in the fields. Then they go to Pets Corner.
"I want to stroke a chipmunk," Luca says.
"This is Lulu. Do you want her on your shoulder?" Berry asks. Box: Voc., p. 201
"Oh, she's very cute!" Ellie says.
"Look!" Adam says.
"Oh no! My shoulder is wet!" Luca says.
Everybody laughs.

1 [əd'ventʃə] 2 ['sliːpəʊvə]

Scene 5 It's 5.30.

"Let's eat," Ellie says.

"But we don't have nice things," Luca says.

"We have lots of nice things," Adam says.

"I want to buy sweets," Luca says. "Where's the village?" Box: Voc., p. 201

"OK, Luca. Go through that field," Berry says.

Scene 6 It's 6.15. Adam, Berry and Ellie are hungry.

"Where's Luca?" Adam asks.

"I want to eat," Ellie says.

Adam gets a text from Luca:

They go to the field.

"Help! It's a bull!" Luca says.

"It isn't a °bull. It's a cow," Berry says. "Cows aren't dangerous[3]!"

Everybody laughs. But Luca doesn't laugh.

Scene 7 It's 11 o'clock. The four friends are in sleeping bags in the barn.

"What's that noise?" Adam asks. He's nervous.

"It's a donkey," Berry says.

"What's that noise?" Ellie asks.

"It's a sheep," Berry says.

"Oh no! What's that noise?" Luca asks.

"Oh, Luca! It's only a chicken," Berry says. "Go to sleep!"

"Good night," everybody says.

Scene 8 On Sunday the friends have lots of fun. They play on the trampolines. They ride Harry, Berry's pony. They feed the animals. In the afternoon Ellie, Adam and Luca go back to Plymouth by bus.

"Thanks Berry. It's great here," Ellie says.

"Yeah, I love the country," Adam says.

"It's nice, but I'm a city boy," Luca says.

"And I'm a country girl," Berry says.

2 The scenes

a) Match the headings with the scenes (1–8) in the story.

A cute chipmunk | Time to go home | Time to eat | Let's go to the country | Noises at night | Come to a sleepover | No sweets! | A dangerous animal?

b) Check with a partner.

3 Questions on the story

Answer the questions in 1–5 words.

1 How do the three friends go to Woolwell?
– By ...

2 What's in Adam's bag?

3 What animals do they see on the farm?

4 What animal does Luca meet in the field?

5 Who's nervous at night?

6 Who's a country girl?

More practice 4 p. 138

4 THEATRE TIME

Work in groups of five. Pick a scene from the story. Read and act the scene.

More help p. 138

3 [ˈdeɪndʒərəs]

▸ IAT 4.2

1 READING Signs in Plymouth

Look at the signs. Then match the sentences (1–5) with the signs (A–E).

1 You can get the bus here. → Sign ...
2 You can find this sign at a restaurant.
3 This sign is on Berry's farm.
4 This sign is in a park in Plymouth.
5 People in wheelchairs, please go left.

A

B

C

D
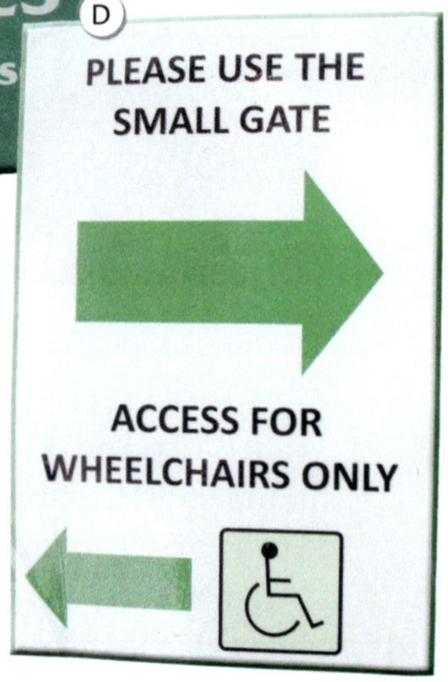

E

Du kannst die Schilder verstehen, auch wenn du nicht jedes Wort kennst.

2 MEDIATION Understanding the signs

a) Partner A: Imagine you're in Plymouth. Answer partner B's questions – in German.
Partner B: You can't understand the signs in Plymouth. Ask partner A three questions. Then swap roles.

1 Schild A: Warum steht der Hund hinter Gittern? Ist er im Gefängnis?
2 Schild A: Was bedeutet „No smoking"?
3 Schild B: Ich habe Hunger. Können wir hier gleich frühstücken?
4 Schild C: Es geht um *animals*, also Tiere. Was dürfen wir nicht tun?
5 Schild D: Können wir hier hineingehen?
6 Schild E: Wie können wir herausfinden, wann der nächste Bus kommt?

b) Pick a sign and talk about it with your partner – in German.

Ich denke, man findet so ein Schild ...

Ja, und ...

So kannst du über Schilder sprechen:
– Man findet so ein Schild an einer Bushaltestelle / in der Stadt / ...
– Das Schild ist für Leute mit Hunden / Leute, die ...
– Du darfst / kannst / darfst hier nicht ...

▸ Workbook 21–22, p. 58

▸ DFF 4.9

1 A poem[1]

2.29

Read or listen to the poem and find out:

1 What's the title of the poem? Can you say it?
2 What does the writer want?
3 Who's the writer? A mum, a dad or a child?

2 Do you need a dictionary[2]?

a) Find the English words for these animals in the poem.

Du kennst schon viele Tierwörter, andere sind neu, aber du kannst sie erraten.

b) Write these animal words on small cards. Then put them in alphabetical order.

stoat | budgie | owl | guinea pig | parrot | kitten | horse

Einige Tierwörter musst du im Wörterbuch nachschlagen (ab S. 208). Bringe die Wörter zuerst in eine alphabetische Reihenfolge, dann findest du sie schneller.

c) Now write these animal words on cards too. Put all the words from 2b and 2c in alphabetical order.

goat | peahen | stick insect | gibbon | puppy

d) Which animal words do you need to look up? Find the words in the Dictionary (pp. 208–218). Write the German words under the English words or on the back of the cards.

Box: Voc., p. 202

Muuuuuuummmmmm

Can we have a °kitten
Can we have a dog
Can we call her Frisky
Can we call him Bob?
I can take him out each day
I can brush his fur
I will buy the dog meat
And milk to make her purr
Mum!!

Oh … no … well –

Can we have a donkey
Or can we have a °horse
A monkey or a °parrot
Hamster or a snake?
Can we have a °guinea pig[3]
A °peahen[4]
Or a °stoat[5]
°Llama[6] or a °budgie[7]
A rabbit or a °goat?

Can we have a crocodile
°Gibbon or an °owl
All the zoos are closing
There's lots and lots around …
A °penguin[8] would be really good
Keep it in the bath
A °hyena[9] in the garden
To make the milkman laugh.

No, WE DON'T WANT °stick insects
And °goldfish aren't much fun …
Oh can we have a °puppy …
Mum, mum, muuuuuuummmmmmm.

Peter Dixon

▸ Skills file 4, p. 164

1 [ˈpəʊɪm] 2 [ˈdɪkʃənri] 3 [ˈgɪni pɪg] 4 [piːhen] 5 [stəʊt] 6 [ˈlɑːmə] 7 [ˈbʌdʒi] 8 [ˈpeŋgwɪn] 9 [haɪˈiːnə]

▸ Text file 5, pp. 156–158

1 The kids from Harbour Road: A class project

a) Watch the film.
Then complete the captions.

1 The kids meet outside the ...

2 Paul is busy with his ...

3 First they look at the ...

4 Then they ask lots of ...

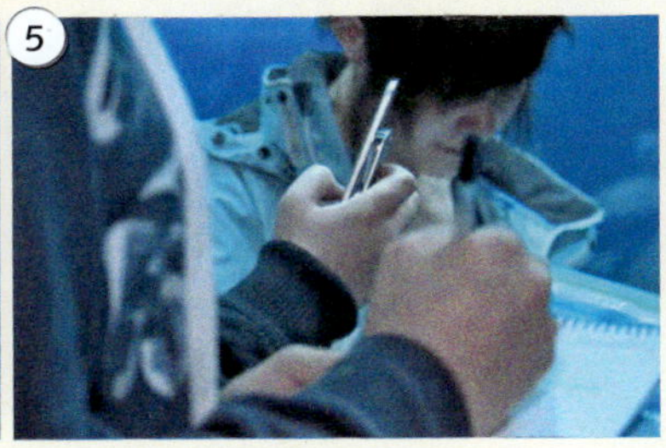
5 Sarah and Anna write notes, but Paul uses his ...

6 Paul has a big problem with his ...

b) Watch the film again. Try to remember: Who says it – Anna, Paul, or Sarah?

1 Let's do our project on sharks[1].
2 You're no help!
3 I love my new mobile.
4 Do sharks eat other fish in the tank[2]?
5 Do you think we have all the information?
6 Pens and paper are better than[3] mobile phones.

2 People and places: A normal day at school

a) Watch the film. Then talk about how Emily feels in the scenes: In scene A / B / ...

A Emily feels ... when she can't do things alone.

B Emily feels ... when her friends help her too much[4].

C Emily feels ... when people don't listen to her.

D Emily feels ... when Laura invites her.

b) Watch the film again. Is it a good or bad day for Emily?

[1]shark [ʃɑːk] *Haifisch* [2]tank [tæŋk] *Aquarium* [3]better than ['betə ðæn] *besser als* [4]too much *zu viel*

STOP! CHECK! GO!

▸ KV 42 ▸ DFF 4.1 ▸ DFF 4.2 ▸ INKL 4.12 A/B

Ein Lösungsblatt für die Aufgaben 1 bis 5 kannst du von deiner Lehrerin / deinem Lehrer erhalten. Den Hörtext (S. 86) findest du auch auf der Audio-CD im Workbook.

1 WORDS On Merryweather Farm

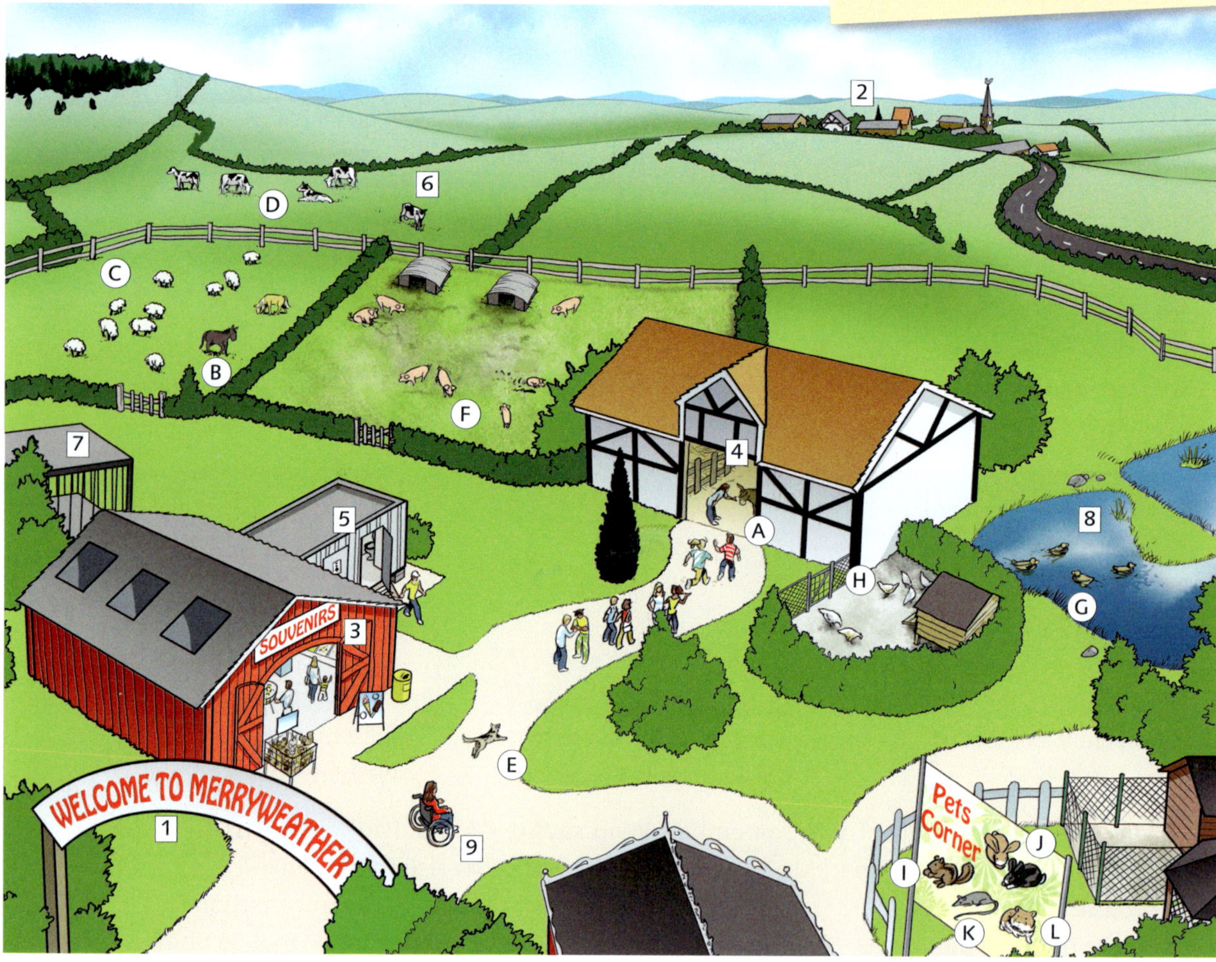

a) Match the things (1–9) in the picture with the words in the green box.

barn • cage • farm • field • pond •
toilet • shop • village • wheelchair

b) Name the animals (A-L) in the picture.

c) Close your book. What things and animals can you remember? Make a list – write as many as you can.
Compare with a partner.

2 WORDS Visitors at the farm

2.30

a) Listen to the phrases (1–8). Who's the speaker? Berry or a visitor? – *1 visitor, 2 …*

b) Listen again. Finish the sentences.

1 Excuse me, please. We want to visit …
2 When do you feed the …?
3 We feed the ducks at …
4 Excuse me, please. Where are the … ?
5 What's that …?
6 It's only a donkey. Don't …
7 Look at the hamsters. They're really …
8 Come on, Sam. Let's go …

c) Listen again and repeat.

3 REVISION A day with my family

a) Complete the text.

Every morning mum, dad and I ... (get up) at 6 o'clock.
After breakfast I ... (go) to school by car with my dad.
At about 9 o'clock the first visitors ... (come).
Mum and dad ... (have) lunch at 1 o'clock. After lunch dad usually ... (stay) in the shop and mum ... (work) with the ponies.
I ... (come) home from school with dad before 4 o'clock.
Dad ... (have) something to eat with me. Then we ... (go) outside. Sam ... (come) with me. We ... (look) after all the animals.
There's lots of work on a farm every day.

b) Make a table like this for a day with your family.
Then tell your partner.

When?	Who?	What?
every morning / before 6 o'clock	mum, dad and I	get up

More help p. 138

4 LANGUAGE An interview with Cyril and Sandy

// ● p. 139

a) Complete the reporter's questions with *do* or *does*.

1 ... you like Plymouth?
2 ... you have a best friend?
3 ... you and Sandy live on the beach?
4 ... Sandy like Plymouth too?
5 ... Sandy have a best friend?

– Yes, it's great.
– Yes, I do. Her name is Sandy.
– Yes, we live in Kingsand.
– Yes, she loves Plymouth.
– Yes, she does. I'm her best friend!

b) Complete Cyril's answers with *don't* or *doesn't*.

1 Do you like Mr Johnson?
2 Do you live in a big house?
3 Do you and Sandy go to school?
4 Does Sandy have a car?
5 Does Sandy eat crabs?

– No, I ... like Mr Johnson. He's terrible.
– No, I ... live in a big house. I like small houses.
– No, we ... go to school.
– No, she ... have a car. But she has a bike.
– No, she ... eat crabs. I'm a crab!

c) Match the questions with Sandy's answers.

1 Where do you live?
2 When do you get up?
3 Where do you have breakfast?
4 What do you do after breakfast?
5 Why do you like Cyril?

– Very late – after 10 o'clock.
– I always have breakfast on the beach.
– Because he's friendly and he's fun!
– In Kingsand.
– I often go to Plymouth.

STOP! CHECK! GO!

▸ *KV 42* ▸ *DFF 4.4* ▸ *INKL 4.12 A/B*

5 WORDS °Useful phrases

at • by • in • through • to (3x) • with

a) Find the right word for these phrases from the box.

1 Help! I'm ... trouble!
2 I want to go ... the toilet!
3 I get up ... 6 o'clock.
4 I go to school ... bus.
5 I listen ... music every evening.
6 I feel great when I'm ... my friends.
7 Go ... that field.
8 Go ... sleep. Good night!

b) ○ Match the phrases in a) with the pictures (A–H).

6 WRITING Luca and you

a) Write the dialogue with Luca in your exercise book. Write as many sentences as you can.

Luca	You
Hi, I'm Luca. What's your name?	– Hi, Luca. I'm ...
Do you live in England?	– No, I live in ...
Do you live in the country?	– ...
Do you like English?	– ...
Do you have a pet?	– ...
When do you feel fed up?	– ...
When do you feel great?	– ...
Do you want to come to Plymouth?	– ...

More help p.139

b) ● Write a dialogue between you and Luca.
Now you ask the questions – as many as you can.

7 SPEAKING An interview with a student in your class

a) Think of good questions for your interview. Write your six best questions on a piece of paper.

Example: *What do you ...?*
Where do you ...?
When do you ...?

More help p.140

b) Walk around: Find a partner.
Ask and answer your questions.
Then swap questions and find a new partner.

8 °PROJECT[1] Interesting animals

Find out about an interesting animal. You can work alone, with a partner or in a small group.

STEP 1: Pick an animal for your project.

budgie

elephant

guinea pig

tiger

polar bear

STEP 2: Pick five questions – or more – for your project.

Where do the animals come from? (what country) • What do they look like? (colour/furry) • Are they big or small? • How long[1] are they? • Where do they live? (cage/nest[2]) • Do they live inside/outside? • What do they eat? • What can they do? (run/swim/talk) • How long[1] do they live? (1 year/2 years) • Are they good pets?

STEP 3: Find the information on the internet. Go to www.cornelsen.de/lighthouse and put in the webcode LH-1-89.

STEP 4: Make a mind map like this:

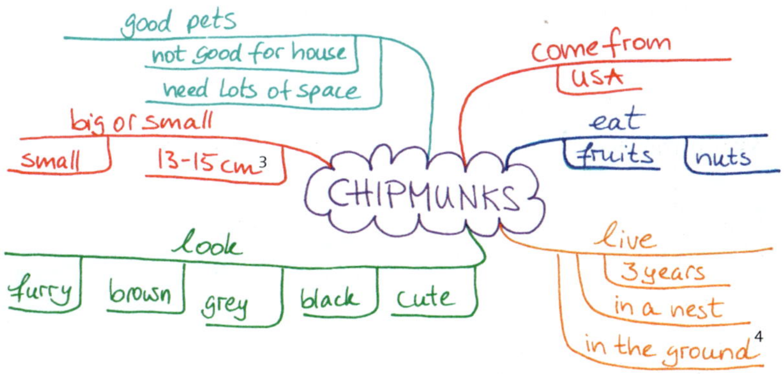

STEP 5: Pick a) OR b).

a) Talk about your animal for 1 minute.

b) Write a text about your animal. Find photos for your text. Then put the text on the wall. More help p. 140

9 My learner log

Copy and complete your learner log. You can put it in your DOSSIER.

My learner log

Now I can ...
- say the names of lots of animals: ...
- say the time: ...
- ask questions in an interview: ...
- say when I feel great or fed up: ...
- write an invitation:
- use a dictionary:

In Unit 4 ...
- my favourite text is on page ...
- my favourite words are ...
- my favourite phrases are ...
- my favourite people are ...
- difficult words are ...

My progress in English is: GREAT! / OK / NOT VERY GOOD

[1] how long? [haʊ 'lɒŋ] *wie lang? / wie lange?* [2] nest *Nest* [3] cm = centimetre ['sentɪmiːtə] *Zentimeter*
[4] ground [graʊnd] *Erde*

Unit 5 All about Adam

► Folie 1 ► IAT 5.1

1 The harbour[1] in Plymouth

a) Do you know the people in photos A–D? Who are they? Can you guess?
Example: I think the boy in photo C is ...

b) What can you see on pages 90–91? Name ten things. Write a list. More help p. 140

c) Choose one of the photos and talk about it with your partner.

In the big photo / In photo A / ... On the left / On the right / In the middle	there's a ... I can see ...

1 ['hɑːbə]

2 Adam's family

2.31

a) Adam is talking to Ellie. Listen and look at the small photos. Write the letters (A–D) in the right order.

b) Listen again. Answer the questions.

1 Where is Adam going?
   A To school. B To the cafe. C Home.
2 Where is Adam's dad working now?
   A In the cafe. B On the ferry.
   C In France.
3 What does Adam want to do?
   A Help in the cafe. B His homework.
   C Nothing.
4 Where is Adam's brother in the afternoons?
   A With his mum. B At school.
   C With his babysitter.

► Workbook 1, p. 65

In the cafe

1 Can I help you?

2.32 **a)** It's 4 pm in the cafe. Adam's mum is busy. Listen. Look at the photos. What things (A–J) do the customers want?

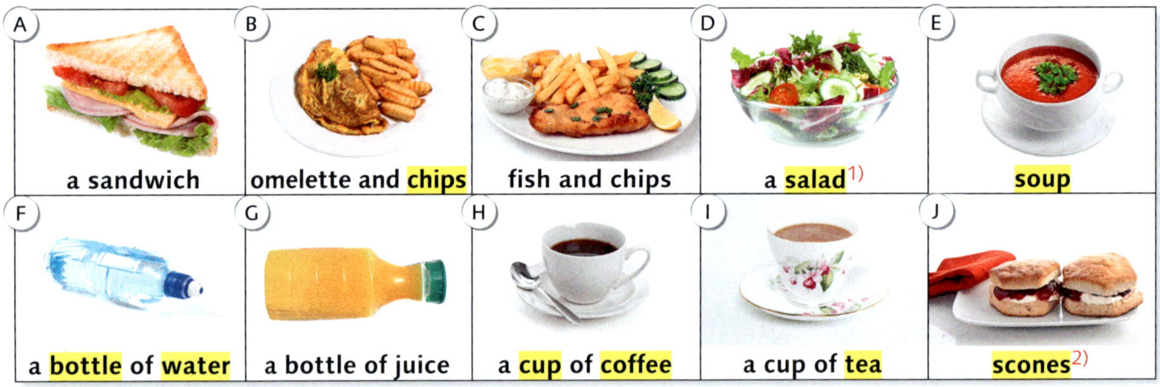

b) Listen again. Who says this – mum (write M) or a customer (write C)?

1 Can I help you?
2 One fish and chips, please.
3 Something to drink?
4 A bottle of water, please.
5 That's £10.50, please.
6 Next please.
7 Anything else?
8 No thanks. That's all.

2.33 **c)** Listen and repeat.

d) Make a dialogue in a cafe. Use words and phrases from a) and b).

More help p. 141

2 How's it going?

2.34 **a)** Does Adam's dad like his new job? Read and find out.

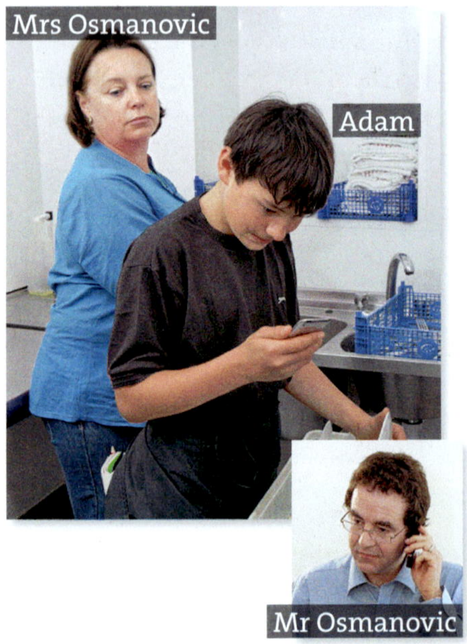

Adam is helping in the cafe. His mobile is ringing.

Adam Hey dad, how's it going?
Dad Fine, thanks. How's it going at home?
Adam Oh, OK. But I miss you! How's your new job on the ferry?
Dad It's great. But I miss you all too. Is mum busy[3)] now? Is she working?
Adam She's cooking. She can't talk to you. The cafe is busy.
Dad Oh, OK. Are you helping mum?
Adam Yeah, I'm washing up.
Dad That's great. But you must work hard at school too.
Adam Yeah, dad. Sorry, I must go. We're very busy here.
Dad OK. Say hi to everybody. Bye, Adam.
Adam Bye, dad. See you at the weekend.

b) Who's doing what? Write five sentences.
1 Dad is ... 2 Mum is ... 3 Adam is ... 4 ...

cooking • talking to Adam • washing up • working on a ferry • helping in the cafe

1 ['sæləd] 2 [skɔnz] 3 ['bɪzi]

▸ Workbook 2–3, p. 66

3 A letter from school

a) Read the letter. Is it good news for Adam?

Eggbuckland Community College
A DCSF Designated Technology College • **Principal : Katrina Borowski**
LEARNING - CARING - ACHIEVING

Dear Mr and Mrs Osmanovic

I'm a bit worried about Adam. I don't think he's very happy at the moment. He isn't working very hard at school. He isn't doing his homework and he's often tired. Please phone me and we can talk about it.

Best wishes

R Lee

Class 7 teacher

b) What do you think Adam's mother says?

1 Ms Lee is ... about you, Adam.
2 Miss Lee thinks that you aren't very ... at the moment.
3 You aren't working very hard ...
4 You are ... tired at school.
5 I'm ... about this letter, Adam. More practice 1 p. 141

4 What's happening?

a) It's 7 pm. Look at Adam's family and friends. What are they doing?
Look at the box and complete the sentences.

doing homework • eating • playing a game • reading a book • riding a bike • riding a pony • watching TV • working

1 Mum is ...
2 The boys are ...
3 Dad is ...
4 Berry is ...
5 Luca is ...
6 Ellie and Zoe are ...

b) One student mimes one of the activities in the green box. The other students guess. Then swap roles.

You're doing homework.
Wrong.
You're reading a book.
Right.

It's boring at home!

1 Trouble for Adam

2.35

a) Look at the pictures. Where's Adam? Who is with Adam?

1

It's Tuesday, after school. Adam is in his mum's cafe. He's helping.
"Go home, Adam. You can't stay here. You must do your homework," his mum says.

2

Adam thinks, "It's so boring at home! No mum, no dad, and Zack is with his new baby-sitter." But then he has an idea. Now he's phoning his friends. "Hey, come to the harbour."

3

Adam is diving. His friends are diving too. They're having lots of fun. But diving in the harbour is dangerous.

4

Zack and Alisha are walking in the harbour.
"Oh no! It's my brother and Alisha. I must hide!" Adam says. But it's too late.

Box: Voc., p. 203

5

Alisha is talking to Adam.
"You can't dive here, Adam. It's very dangerous. Go home."
"It's boring at home," Adam says.
"You need a hobby, Adam."

6

Alisha has a good idea. Her friend Josie works at the PMZ music club. And Adam likes music.
"Hi, Josie. Can you send me a brochure for PMZ, please?"

b) What's happening in the pictures? Read the text again and finish the sentences.

1 In picture 1 Adam is ...
2 In picture 2 Adam is ...
3 In picture 3 Adam and his friends are ...
4 In picture 4 Zack and Alisha are ...
5 In picture 5 Alisha is ...
6 In picture 6 Alisha is ...

- phoning his friends.
- helping in the cafe.
- talking to Adam.
- walking in the harbour.
- phoning Josie.
- diving in the harbour.

► Workbook 6, p. 68

kein Sporttag am 29.7.

Feris	Simon Lamin
Moritz	Benny Amann

▸ INKL 5.3 ▸ DFF 5.3 ▸ INKL 5.4 ▸ KV 44

2 Welcome to PMZ

a) Look at the brochure. Find out: What does PMZ mean? What can you do there?

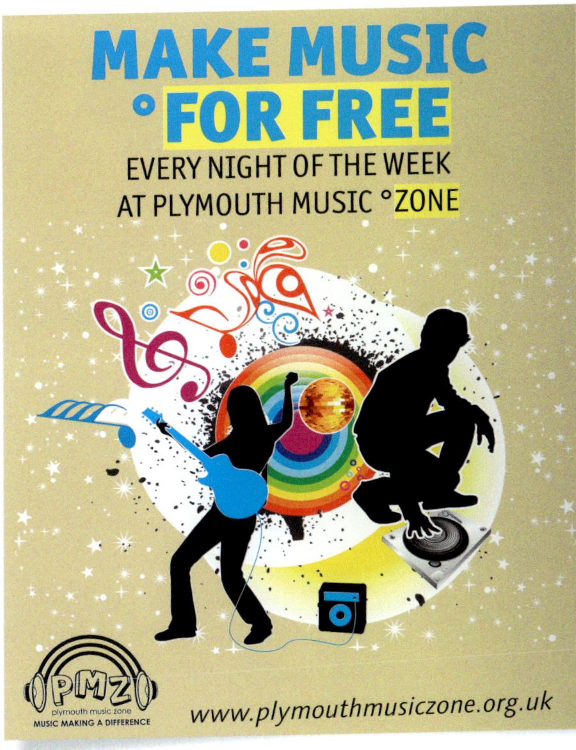

MON — **THE PMZ GUITAR CLUB**
4 pm – 6.15 pm ¦ Everybody welcome! Learn to play the guitar.

TUE — **THE BIG BASH**
5 pm – 6 pm ¦ 8–18 yrs
Play the drums in a group.

WED — **JAM BAND**
4 pm – 5 pm ¦ 8–18 yrs
Bring your instrument. Play in a band.

THUR — **°BEATS PER MINUTE (BPM)**
4.30 pm – 5.30 pm ¦ 11–25 yrs
Instrument workshop for young °disabled musicians. Make some new music.

FRI — **STREETBEATZ**
4 pm – 6.15 pm ¦ 12–19 yrs
For all young rappers.
Make your music in the PMZ studio.

SAT — **THE ROOF RAISERS**
10 am – 12.30 pm ¦ 11–18 yrs
For young singers. Sing with a real band.

2.36

b) ○ Listen to Adam. Pick A, B, C or D.

1 Who is talking to Adam? A His mum. B His dad. C Josie. D Alisha.
2 What does Adam like? A The drums. B Rapping. C The guitar. D The piano.
3 Where is PMZ? A At Eggy. B In London. C In a village. D Near the city centre.
4 What does Adam want to join? A The guitar club. B Streetbeatz. C Jam Band. D The Big Bash.

c) ● Copy this table. Listen again and take notes. More help p. 141

PMZ address: …	Times (Sat): … …
Bus number: …	Price: …
Times (Mon–Fri): … …	

3 NOW YOU

a) Appointments: Write the questions in the green box in a table and write your answers. More help p. 142

▸ Wordbank 8, p. 177

b) Make appointments with two partners. Go to your appointments. Take notes.

c) Tell the class about one partner.

d) ● Write a text about you and music. You can put it in your DOSSIER. More help p. 142

- What's your favourite band?
- Who's your favourite singer?
- What's your favourite English song?
- Can you play an instrument? What instrument?
- Can you sing? Can you rap?
- Are you in a band?

▸ Workbook 7–8, p. 68

▸ INKL 5.5 ▸ Folie 29

1 Photos on Adam's mobile

2.37

a) Read the dialogue. Put the photos in the right order.

Ellie — Let's see the photos on your mobile then. ... That's your mum. What's she doing?

Adam — Good question. She's in the cafe. She's making sandwiches, I think. This is me.

Ellie — Oh, yes. You're in the cafe too. What are you doing? Box: Voc., p. 203

Adam — Let's see. I'm setting the tables. Or I'm cleaning the tables. I'm not sure.

Ellie — This must be your little brother Zack. He's with my stepmum, Alisha. What are they doing?

Adam — They're sitting in a park. I think it's near our house, or maybe it's the Hoe.

Ellie — And this must be your dad. What's he doing?

Adam — He's cooking. He's a great cook. And this is me with my group at PMZ.

Ellie — Cool. Let's see. What are you doing?

Adam — We're rapping.

Ellie — You're rapping? Really? Can you rap?

Adam — Well, I'm learning!

b) Find a sentence from the dialogue for each picture.

2 Questions and answers with 'ing'

a) Copy and complete the tables with questions and answers from 1.

Question word	form of 'be'	Pronoun	verb + -ing
What	's	she	doing?
What	...		...

Pronoun	form of 'be'	verb + -ing
She	's	making sandwiches.
I	'm	...

b) Look at the tables again. Complete the rule.

FOCUS

Das *present progressive* wird gebildet mit:

I + 'm	+	verb + ing
he / she / it + ...	+	verb + ing
you / we / they + ...	+	verb + ing

Man benutzt die Verlaufsform in der Gegenwart (*present progressive*),
a) um Bilder zu beschreiben und
b) um zu sagen, was gerade passiert.

▸ Language file 10, p. 171

► KV 45 ► KV 46 ► DFF 5.1 ► Folie 30

3 What are you doing?

a) It's Saturday. Ellie is talking to Adam on the phone. Complete the sentences with *'m • is • 's • are • 're.*

Ellie

1 What am I doing? I'm with my family. My stepdad is making breakfast. He... cooking omelettes. My favourite food! I... making toast.
2 My sister Zoe ... feeding the cats. They... making lots of noise. They're hungry!
3 Mum ... sitting at the table. She... writing an email.
4 My brother Conor ... watching TV. What ... you doing now, Adam?

Adam

More practice 2 p. 142

b) Adam is talking to Ellie. Complete the sentences with the *present progressive*.

1 Today is a nice day because dad is home. Mum ... (sit) in the garden. Zack ... (ride) his bike there. Mum ... (look) after him. Box: Voc., p. 204
2 I... (look) at them through the window. Can you hear that noise? That's Zack with mum. They... (laugh).
3 Dad and I ... (work) in the kitchen. Dad ... (make) something special because it's mum's birthday. I... (set) the table.
4 OK Ellie, Dad ... (talk) to me. I must go now. See you on Monday.

More practice 3 p. 143

4 What's Cyril doing?

2.38

a) What's Cyril doing now? p. 143
Write the numbers 1–5. Then listen and choose an answer from the box:

1 Cyril is swimming, 2 ...

playing football • playing tennis • rapping • reading a story • riding a bike • swimming • talking on the phone • washing up • watching TV • writing a text • writing an email

b) Listen again. Compare answers with a partner.

I think Cyril is swimming.

Me too. / No, I think Cyril is ...

5 NOW YOU

What is your father / mother / sister / friend / ... doing now?
Write sentences about your family and friends – as many as you can.

I think my	best friend mum dog ...	is working is doing homework is playing ...	now.

6 What are they doing?

a) Look at the photos. Discuss what you think the people are doing. Then write sentences.
A: I think the boy in photo 1 is ...
B: Really? I think he's ...
C: OK. Let's write: 1 He's ...

b) The groups tell the class.
In photo 1 we think she's ...

Check on page 120.

1 Before you read

2.39

Listen to the songs. Do you like them?

I like / don't like song number …
– It's great / OK / terrible!
– I love it! / I don't like it. / I hate it!

Music makes a difference[1]

2.40

Box: Voc., p. 204

It was Friday afternoon. Adam was on the bus, on the way to PMZ. Some other kids were on the bus too. Box: Voc., p. 205

"Hey you," one boy said to Adam. "You're sitting on my seat!"

The other boys and girls laughed.

"Hey babyface, how old are you? Five?" a girl asked.

They all laughed again. Adam said nothing.

Adam was at PMZ with his rap teacher, Josie.

"Are you feeling OK, Adam?" Josie asked.

"I had a bit of trouble on the bus," Adam said. "Some kids were mean. I'm fed up."

"That's terrible," Josie said. "But you can use that feeling in your rap."

In the lesson, Josie said, "When you rap, you must rap about your life." Josie asked, "What's important in your life?"

"Friends … my girlfriend … TV … my family … music." Everybody had different ideas.

"Cool," Josie said. "And you can rap about problems too. Any ideas?"

"Trouble at school … trouble with parents … trouble with other kids …," they said.

"OK. We have a rap °battle here at PMZ next week. You can write a rap," Josie said.

On Monday morning Adam was at school.

"How's it going at PMZ?" Luca asked.

"It's great. I'm writing a rap. But it's hard," Adam said.

"Can we listen to it?" Ellie asked.

"Sure. You can all come to the rap battle on Friday," Adam said.

1 ['dɪfrəns]

On Friday evening lots of people were at PMZ. And Adam was very happy because his dad was there.
"Welcome to PMZ everybody. And welcome to our rap battle," Josie said.
Adam was nervous. His friends were excited.
"Go, Adam, go!" ...

Adam's rap was great. He was second in the rap battle.
"Well done, Adam," his mum said.
"I'm very proud of you, Adam," his dad said.
"Thanks," Adam said. "Music really makes a difference for me."

Music makes a difference

°Chorus
Music makes a difference, a difference, a difference.
Yes, music makes a difference – for me.

Trouble at school, trouble on the bus,
Trouble at home, but °I don't make a fuss.
There's °one thing that I know
And now I'm °telling you,
I need music – and you need it too.
Chorus

Trouble with my mum, and trouble with my dad
°Nobody understands, when I'm feeling so bad.
But there's one thing that I know
And now I'm telling you,
I need music – and you need it too.
Chorus

I'm not like you, and you're not like me
Everybody's different – everybody's free.
There's one thing that I know
And now I'm telling you,
I need music – and you need it too.
Chorus

Adam Osmanovic

2 Can you remember?

Who said this in the story?
1 "You're sitting on my seat!" (lines 4–5)
2 "Are you feeling OK, Adam?" (line 12)
3 "I'm fed up." (l. 14)
4 "How's it going at PMZ?" (l. 29)
5 "Go, Adam, go!" (l. 43)
6 "Music really makes a difference for me." (ll. 48–49)

3 True, false[2] or not in the text?

1 The boys and girls on the bus were nice.
2 Adam's rap teacher is Josie.
3 Josie is from Plymouth.
4 The rap battle was on Friday.
5 Adam's dad wasn't there.
6 Adam was first in the rap battle.
7 Adam's mum listens to rap every day.
8 Music is important for Adam.

2.41 2.42 4 RAP Music makes a difference

a) Listen to Adam's rap. Do you like it?

b) Who wants to be a rapper? You can have a rap battle in your class. Pick one verse of Adam's rap. Learn it. Rap for the class. Who's the best rapper?

More practice 4 p.144

▸ Text file 6, p. 159 ▸ Workbook 15–18, p. 71

2 [fɔls]

▸ IAT 5.2 ▸ INKL 5.8 ▸ KV 47 ▸ INKL 5.9 ▸ DFF 5.2 ▸ Folie 31

1 In the park

On the left | On the right

next to | on | between | In the middle | behind | under | in front of

Box: Voc., p. 205

a) What can you see? Match the sentences.

1 On the left I can see a bike.	A They're **on** the table.
2 On the right there's a baby.	B It's **in front of** the baby.
3 There are apples.	C He's **between** the boys.
4 I can see a red ball.	D It's **next to** the apples.
5 There are two dogs.	E It's **behind** the tree.
6 There's a seagull.	F They're **under** the table.

c) Look at the picture and listen. (2.43)
Say what's right or what's wrong.

b) What are they doing?
Make sentences – as many as you can.

On the left In the middle On the right	two dogs … a boy … three girls … children … a girl … a baby … two men …

More help p. 144

2 NOW YOU

Partner A: Go to page 147.
Partner B: Go to page 120.

Wenn du ein Bild beschreibst, nenne die Gegenstände und Personen auf dem Bild nicht einfach, sondern sage, **wo** sie sich befinden.
Wenn du sagen möchtest, was die Personen auf dem Bild machen bzw. was gerade auf dem Bild passiert, benutze das *present progressive*:
– *The kids **are playing** football. / The baby **is sleeping**.*

▸ Skills file 5, p. 165

▸ Workbook 19–21, pp. 72–73

1 Four text messages

a) Look at the four text messages. Are they from Adam, Adam's mum, Luca or Josie? Example: I think text message A is from ...

Text message language
+ = and
U = you
C = see
2 = to / too / two
gr8 = great
R U = are you
L8r = later
X = kiss

b) Read the text messages aloud.

2 MEDIATION What's that in German?

You and your partner get a text from an English friend, Amanda. She's in Germany at the moment. Work with your partner. How do you say it in German?

Amanda fragt, wo ...?

Ja, sie schreibt, dass sie ...

3 WRITING A text to Amanda

Write a text message to Amanda. More help p. 144

▸ INKL 5.11 ▸ DFF 5.4 ▸ DFF 5.9

1 A recipe[1] for scones

a) Look at the picture in the recipe. Try to explain these words in German: *scone*, *jam*, *cream*.

What are scones?

In England people often eat them in the afternoon with tea, coffee or °milk.

How do you make scones?

1 Put °butter (50g), °flour[2] (225g), °sugar[3] (50g), °baking powder (3 °teaspoons) and °salt[4] (half a teaspoon) in a °bowl.
2 Rub the butter into the flour with your fingers.
3 Add milk (75ml) and one °egg.
4 Mix everything together.
5 Make 12 scones with a °glass.
6 Put the scones in the °oven[5] (230°C) for 8 – 10 minutes.
7 Cut a scone.
8 Put cream and jam on it – and eat it!

b) Read the recipe for scones and put the pictures (A–H) in the right order (1–8).

2 New words in the recipe

a) Work with a partner. Find these eleven words in the recipe. What do you think they mean in German?

milk, flour, butter, sugar, teaspoon, egg, baking powder, bowl, oven, glass, salt

▸ Skills file 3–4, pp. 163–164

b) Check in the Dictionary (pages 208–218).

You can often guess the new words.
Remember:
Some words are like German words: *butter, milk, glass, oven, salt.*
Look at the pictures in 1b for help:
– *bowl (picture B)*
– *teaspoon, flour, baking powder (picture D)*
– *egg (picture H)*

1 [ˈresəpi] 2 [flaʊə] 3 [ˈʃʊgə] 4 [sɔːlt] 5 [ˈʌvn]

▸ Workbook 23, p. 74

► KV 48 ► KV 49

1 The kids from Harbour Road: What's your talent[1]?

a) What's your talent? – I can ...

Then watch the film and find out what Anna, Paul and Sarah can do.

b) Look at the picture. Put the sentences in the right order. Then watch part 1 again and check.

A That's four pounds for you, and four pounds for you, please.
B I'm hungry! Can I have a muffin, and ... a hot chocolate[2], please.
C Hi!
D Thanks. / Thank you!
E Chocolate or blueberry[3]?
F Hi, Anna!
G I'll have a chocolate muffin, please.
H And yourself[4]?
I A hot chocolate and a blueberry muffin, please.
J We're here!

c) Match the sentence parts. Then watch part 2 and check.

1 In the cafe Anna	cool dance for Anna.
2 She has no idea	wants to sing.
3 Paul wants to	isn't happy.
4 And Sarah	play the guitar.
5 But then Sarah	for the class party.
6 She knows a	has an idea.

d) Watch part 3. Do Anna's dance.

► Text file 6, p. 159

2 People and places: A visit to PMZ

a) Watch the film. Talk about PMZ with a partner.
– I think PMZ looks interesting / boring / ... What about you?
– I think Jimmy is a good / great / terrible / ... rapper.
– I think the Jam Band's music is ...

b) Answer these questions. Watch again and check.
1 Who works at PMZ?
2 How many people come to PMZ every week?
3 What instrument does Jimmy play?

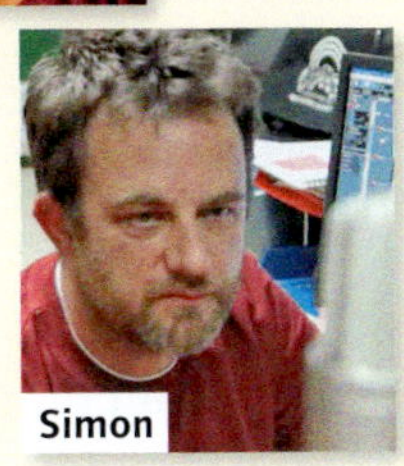

[1] talent ['tælənt] *Talent* [2] hot chocolate [hɒt 'tʃɒklət] *heiße Schokolade* [3] blueberry *Heidelbeere, Blaubeere*
[4] And yourself? *Und du?*

STOP! CHECK! GO!

▸ KV 49 ▸ DFF 5.1 ▸ DFF 5.2 ▸ INKL 5.12

Ein Lösungsblatt für die Aufgaben 1 bis 5 kannst du von deiner Lehrerin / deinem Lehrer erhalten. Den Hörtext (S. 105) findest du auch auf der Audio-CD im Workbook.

1 REVISION Questions and answers

a) What do you know about crabs? Do this crab quiz.
Write the answers: *1 No, they don't. 2 Yes, ...*

1 Do crabs live in towns?
2 Do crabs live on the beach?
3 Do crabs eat fish?
4 Do normal crabs sing?
5 Does Cyril live in a house?
6 Does Cyril talk?
7 Does Cyril walk fast?
8 Does Cyril like people?

b) Now make a seagull quiz. Write the questions.

1 seagulls / live near the sea?
2 seagulls / live in towns?
3 seagulls / eat crabs?
4 seagulls / sing or make a noise?
5 Sandy / live in a house?
6 Sandy / eat crabs?
7 Sandy / talk?
8 Sandy / like °pizza?

c) Now answer the questions about seagulls.

d) Make a quiz about another animal. Put it on the board. Who knows the answers?

More help p. 145

2 LANGUAGE Describing pictures

a) Say what Cyril is doing. Finish the sentences with the verbs in the box.

ringing • playing • sitting • watching • listening

Cyril is ... (1) on a chair, on the beach. He's ... (2) to music. He's ... (3) three kids. They're ... (4) football. His mobile is ... (5).

b) Say what Sandy is doing. Finish the sentences with *'s* or *'re*.

Sandy is on the beach too. She... (1) watching Mr Johnson. He... (2) walking on the beach. Mrs Johnson is there too. They... (3) looking at Cyril. They... (4) feeling hungry! Sandy has a mobile. She... (5) phoning Cyril.

c) Look at the pictures in 2a and 2b again. Finish the dialogue between Sandy and Cyril.

Sandy	Cyril
Hi, Cyril. Where are you sitting?	1 ... on my favourite chair.
What are you doing?	2 ... to music.
What are you watching?	3 ... kids.
What are the kids doing?	4 ...
Cyril, look! The Johnsons ... coming!	5 Help! I... going!

3 LANGUAGE People on the ferry

2.44

a) Copy the table. Then look at the picture and listen to Adam and his dad. Match the people (A–I) in the picture with the names.

Sam	*D*	*Linda*	...	*David*	...
Anna	...	*Toby*	...	*Uma*	...
Rick	...	*Gemma*	...	*Adam's dad*	...

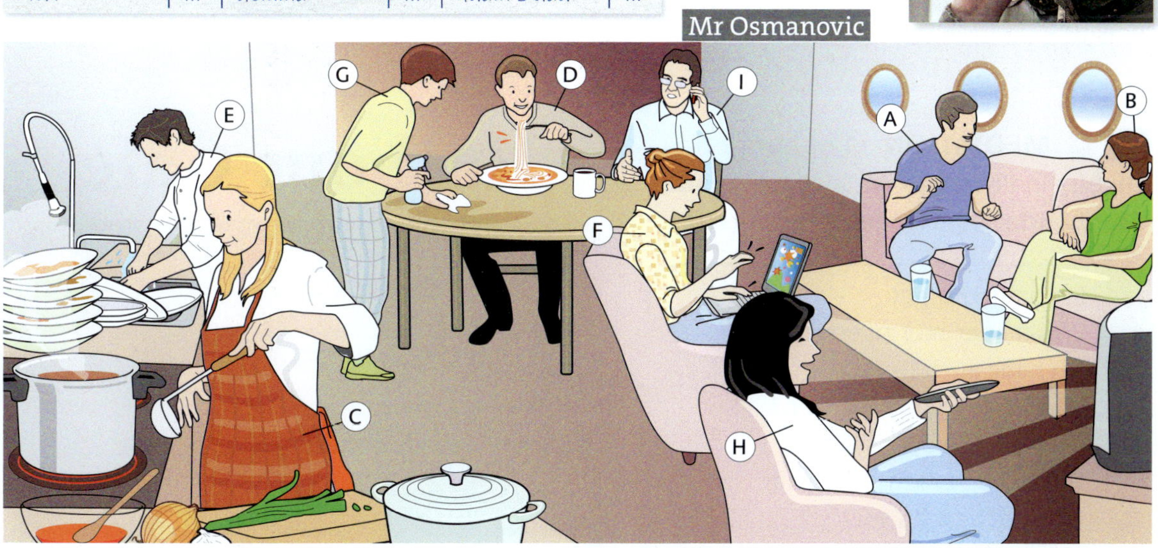

b) Look at the picture again. What are the people doing? Write sentences like this:
Sam is eating. Anna ...

clean the table • cook • do nothing • eat • laugh • play a game • talk • talk on the phone • wash up • watch TV

4 READING A picture

a) Look at the picture. Read the text. Are the sentences true (T) or false (F)?

1 There are lots of people in the park.
2 On the left I can see a boy and a girl.
3 The boy is talking on the phone.
4 The girl is reading.
5 On the right I can see a family.
6 They're eating lunch.
7 There's a big dog in front of a yellow bag.
8 It's looking at the sandwiches.
9 In the middle I can see a red chair.
10 A boy is sitting on the chair.
11 There's a cat under the chair.
12 I can see a big red ball next to the chair.

b) Describe the picture. You can use the ideas in a).

STOP! CHECK! GO!

► KV 43 ► KV 49 ► DFF 5.5 ► DFF 5.6

5 WORDS Food and drinks

a) Find the odd word out.

1 sweets, tea, sandwich, cafe
2 breakfast, soup, lunch, dinner
3 tea, juice, water, chips
4 coffee, chicken, fish, omelette
5 fruit, salad, scones, vegetables

b) Complete the sentences with answers from a.

1 You can buy food and drinks in a ...
2 I often have vegetable ... for lunch.
3 My favourite food is fish and ...
4 Some people drink ... for breakfast.
5 We often have tea and ... in a cafe at the weekend.

6 MEDIATION I'm hungry!

Du bist in Plymouth mit einem Freund. Beantworte seine Fragen auf Deutsch.

1 Ich habe Hunger. Was gibt es hier zu essen?
2 Ich habe auch Durst. Was kann ich hier trinken?
3 Gibt es auch etwas Süßes?
4 Wir haben £10 für uns beide. Was schlägst du vor?
5 Müssen wir alles hier essen oder können wir es auch mitnehmen?

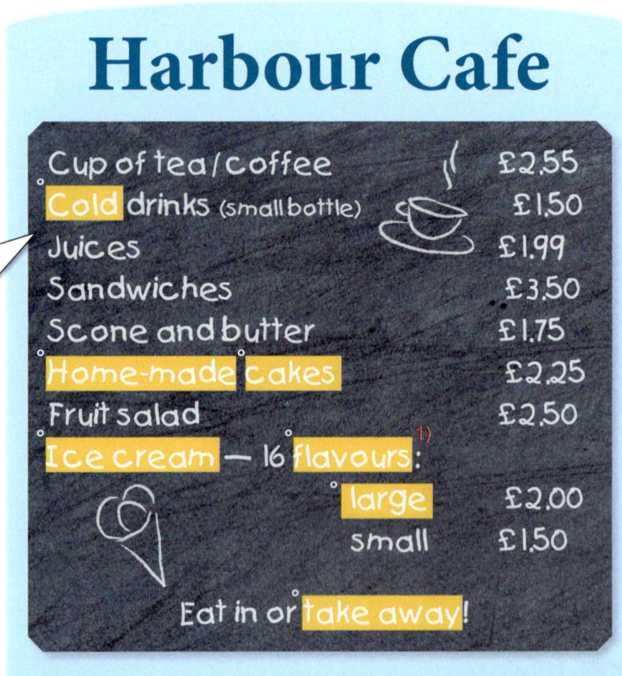

7 WRITING and SPEAKING In the Harbour Cafe

a) Write a dialogue in your exercise book. Here are some ideas.

Frage, was der Kunde möchte.

You work in the cafe:
- Hello. Can I ... ?
- OK. Anything ...?
- ... to drink?
- ... else?
- That's £ ...
- Thanks. ...

Rufe den nächsten Kunden auf.

Schau auf die Speisekarte in Aufgabe 6 und bestelle etwas zu essen und zu trinken.

You are hungry:
- Hello. Yes, please – ..., please.
- Yes, ..., please.
- Oh, yes, ..., please. And ...
- No, thanks. ...
- OK. Here ...

Bestelle noch mehr, z.B. etwas Süßes.

Wenn du genug bestellt hast, sage, dass das alles ist.

Bezahle alles.

b) Practise your dialogue with a partner.

1 ['fleɪvə]

8 READING and WRITING On Saturday morning …

a) Read the story. Put the phrases (A–G) with the photos (1–7).

1 The cafe was very busy.

2 Ms Lee was in the cafe.

3 She was hungry.

4 Adam was very fast.

5 Oh no! Trouble?

6 It was Adam's rap!

7 Ms Lee was happy.

A Can I help you?

B I'm washing up.

C That's a great rap!

D You're welcome. Bye.

E Hello, Ms Lee. I'm fine, thanks.

F Here you are. One tea and a scone.

G Yes, Adam is working very hard at school now.

b) Draw another picture for the story and write speech bubbles for it. More help p. 145

9 My learner log

Copy and complete your learner log. You can put it in your DOSSIER.

My learner log

Now I can …
- use the present progressive and say what's happening. Example: …
- describe a picture 😀 😐 ☹
- buy something to eat and drink in a cafe: 😀 😐 ☹
- understand a text message: 😀 😐 ☹
- understand a recipe: 😀 😐 ☹

In Unit 5 …
- my favourite text is on page …
- my favourite words are …
- my favourite phrases are …
- my favourite food is …
- my favourite people are …

My progress in English is: GREAT! 👍 / OK / NOT VERY GOOD 👎

▸ Workbook pp. 75–78

Unit 6

°School is out – for summer

▸ KV 51 ▸ DFF 6.1

1 Summer sounds

3.02

Listen to the summer sounds (1–4) and match them with the brochures (A–D).

Summer sounds 1: Brochure ...

Summer sounds 2: ...

Summer sounds 3: ...

Summer sounds 4: ...

A

The Cawsand Ferry Co.[2]

Visit the smuggler villages of Cawsand and Kingsand. Great beaches, walks, restaurants, shops and cafes.

Smuggler's cave in Cawsand

Ferry times:

Plymouth
10.30 am, 12.00 pm, 2.30 pm, 4.00 pm

Cawsand
9.30 am, 11.00 am, 12.30 pm, 3.00 pm, 4.30 pm

Tickets:
Adults £4 one way
Children £2 one way
Dogs free

B

Canoe Tamar[1]

Experience .... discover .... enjoy ....

Canoe trips: 3–3½ hours with picnic stop

Trips cost: £22 per person

Everybody welcome – dogs too!

2 Four trips

3.03

a) Ellie, Luca, Adam and Berry are at school. Listen. Which trip do they pick – A, B, C or D?

b) Listen again. Match the ideas (1–4) with the answers (A–D).

1 What about a trip to Dartmoor?	A Yes, but they're expensive.
2 Well, °I'd prefer a °canoe trip.	B Oh no! That's boring!
3 I love °theme parks.	C I think that's a great idea!
4 I really want to go to the beach!	D But I can't swim very well!

1 [kəˈnuː ˈteɪmɑː] 2 [ˈkɔːsænd]

▸ IAT 6.1 ▸ DFF 6.2

C

D

3 NOW YOU

a) Think: Look at the brochures. Pick your favourite trip.
Example: My favourite trip is ...

> the canoe trip • the ferry trip • the camping trip • the trip to a theme park

b) Pair: Talk to a partner. Agree on one trip.

- What about a ...?
- I'd prefer a ...
- I really want to do a ...
- I love ...

- I think that's a great / terrible idea.
- Oh no! That's boring / expensive / ...
- Me too. I really like walking / ferry trips / the beach / ...

c) Share: Now work in groups of four. Agree on one trip in your group. Tell the class what your group wants to do.

We want to do a ...

A trip to the beach

3.04

1 Planning a trip

a) What things do you need on the beach? Read the text for ideas. Then start a network. More help p. 145

It's Friday, the last day of school. The four friends want to plan the trip to Kingsand.

Berry — OK, guys! When are we going to Kingsand?

Luca — What about next Monday – the first day of the summer holidays?

Ellie — That's a great idea. What can we bring?

Adam — Well, we need beach things, like °swimsuits[1] and °swimming trunks and °towels.

Box: Voc., p. 206

Ellie — And °sunglasses ... and °hats ...

Luca — Yeah, and we need things for a picnic – like sandwiches.

Ellie — And water – lots of water ...

Berry — Yeah. My dad is coming in the car, he can bring our things. Mum is staying on the farm because she's busy.

Luca — Is Sam coming too?

Berry — No. He's staying with mum.

Ellie — Oh, °that's a pity.

Luca — Now let's talk about food!

b) True or false?

1 The friends are going to Kingsand on Friday.
2 Berry's parents are coming too.
3 Her dog Sam is staying at home on the farm.

3.05

2 Shopping for the picnic

a) Listen and take notes.

Partner A:
Make shopping lists for Adam and Luca.

Partner B:
Make shopping lists for Ellie and Berry.

Adam
...
...

Luca
...
...

Ellie
...
...

Berry
...
...

b) Swap lists with your partner. Listen again and check your partner's lists.

c) Look at the four lists. Agree on more things you can bring for the picnic.

What about ...?

Yes, good idea. / No, I don't like ...

d) Add more words to your network in 1a.

1 ['swɪmsu:ts] 2 ['tʃɒklət] 3 ['bɪskɪts] 4 [ɒrɪndʒɪz] 5 ['sɒsɪdʒɪz]

3 Things for the beach

a) It's Sunday – the day before the Kingsand trip. Look at the pictures and guess what the friends want to bring.

b) Then read the text messages and find out. What are the friends bringing?
Example: They're all bringing ... Ellie / Luca / ... is bringing ...

Hi everybody. Don't °forget suncream for the beach.
Berry

Right! + don't forget swimming things + shorts. :)
Ellie

OK. I'm bringing my bodyboard.
Luca

Gr8! I'm bringing a football. Who has a tube?
Adam

I have a big tube. I can bring it. :)
Berry

Gr8. R U bringing ur frisbee, Ellie?
Luca

Yes + speakers for my phone. C U.
Ellie

OK. Don't forget towels. C U at the ferry! XXX
Berry

c) Add more words for the trip to the beach to your network from 1a.

4 °Chain game

Imagine that you're going to the beach. What do you want to bring?

I want to bring a tube.

I want to bring a tube and sandwiches.

I want to bring a tube, sandwiches and a ...

5 A summer song

3.06

a) Listen to Adam's favourite summer song. Do you like it?

It's great!

It's OK!

It's ...

b) Listen and sing along.

Magic Summer Night

Come on happy people get on the floor,
Do you feel it so right?
So come on raise your hands up, hands in the air,
Magic summer night – shakalakaboom!

School is out, that's all what we need,
Stars are shining so bright.
So come on raise your hands up, hands in the air,
Magic summer night – shakalakaboom!

by Oliver Boehm & Thomas Schleh

▸ Workbook 1–3, p. 81

▸ DFF 6.4

1 Before you read

Look at the pictures on this page. Talk to a partner. Who can you see? Where are they?

A

B

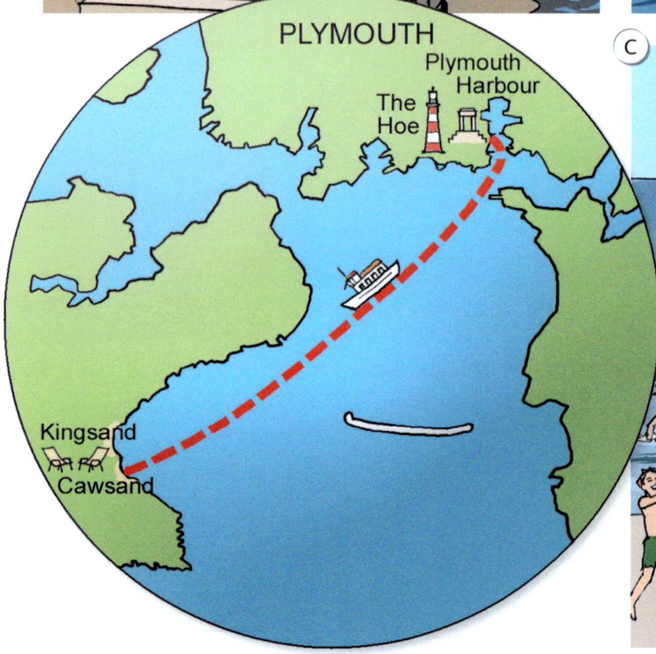

C

2 You're going on a ferry trip!

a) Close your eyes. Listen. Enjoy the ferry trip.

3.07

b) Talk to a partner.

What's the ferry trip like?

What do you see?

What do you hear?

What do you feel?

More help p. 146

All °aboard!

3.08

Scene 1 A °message in a bottle

Berry — Where's my dad? He's late.
Adam — Don't worry, Berry.
Berry — But he's never late.
Luca — And he has our picnic!
Ellie — Look at that old °woman. She looks like a °smuggler from an old story! What's she doing?
Adam — She's °putting something in a bottle. I think it's a message!
Luca — A message? Maybe it's for us!
Ellie — She's going away ... Let's go and look!
Luca — The message is for you, Berry.
Berry — For me? What? Oh!

To Berry and her friends!
Cawsand is great,
But Kingsand is °better.
Find the next bottle
And read the letter!

We have your dad,
°The sea's coming in.
You have 30 °minutes -
But °hurry! He can't swim!

Walk for two minutes
And then stop.
You're in a °square
Now find a shop.

From a Kingsand smuggler

Berry — We must find dad!
Ellie — But how?
Berry — First we must find a shop.
Luca — This is exciting!
Adam — Look at the big °map. There's a shop near here, THE SHOP IN THE SQUARE!
Ellie — That's it. Let's go.

Scene 2 We only have 30 minutes!

Luca — Here's the shop. Can we stop and buy some sweets? I'm hungry.
Adam — Don't be stupid, Luca. We only have 30 minutes.
Ellie — Where's the next message?
Berry — Maybe there's °another bottle?

Luca — I see one. Look, on that chair.
Ellie — I have it. And here's the message.
Adam — Oh, great!

Smugglers are hungry
They want to eat.
Find a cafe
Where smugglers meet.

Luca — We must find a cafe. But where?
Adam — Look, there's the old woman.
Ellie — Let's °follow her. Come on, Berry!
Berry — I'm coming!

Scene 3 We only have 20 minutes!

Luca There's the old woman again. Let's go!

Adam Are you OK, Berry?

Berry It's hard work!

Ellie We can °push you.

Berry Yes, please!

Ellie Come on, guys. Push!

Berry That's great! Thanks!

Adam Look, a cafe!

Ellie The *Smuggler's Rest*. That's it – a cafe where smugglers meet!

Adam Look, there's another bottle.

> What's the time?
> You don't know?
> Find a big °clock.
> Go, go, go!

Berry What's the time? I can look at my phone.

Luca No, it says: Find a big clock.

Ellie I can't see a clock. Can you see the old woman?

Adam No, she isn't here. What can we do?

Luca °Quick. We're too °slow. We only have twenty minutes. °Look for a big clock.

Scene 4 We only have 10 minutes!

Ellie Look, there's the clock!

Berry Oh, yes! A really big clock!

Ellie There's the bottle!

Adam Quick. We only have ten minutes.

Luca I have the bottle. And here's the message.

> Feeling °hot?
> Want an °ice cream?
> Look for the cows
> And find your dream.

Berry Well, I'm feeling very hot.

Luca And I really want an ice cream.

Adam But what are we looking for?

Ellie Cows?

Adam Cows on the beach?

Berry Look. I can see cows.

Ellie Me too.

Luca And a bottle. Quick.

Scene 5 *We only have one minute!*

Luca — There's a message in the bottle.

> **O**nly one minute,
> Look near the water.
> A dad is °waiting
> For his °daughter!

Adam — Let's look on the beach.
Ellie — I can see the old woman.
Luca — But where's Berry's dad?
Adam — Quick! We only have one minute!
Berry — There he is – in the sand! Hey Dad!
Dad — Help! I can't °get out!
Luca — We're coming! Don't worry!
Mum — Hello, everybody.
Berry — Mum! You are the Kingsand smuggler! – Dad, let's get you °out of there.
Ellie — That was a great game!
Adam — Yeah, it was really good.
Berry — But a bit °scary too.
Mum — Are you OK now? Are you hungry?
Luca — Yes!
Dad — Your picnic is °over there. Sam is looking after it.
Luca — I can see Sam.
Adam — He's eating something.
Berry — Oh no! He's eating our picnic! Sam! Stop!

Scene 6 *Berry's news*

3 The last scene

3.09

Listen to Scene 6. Answer the questions:

1 Where is Berry going in August?
2 Is she happy?
3 Why? Why not?

4 THEATRE TIME

a) Pick a scene. Make groups of five to six students: Ellie, Berry, Luca, Adam, Berry's mum and Berry's dad. Read the scene together.

b) Act your scene for the class.

► Workbook 4, p. 82

► Folie 34 ► IAT 6.2 ► DFF 6.5 ► KV 55 ► KV 56

1 Talking about summer plans

3.10

a) The four friends are talking about summer plans.
Listen. Match the names (Luca, Ellie, Adam and Berry) and the tickets (1–4).

b) Listen again. Who says what – Luca, Berry, Adam or Ellie?

1 We're °flying from London.

2 Nothing special. I'm staying at home all summer.

3 I'm staying at home in July.

4 I'm going to Spain for a week with dad.

5 Mum and dad are working.

6 My granny from Ghana[2] is visiting us.

2 What are your summer plans? //● p. 146

Work with a partner. Talk about your summer plans. Use the ideas in the green boxes.

A: Begrüße deinen Partner / deine Partnerin. Frage, wie es ihm / ihr geht.
- Hi.
- Hello Anna / …
- How are you?
- Are you OK?

B: Grüße zurück. Sage, wie es dir geht.
- Hi …
- I'm fine, thanks.
- I'm OK.

A: Frage, was er / sie im Sommer vorhat.
- What are your summer plans?
- What are you doing in the summer?

B: Sage, was du vorhast. (2 oder 3 Ideen)
- Nothing special!
- I'm going to Turkey / …
- I'm staying at …
- I'm flying to …
- My uncle / cousin / friend / … is visiting us.

A: Sage, wie du die Pläne deines Partners / deiner Partnerin findest.
- That's interesting / nice / cool / …
- Really? Can I come too?
- Wow! Great!

B: Nun frage deinen Partner / deine Partnerin, was er / sie vorhat.

A: Sage, was du vorhast.

B: Sage, wie du die Pläne deines Partners / deiner Partnerin findest.

1 ['mæləgə] 2 ['gɑːnə]

► Workbook 5–6, pp. 83–84

▸ KV 57

1 The kids from Harbour Road: Summer holidays

a) The kids are going on a camping trip. What do you think they take? Watch the film and find out.

1  ice cream

2  a tent[1]

3  sandwiches

4  sausages

5  a can of beans[2]

6  a bike

7  matches[3]

8  a can opener[4]

b) Put the photos in the right order.

A 

B 

C 

D 

c) Are these sentences true or false? Watch the film again and check your answers.

1 First the three friends are in a park.
2 They want to sleep in a holiday flat.
3 They want to eat beans and sausages.
4 They need a can opener.
5 They can't find the can of beans.
6 Anna's father helps the kids.

d) Talk to a partner about the kids from Harbour Road.

I like Paul because ...

Yes, Paul is nice. But I prefer ... because ...

I think ... is fun / cool / ...

2 People and places: A ferry trip to Cawsand

a) You're going on a ferry trip to Cawsand. What do you think you can see? Make a list.

More help p. 146

b) Watch the film. What things on your list do you see?

[1] tent [tent] *Zelt* [2] can of beans [kæn əv 'bi:nz] *Dose mit Bohnen* [3] matches ['mætʃɪz] *Streichhölzer*
[4] can opener ['kæn əʊpnə] *Dosenöffner*

Unit 1 Stop! Check! Go!

10 SPEAKING A timetable ▸ Unit 1, p. 33

a) Copy this timetable into your exercise book. Some lessons are missing. Answer partner A's questions. Then ask partner A. Complete the timetable.

Lesson	Monday	Tuesday	Wednesday	Thursday	Friday
1	....	music	technology	geography	PE
2	maths	English	history	German	....
3	science	....	PE	....	English
4	art	maths	....	science	German
5	....	German	maths	....	....

Unit 2

5 What's different? ▸ Unit 2, p. 39

Look at room B. Your partner looks at room A.

You start. Describe your room to your partner.
Find four different things or more.
Make notes about the different things.

Partner B There's a bed in room B.
Partner A There's a bed in room A too.
Partner B OK. There are three cushions in room B.
Partner A There are no cushions in room A. That's different!

bed • chair • cushions • desk • lamp • mirror • posters • rugs • shelves • table • TV • wardrobe

Room A	Room B
no cushions	3 cushions
...	...

7 SPEAKING Good shops

▸ Unit 2, p. 50

a) Answer partner A's questions about this shop:

b) Imagine you're in Plymouth. You want to find a good sports shop. Ask partner A these questions. Write down:
- the name of the shop
- the address
- the phone number.

Unit 3

3 ROLE-PLAY A garage sale

▸ Unit 3, p. 63

You have a garage sale in Plymouth. Listen to your partner's questions. Pick the best answer.

It's £ ...
It's a special offer.
It isn't expensive.
It's good value.
Good. That's £..., please.
Thank you.

Swap roles.

PARTNER B

Unit 5

2 NOW YOU ▸ Unit 5, p. 100

Partner B

a) Listen to your partner. He/She is talking about *picture 1*. There are five differences in your picture. When you hear a difference, tell your partner.

In my picture the car is ...
In my picture the boy is ....

b) Now describe *picture 2* to your partner. Say what you can see, where the things and people are, and what they're doing.

On the left / In the middle / On the right I can see ...
There's a ... next to / in front of ...
He's / She's playing ...

Your partner listens and looks at his/her picture. Some things are different in your picture. He/She must find five differences.

1

2

Lösung:

Unit 5

6 What are they doing? ▸ Unit 5, p. 97

Look at the photos and check your answers.

Unit 1

More practice 1 The new timetable ▸ Unit 1, p. 21

a) Write right and wrong sentences about the timetable on page 21 – as many as you can.

Lesson one on Friday is …
Lesson … on Thursday is science.
Lesson three on … is …
Lesson … on … is …
…

b) Read your sentences to your partner. He / She says 'right' or 'wrong'.

//● 4 At Eggy ▸ Unit 1, p. 23

Put in: *He's • She's • It's • They're*

1 Eggy is my new school. … big.
2 Ellie is a new student at Eggy. … cool.
3 Mr Brown is at Eggy too. … our ICT teacher.
4 Mrs Ford isn't our English teacher. … our art teacher.
5 Adam and Berry aren't in the classroom.
… in the sports hall.
6 Look at our new books. … nice.

More practice 2 °Photos from Eggy ▸ Unit 1, p. 23

he • she • it • they

Match the words in the box with the photos: *1 it, 2 …, 3 …*

1 

2 

3 

4 

5 

6 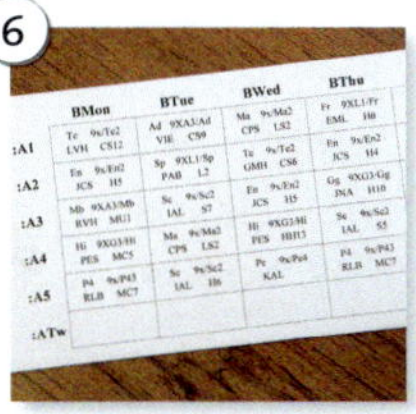

7 

8 

9 

10 

Unit 1

More help 5 Pets and friends ▸ Unit 1, p. 23

b) Write about your friend or pet. You can write:

(Name) is my pet.
He's / She's a dog / cat / ...
He's / She's four / six / ...
He's / She's big / small / ...
He's / She's brown / black / ...
He's / She's nice / fun / great / ...

(Name) is my friend.
He's / She's ten / ...
He's / She's from ...
He's / She's nice / fun / great / ...
My friend is / isn't at my school.
... is / isn't in my class.

More help 6 People and places in Plymouth ▸ Unit 1, p. 23

b) Match the sentences.

1 Plymouth isn't in Germany.
2 Eggy isn't in London.
3 Cyril isn't a seagull.
4 Sandy isn't a crab.
5 Mr Brown isn't a maths teacher.
6 The four friends aren't from Germany.
7 Ellie and Berry aren't teachers at Eggy.
8 Luca and Adam aren't girls.
9 Ms Lee and Mr Brown aren't students.

A He's a crab.
B They're teachers.
C It's in Plymouth.
D They're boys.
E They're from England.
F It's in England.
G She's a seagull.
H They're students at Eggy.
I He's an ICT teacher.

More help 7 Make a quiz for the class ▸ Unit 1, p. 23

a) Pick some quiz cards. Complete the cards with the ideas in the green boxes.

big • small • black • a pet • a wild animal • ... →

It's an animal.
It's ...
It isn't ...
What is it?

He's / She's a boy / girl.
He's / She isn't ...
He's / She's ...
Who is she?

← eleven • my best friend • my brother / sister • in my class • ...

big • small • black • great • cool • fun • new • ... →

It's a thing.
It's ...
It isn't ...
What is it?

They're students.
They're ...
They aren't ...
Who are they?

← twelve • my best friends • from ... • in my class • at my school • ...

fun • cool • my favourite sport / hobby • ... →

It's a sport / hobby.
It's ...
It isn't ...
What is it?

He's / She's a teacher.
He's / She isn't ...
He's / She's ...
Who is she?

← nice • cool • my class teacher • PE teacher • from ... • at my school • ...

More practice 3 **The story** ▸ Unit 1, p. 25

Put the sentences in the right order and tell the story.

°Part 1

1 Miss Borowski is in the assembly hall.
2 But Ellie has no tie.
3 It's assembly at Eggy.
4 The students are in the assembly hall too.
5 Miss Borowski says, "The uniform is important!"

It's assembly at Eggy.
...

Part 2

1 Now Ellie has a tie.
2 Class 7Y is in the art lesson.
3 They need paper, scissors and colours.
4 It's a very nice tie. But it isn't the school tie.
5 Luca has an idea.

Luca has an idea.
...

More practice 4 **ACTIVITY** **Make a school tie** ▸ Unit 1, p. 25

1 °Pick your colours.

2 Make the tie.

3 Pick the best tie.

Unit 1

More help **1** **Make networks** ▸ Unit 1, p. 27

b) Copy this school network and add the words from the box to your network.
Can you add more words?
Then compare networks with your partner.

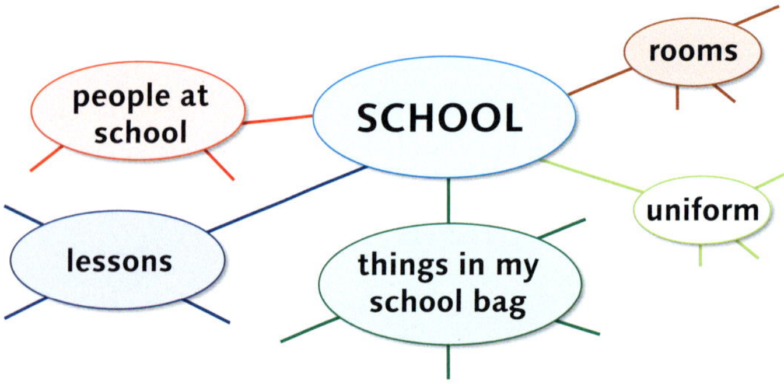

art room • blazer • classroom • class teacher • computer room • diary • English • French • history • hole punch • maths • PE • pencil case • rubber • ruler • skirt • sports hall • student • sweatshirt • teacher • tie • trousers • …

2 **NOW YOU** ▸ Unit 1, p. 28

Write the dialogue with a partner. Then practise with your partner.

A	B
Begrüße B. Frage, wie es ihm/ihr geht.	Grüße zurück. Sage, wie es dir geht und frage A, wie es ihm/ihr geht.
Sage, wie es dir geht. Frage B nach seinem/ihrem Lieblingsfach.	Nenne dein Lieblingsfach. Frage A, ob du etwas ausleihen darfst.
Stimme zu und gib es B.	Bedanke dich. Frage A nach dem besten Freund/der besten Freundin in der Klasse.
Sage, wer dein bester Freund/deine beste Freundin ist.	Sage, ob du ihn/sie auch magst oder nicht.

Unit 1 Stop! Check! Go!

5 **LANGUAGE** **Remember Ellie?** ▸ Unit 1, p. 31

Ellie is with her dad. She has some pictures on her mobile. Complete the sentences.

1 Look, this ... my new school.
2 It... very big.
3 The students in my class ... OK.
4 The teachers ... OK too.
5 This ... my new friend, Berry.
6 She... great.
7 My friends Ruby and Charlie ... at my school too.
8 But they ... (No) in my class.
9 This ... my new uniform.
10 It ... (No) very nice.

More help **9** **WRITING** **A dialogue with a new student** ► *Unit 1, p. 32*

Put Tamara's sentences in the right order and write the dialogue.

Berry	Tamara
– Hi, I'm Berry. What's your name?	– I'm in class 7D. What's your favourite lesson?
– I'm from Woolwell. I'm in class 7Y. What about you?	– OK. See you.
– I like science. What about you?	– Hi, I'm Tamara. I'm from London. What about you?
– See you later Tamara.	– I like history.

Unit 2

More help **3** **ACTIVITY** **My dream house** ► *Unit 2, p. 35*

a) Draw your dream house.
Here's an example.

b) **Walk around:** Talk about your dream house. Use these phrases:

My dream house is …	new / old big / small
My dream house has …	two bedrooms / … one bathroom / … a nice garden a big garage
The living room is …	pink / red / …

Unit 2

//● 2 Ellie's family tree ▸ Unit 2, p. 37

a) Right or wrong? Correct the wrong sentences for Ellie.

1 My mum and dad are together.
2 I live with my dad.
3 This is Pete. He's my stepdad.
4 Pete has three children.
5 Zoe is my stepsister.
6 Conor is my baby brother.
7 My dad has a new partner. Her name is Jackie.
8 This is Finn, my big brother.

1 Wrong. My mum and dad aren't together.

More practice 1 Katie's room ▸ Unit 2, p. 39

Describe Katie's room.
Write sentences – as many as you can:

- *The room is ...*
- *There's a ...*
- *There are ...*
- *I like / don't like ...*

//● 3 NOW YOU
▸ Unit 2, p. 41

a) Answer the questions. Choose answers from the box.

1 Are you noisy?
2 Are your friends fun?
3 Is your grandmother from Germany?
4 Is your dad strict?
5 Is your mum bossy?
6 Is your room messy?

Yes, I am. / No, I'm not.
Yes, he is. / No, he isn't.
Yes, she is. / No, she isn't.
Yes, it is. / No, it isn't.
Yes, they are. / No, they aren't.

b) Ask your partner the same questions.

More practice 2 More questions
▸ Unit 2, p. 41

Write the correct questions in your exercise book and answer them.

1 from – you – Are – Germany – ?
2 mum and dad – Germany – Are – from – your – ?
3 a – Is – father – teacher – your – ?
4 your – English – school bag – Is – book – your – in – ?
5 your best friend – class – Is – your – in – ?
6 strict – your – Are – teachers – ?

//● 3 Is Ellie happy?
▸ Unit 2, p. 43

Complete the sentences.

1 On Monday Ellie is happy because she can live with ...
2 On Tuesday Ellie is happy because she has a nice ...
3 On Wednesday Ellie is happy because she can watch ...
4 On Thursday Ellie isn't happy because Finn ...
5 On Friday Ellie isn't happy because dad and Alisha ...
6 On Saturday Ellie ... because ...
7 On Sunday Ellie ... because ...

More help 4 A week later
▸ Unit 2, p. 43

Write Ellie's diary for this picture.

Dear Diary
I'm very ... ☺ again.
I'm at mum's ...
I'm in the ... with ...
The cats ... happy.
Mum ... happy.
And Zoe is ... too.
Conor ... here.
Finn isn't ...
That's ... (OK / ...)!

Unit 2

More practice 3 WORDS Favourite phrases ▸ Unit 2, p. 43

a) Put the phrases from the story in two lists: 😃 ☹

b) Check your lists with a partner.

Great news! • I'm lonely. • He isn't very happy. • Finn is very cute! • Be quiet, Finn! • Tuesday is the big day. • I miss mum. • Dad has no time for me. • The best of both worlds!

More help 2 NOW YOU ▸ Unit 2, p. 44

b) Write about your dream house or flat. Use your mind map. You can use sentences like this. Write as much as you can.

My (dream) house / flat is in Hamburg / Dresden / ...
It's near a village / city / ...
The colour is nice. It's yellow / red / ...
It's small / big / great / cool / ...
There are three / four / ... rooms in my house / flat.
There's a kitchen, a living room, a ... / ...
My favourite room is ...
There's a table / ... in the living room / ...
There are lots of chairs / pictures / ... too.
It's messy / noisy / ...!
There's no TV / I share a room with my brother / sister / ...

More practice 4 NOW YOU ▸ Unit 2, p. 45

How do you say these things in English?

1 Wie fragst du nach einem englischen Wort?
2 Wie fragst du, ob du auf die Toilette gehen darfst?
3 Wie fragst du, was ihr als Hausaufgaben aufhabt?
4 Wie bittest du jemanden, etwas noch einmal zu wiederholen?
5 Wie fragst du, auf welcher Seite ihr gerade seid?
6 Wie sagst du, dass dir etwas leidtut?
7 Wie bedankst du dich?
8 Wie fragst du, ob du dir einen Radiergummi borgen kannst?
9 Wie fragst du, was ihr in der nächsten Stunde habt?

More practice 5 Can you spell that?

▸ Unit 2, p. 46

Partner A: Look at the pictures in box A. **Partner B:** Turn the page upside down.

a) Choose one of the words from your box. Spell it for partner B. Partner B listens and writes the word. Check the spelling.

b) Swap roles.

a) **Partner B:** Listen to partner A. Write the word. Then check the spelling.

b) Choose one of the words from box B. Spell it for partner A. Partner A listens and writes the word. Check the spelling. Then swap roles again.

More help 2 Addresses and phone numbers

▸ Unit 2, p. 46

c) Copy the notes. Listen to Berry. Add the missing letters.

M	E	R		Y	W		A		H	E	R

			M

W	O		L		E		

Unit 2 Stop! Check! Go!

4 Questions for Sandy

▸ Unit 2, p. 49

Answer Cyril's questions for Sandy.

1 Hey, Sandy. Are you happy? – *Yes, I am.*
2 Is your family small? – *No, …*
3 Are your parents strict? – *…*
4 Is your mum cool?
5 Are your brothers and sisters mean?
6 Are you and your family noisy?
7 Is your new house messy?

Unit 3

//● 2 NOW YOU ► Unit 3, p. 55

a) Make a table about *your* Saturdays.

buy … • go to … • have … • meet … • play … • ride … • stay … • watch … • …

I always	I sometimes	I never
go shopping	…	…

More practice 1 ACTIVITY A birthday °calendar[1] ► Unit 3, p. 57

You can make a birthday calendar for your family and friends too.

Step 1: Make 12 groups. Pick a month for your group. Write it on a piece of paper.

Step 2: Find out who has a birthday in your month – and the date. Write it on your month.

Step 3: Draw a picture for your month.

Step 4: Put the months together. Put the calendar on the wall of your classroom.

//● 5 Cyril and Sandy's day ► Unit 3, p. 59

Write about Cyril and Sandy's day. Put in the correct forms of the verbs: *get* • *go* • *have* • *meet*

1 In the morning I … up early.

2 Sandy is lazy. She … up late.

3 I usually … breakfast on the beach.

4 I often … my friends.

5 We … swimming together.

6 Sandy often … to Plymouth with her friends.

1 ['kælɪndə]

More practice 2 **Ellie's weekend** ▸ Unit 3, p. 59

Complete the sentences about Ellie.

1 °At the weekend I ... (go) to my dad's flat.
2 He always ... (get up) first.
3 He ... (make) breakfast for me and Finn.
4 Alisha, my stepmum, ... (stay) in bed.
5 Dad, Finn and I sometimes ... (go) shopping at the supermarket.
6 After lunch I ... (meet) my friends in town.
7 In the evening dad ... (watch) TV with Alisha.
8 I sometimes ... (watch) too. I sometimes ... (play) with Finn.
9 °On Sunday evening I ... (go) to my mum's house.

More help **6** **NOW YOU** ▸ Unit 3, p. 59

a) Make notes about your day. You can use a mind map like this:

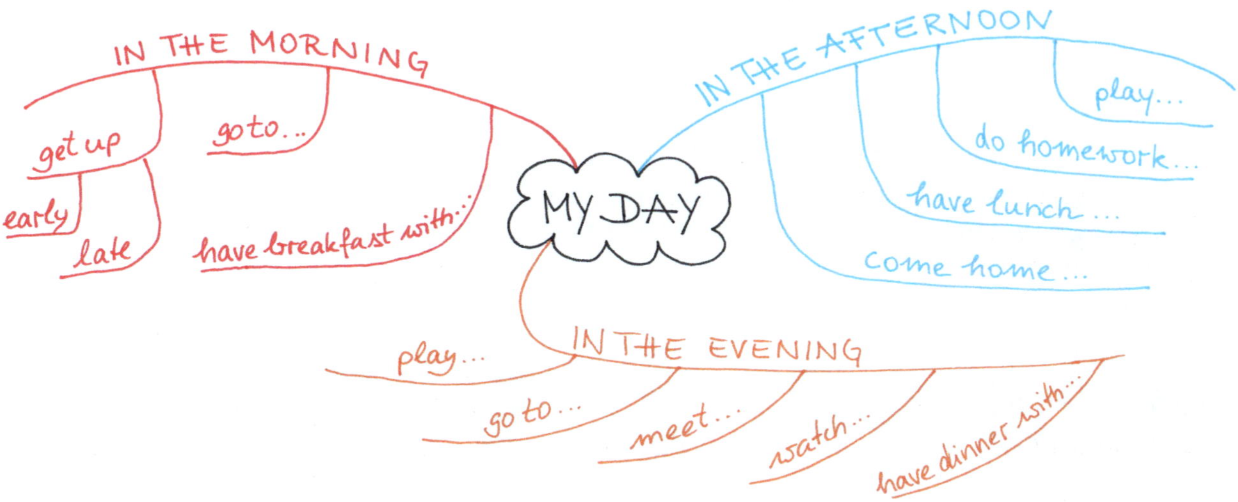

More help **6** **NOW YOU** ▸ Unit 3, p. 59

b) Use your notes and write a text about your day. Use phrases like this:

My day
In the morning I get up (early / late).
I (usually / always) have breakfast (with ...)
Then I (go to school / ...)
In the afternoon I (come home / ...)
I have lunch. Then I (sometimes) ...
In the evening I (make ... / play ... / watch ... / ...)
Then I (go to ... / ...)

Use **always • usually • often • sometimes • never**:
– I usually get up late.
– I always have lunch at school.

You can put your text in your DOSSIER.

Unit 3

More help 3 Luca's birthday ▸ Unit 3, p. 61

Write the story. The sentence parts in the green box can help you.

On Thursday Luca has no ideas for ...
But his mum has ...
On Saturday morning Luca gets ...
Later the boys meet Jack's friends ...
Jack goes ...
Then Luca goes down the hill ...
Jack and Luca go to ...
Luca has ...

... a great idea – a concert!
... down the hill first.
... his birthday.
... the hospital.
... a sore leg.
... at the Hoe.
... but he falls.
... great presents.

More help 1 Luca's garage sale ▸ Unit 3, p. 62

a) What's in Luca's garage sale? Make two lists.
The words in the box can help you.

There's ...	There are
a bike	2 footballs
a ...	3 ...

bike • blazer • books • boxes • calculator • car • cat • computer • computer games • crab • cushion • footballs • hoodie • lamp • mobile phones • pencils • pencil case • pens • picture • posters • rulers • schoolbag • shirt • sweatshirts • ties • ...

2.12 1 Luca's garage sale ▸ Unit 3, p. 62

c) Listen again. How much are the things in the garage sale? Write the prices.

1 The calculator is £...
2 The mobiles are £...
3 The crab is ...
4 The posters are ...
5 The computer is ...
6 The school bag is ...
7 The blazer is ...
8 The footballs are ...

You write:	You say:
£1.50	One pound fifty
50 p	Fifty p

2.13 More practice 3 Jack helps with the °prices ▸ Unit 3, p. 62

Listen and write the prices in your exercise book.

More help 2 A new helmet ▸ Unit 3, p. 63

a) Copy and complete the dialogue. Choose the right words.

Luca — This helmet looks big / nice (1). I like it. Excuse me, please / thank you (2). How much / What (3) is the red helmet?
Man — It's / They're (4) £24.99.
Luca — That's too expensive / big (5)! How much / Where (6) is the white helmet?
Man — It's a stupid / special (7) offer. It's £16.99.
Luca — That's OK. I'll do / take (8) it.

More help 2 Guessing new words ▸ Unit 3, p. 64

a) What are these words in German? Find the words in the adverts on p. 64. Then read the sentences in German here. They can help you.

1	on stage (advert A)	Wo befinden sich bei einer Show die Leute, die singen und tanzen? Schau dir das Bild an.
	fireworks (advert B)	Das Bild hilft dir. Gibt es ein ähnliches deutsches Wort?
2	theatre (advert A)	Das deutsche Wort ist sehr ähnlich, es wird nur etwas anders geschrieben.
	festival (advert B)	Das Wort gibt es auch im Deutschen. Schau auf das Wort davor. Gibt es auch ein *summer festival* bei euch?
3	opening times (advert C)	Was kommt nach diesem Wort im Text? Es sieht aus wie Uhrzeiten, oder? Du hörst oft im Unterricht: *Open your book*. Und dann öffnest du dein Buch. Was könnte *opening times* heißen?
	adult (advert C)	*Adults* müssen £11 Eintritt zahlen. *Children* zahlen nur £6.50. Sind *adults* älter oder jünger als Kinder? Was könnte das Wort heißen?

Unit 3

More practice 4 More words from the adverts ▸ Unit 3, p. 64

a) Work with a partner. One of you open your book at p. 64.
Look together at the adverts and try to guess these words:

In advert A: live, price, book
In advert B: championships, free
In advert C: fantastic, dive show, tiger sharks, tickets

b) What helps you to guess the words?

Unit 3 Stop! Check! Go!

More help 1 WORDS In a town ▸ Unit 3, p. 66

c) Make sentences.
You can use ideas from the box.

1 ... in a park.
→ *You can play games in a park.*
2 ... in a restaurant.
→ *You can ...*
3 ... in a shopping centre.
4 ... in a swimming pool.
5 ... in a mobile phone shop.
6 ... in a bike shop.

- buy a bike / a helmet / a mobile / things
- go swimming / shopping
- have lunch / breakfast
- meet friends
- play football / games
- ride a bike

More help 8 READING Casper the cat ▸ Unit 3, p. 69

Find these words in the text. Guess what they mean in German.
The sentences in German can help you.

1 leaves (line 3)	Schau dir die Wörter davor und danach an. Was macht Casper jeden Morgen?
2 bus stop (l. 4)	Du kennst beide Wörter aus dem Deutschen. Das erste Wort ist klar, aber das zweite Wort musst du etwas anders übersetzen, dort stoppt der …
3 waits (l. 4)	Casper ist an der Bushaltestelle. Was macht er dort zunächst?
4 sits (l. 5)	Das Wort ist auch einem deutschen Wort sehr ähnlich.
5 window (l. 6)	Schau dir das Foto an. Wo sitzt Casper? Wohin schaut er?
6 travels (l. 8)	Es geht um den Bus. Was macht er? Achte auf die Zahl nach dem Wort.
7 bus driver (l. 9)	Schau dir die Wörter davor und danach an. Könnte das eine Person sein? Wer ist das?
8 gets out (l. 9)	Schau auf die Wörter davor. Casper ist wieder an seinem Haus. Was macht er?

Unit 4

More practice 1 Animal words

► Unit 4, p. 71

Collect as many animal words as you can.
Copy this diagram and complete it.

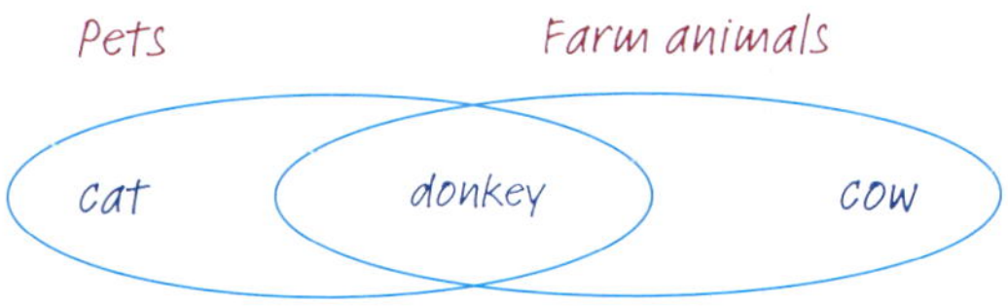

Or write two lists, like this:

Pets	Farm animals
...	...

More help 2 NOW YOU

► Unit 4, p. 72

a) Write sentences. You can use the ideas in the brackets.

1 Every morning ... (my mum / my sister / my alarm clock / ...) wakes me.
2 Before breakfast I ... (go to the bathroom / get ready for school / ...)
3 I go to school by ... (bus / car / bike) / I walk to school with ...
4 I come home before / at ... (one o'clock / two o'clock / ...)
5 In the evening I ... (watch TV / do my homework / do sport / listen to music / ...)

More practice 2 On school days

► Unit 4, p. 73

a) Copy and complete the table for you.

b) Appointments: Make appointments with two partners. Then talk to your partners like this:

> I get up at 6 o'clock. What about you?

Listen to their answers and complete the table.

	Me	1 o'clock ...	2 o'clock ...
get up	6.00	...	...
have breakfast	6.15	...	...
go to school	...		
come home			
have lunch			
do my homework			
have dinner			
go to bed			

More help 2 NOW YOU

► Unit 4, p. 74

a) Find more ideas when you feel great or when you feel fed up. Look at the box for help.
Make notes like this:

I feel great ...	I feel fed up ...
when I play football	when my dad is bossy.
when I ...	...
...	

- when I'm with my family / ...
- when I (don't) have school
- when my best friend / ... doesn't text me
- when my parents / teachers are strict
- when my brother / ... borrows my things
- when my mum / ... doesn't have time for me

Unit 4

More help 3 Berry's homework ▸ Unit 4, p. 75

d) Write a short text about your feelings. Use your notes from exercise 2 on p. 74. Write more than one sentence. Here are some ideas:

I feel great when I do sport.
My favourite sport is …
I often play with …

I feel great when I'm with my animals.
My (dog/cat/…) makes me happy.
We play every evening.

I feel fed up when my parents are strict.
They say: Do your homework!
Go to bed early!
You can't … (watch TV / go to the cinema with your friends/…)!

I feel fed up when my sister borrows my things.
She always borrows (my pullovers/…).
She never asks me.

//● 4 That's wrong! ▸ Unit 4, p. 77

a) Correct the sentences. Use *doesn't* or *don't*. Then write the right sentences.

1 Berry lives in the city. – That's wrong! She doesn't live in the city. She lives in a village.
2 Berry's parents have a pet shop. – That's wrong! They don't … They have …
3 Berry rides a donkey. – That's wrong! … …
4 Berry has a cat. – That's wrong! … …
5 Berry's mum and dad have cows on the farm. – That's wrong! … …
6 Sam the dog lives in the field. – That's wrong! … …
7 Berry goes to school in Woolwell. – That's wrong! … …
8 Luca and Adam have dogs. – That's wrong! … …
9 Ellie has two ponies. – That's wrong! … …
10 Chipmunks like cats. – That's wrong! … …

//● 5 My interesting pets ▸ Unit 4, p. 77

Complete the text. Put the verbs in brackets in the right form.

1 I … (live) in a small flat and we … (have) a garden.
2 My mum … (like) small pets. She … (want) a big pet.
3 I … (have) a 'normal' pet, like a dog. I … (have) three degus.
4 A degu … (come) from England. It … (come) from Chile.
5 A degu … (need) a friend. It … (like) to be lonely.
6 Degus … (need) lots of space. They … (like) small cages.
7 And degus … (like) other animals. They … (hate) dogs and cats.
8 I often … (play) with Pip, my favourite degu. But we … (go) outside.

Me and my degu

More practice 3 More questions about pets ▸ Unit 4, p. 78

With your partner think of three more questions for your dialogues on page 78.
Use the ideas in the boxes or your own ideas.

Questions for partners with a pet:

Do you ... play with your pet?
talk to your pet?
go outside with your pet?

Where does your pet sleep?
Does your pet ... sleep in your room?
have a cage?

Questions for partners with no pet:

Does your mum / dad / ... like animals?
want a pet?
Does your grandmother / your friend/ ... have a pet?

Do you play with the pet?

More help 11 Talking about pets ▸ Unit 4, p. 78

b) Write about your favourite pet or a friend's pet. Use the ideas in the boxes.

My favourite pet
I like / don't like ....
I have / don't have ...
My aunt / friend has a dog / ...
It lives inside / in the garden /
It eats ...

Martin's pet
Martin has a dog / cat / ....
It lives in the house / a cage / ...
It eats ...
It likes games / ...
It doesn't like dogs / children / cars / ...

Pia's favourite pet
Pia wants a pet.
She doesn't want a cat / crocodile / ...
She wants a degu / a hamster / ...
Hamsters / ... are cute / nice.
They eat ...
They live in a cage / outside / ...

▸ Wordbank 7, p. 177

More help 13 Find someone who ... ▸ Unit 4, p. 79

b) Ask questions like this:

Find someone who ...	Questions
... has an interesting pet.	Do you have an interesting pet? What pet do you have?
... has an interesting hobby.	Do you have an interesting hobby? What hobby do you have?
... gets up very early.	Do you get up very early? When do you get up?
... goes to a nice place in the holidays.	Do you go to a nice place in the holiday? Where do you go?
... likes an English football team.	Do you like an English football team? What team do you like?
... likes homework.	Do you like homework? What homework do you like?

Unit 4

More practice 4 ● **More questions on the story** ▸ Unit 4, p. 81

Answer the questions.

1 Why are the three friends excited? – Because …
2 Why is Luca unhappy? – Because …
3 Why does Luca go to the village? – Because …
4 Is Luca really in trouble? Why / Why not? – …
5 What do the friends do on Saturday evening? – …
6 What do they do on Sunday? – …

More help **4** **THEATRE TIME** ▸ Unit 4, p. 81

Here are some ideas to help you to act the story:

1	Die Geschichte soll spannend klingen, deshalb solltet ihr die Sätze mit Betonung sprechen.	→ For ideas, listen to the story on the CD.
2	Lest nicht alles vor. Anweisungen und Beschreibungen wie "Ellie says" oder "Adam says" könnt ihr weglassen.	→ In your group read through your scene. Which words can you leave out?
3	Andere Dinge könnt ihr weglassen, weil ihr schauspielert. Im Text steht z.B. "Everybody laughs. But Luca doesn't laugh." Also hier lachen alle, außer Luca!	→ Are there more parts in your scene like this?

Unit 4 Stop! Check! Go!

More help **3** **REVISION** **A day with my family** ▸ Unit 4, p. 87

b) Make a table like this for a day with your family. You can use some ideas from the boxes.
Then tell your partner.

When?	Who?	What?
every morning / before 6 o'clock	mum, dad and I	get up

When?
- Every day / morning / afternoon / evening
- Before breakfast / lunch / dinner / school
- After breakfast / lunch / dinner / school
- In the morning / afternoon / evening
- At 10 o'clock / 11.15 / 12.30 / 1.45

Who?
- I
- my mum
- my dad
- my brother
- my sister
- my aunt
- …

What?
- get up / have breakfast / feed my hamster / …
- go to school / go to work
- stay at home / work at home
- go shopping / have lunch
- come home from work / from school
- do homework / do sport / play a game
- watch TV / meet friends / read a book
- make / have dinner with …
- go to bed

//● 4 LANGUAGE An interview with Cyril and Sandy ▸ Unit 4, p. 87

a) Make the questions for the reporter.

1 Plymouth / you / ... / like / ?
2 you / ... / a best friend / have / ?
3 you and Sandy / live / ... / on the beach / ?
4 like / ... / Sandy / Plymouth too / ?
5 Sandy/ have / a best friend / ... / ?

– Yes, it's great.
– Yes, I do. Her name is Sandy.
– Yes, we live in Kingsand.
– Yes, she loves Plymouth.
– Yes, she does. I'm her best friend!

b) Complete Cyril's answers.

1 Do you like Mr Johnson?
2 Do you live in a big house?
3 Do you and Sandy go to school?
4 Does Sandy have a car?
5 Does Sandy eat crabs?

– No, I ... (~~like~~) Mr Johnson. He's terrible.
– No, I ... (~~live~~) in a big house. I like small houses.
– No, we ... (~~go~~) to school.
– No, she ... (~~have~~) a car. But she has a bike.
– No, she ... (~~eat~~) crabs. I'm a crab!

c) Complete the questions for Sandy.

1 ... do you live?
2 ... do you get up?
3 ... do you have breakfast?
4 ... do you do after breakfast?
5 ... do you like Cyril?

– In Kingsand.
– Very late – after 10 o'clock.
– I always have breakfast on the beach.
– I often go to Plymouth.
– Because he's friendly and he's fun!

More help 6 WRITING Luca and you ▸ Unit 4, p. 88

a) Write the dialogue with Luca in your exercise book.
Write as much as you can.

Luca
Hi, I'm Luca. What's your name?
Do you live in England?
Do you live in the country?
Do you like English?
Do you have a pet?
When do you feel fed up?
When do you feel great?
Do you want to come to Plymouth?

You
– Hi, Luca. I'm ...
– No, I live in ...
– Yes / No, I live in a city / town / village.
– Yes, it's great. / No, it isn't easy.
– Yes, I have a ... / No, I don't. But I want a ...
– I feel fed up when my friend doesn't text me / when I have lots of homework / ...
– I feel great when I do sport / when I'm with my friends / when I have holidays / ...
– Yes, I do. Great! / No, thanks.

Unit 4 Stop! Check! Go!

More help **7 SPEAKING** **An interview with a student in your class** ▸ Unit 4, p. 88

a) Here are some more ideas for your interview questions:

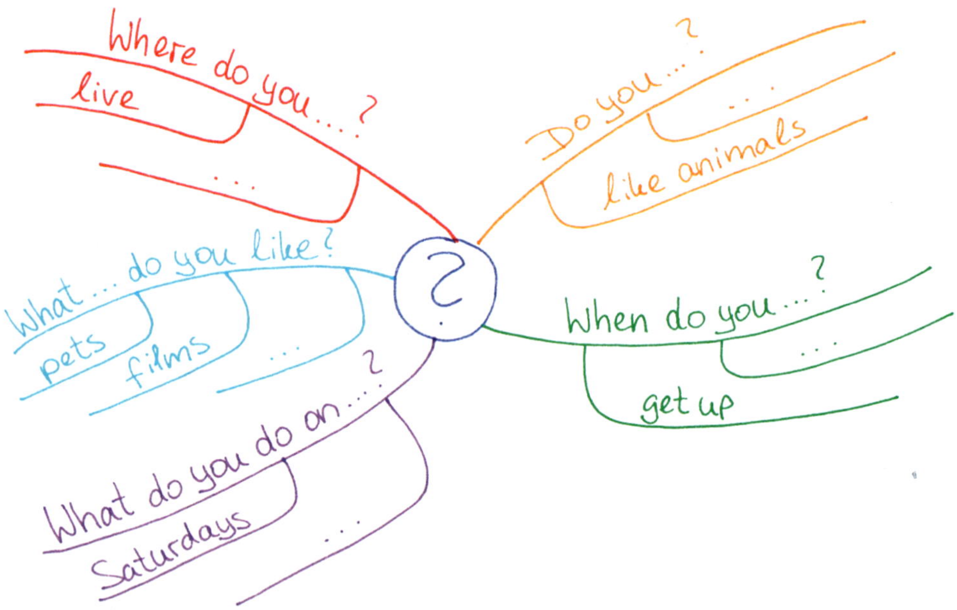

More help **8 PROJECT** **Interesting animals** ▸ Unit 4, p. 89

b) You can write a text like this about your animal.

My project is about chipmunks.
Chipmunks come from the USA. They're brown, grey and black. They're furry and very cute.
They're small – 13 to 15 cm long.
They live in a nest, in the ground.
They eat fruit and nuts. They usually live for three years[1].
Chipmunks are fun, but they aren't good pets.

Unit 5

More help **1** **The harbour in Plymouth** ▸ Unit 5, p. 90

b) How many of the things in the box can you find on pages 90–91? Write a list.

baby • beach • bike • blazer • bus • car • chair • child/children • city • dog • garden • helmet • house • kid • man • park • people • phone • restaurant • road • sea • seagull • shop • sign • swimming pool • table • teenagers • tree • visitors • …

[1] for three years *drei Jahre lang*

More help Can I help you? ▸ Unit 5, p. 92

d) Make a dialogue in a cafe.
Here are some useful words and phrases.

What can you eat?
a sandwich • a chicken sandwich • omelette and chips • fish and chips • a salad • soup • scones • ...

What can you drink?
- a bottle of water/juice
- a cup of coffee/tea
- a bottle of orange/banana/... juice

Can I help you?
↓
..., please.
↓
Something to drink?
↓
..., please.
↓
Anything else?
↙ And ..., please. | ↓ | ↘ No, thanks. That's all.
↓
That's £..., please.
↓
OK. £... – Here you are.
↓
Thanks. Next, please.

More practice 1 Adam and his family ▸ Unit 5, p. 93

Finish the sentences about Adam and his family. You can use the ideas in the box.

1 Adam's dad works on ...
2 Adam's dad likes ...
3 But Adam misses ...
4 The cafe is often ...
5 Adam's mum works ...
6 Adam sometimes helps in ...
7 At school Adam isn't very ...
8 And he isn't doing ... at the moment.

a ferry • happy • his dad • his homework • his new job • the cafe • very busy • very hard

More help 2 Welcome to PMZ ▸ Unit 5, p. 95

c) Copy this table. Listen again and put in the notes from the box.

PMZ address: ...	*Times (Sat): ... ...*
Bus number: ...	*Price: ...*
Times (Mon–Fri):	

- From 4 pm to 7 pm
- From 10 am to 12.30 pm.
- Raglan Road
- Free
- 34

Unit 5

More help 3 NOW YOU ▸ Unit 5, p. 95

a) Appointments: Copy this table and write your answers.

	Me	1 o'clock …	2 o'clock …
What's your favourite band?			
Who's your favourite singer?			
What's your favourite English song?			
Can you play an instrument? What instrument?			
Can you sing? Can you rap?			
Are you in a band?			

▸ Wordbank 8, p. 177

More help 3 NOW YOU ▸ Unit 5, p. 95

d) Write a text about you and music. Here are some ideas.
You can put your text in your DOSSIER.

I love pop / rap / … music
My favourite band / singer is …
My favourite English song is …
I (can't) play an instrument.
My favourite instrument is the guitar / drums / …
I play the guitar / piano / …
I can sing / rap / …
I'm in a band. / My friend is in a band.
The name of the band is …

More practice 2 What's the fourth word? ▸ Unit 5, p. 97

a) ○ Just add 'ing'.

1 read – reading
clean – …

2 eat – eating
do – …

b) There's no 'e' with -ing!

1 ride – riding
make – …

2 come – coming
write – …

c) Look at the examples!

1 rap – rapping
get – …

2 swim – swimming
sit – …

More practice 3 What are they saying? ▸ Unit 5, p. 97

Finish the sentences A–F. Use the *present progressive*.

A

Berry — It's 2 o'clock. We're late, Ellie!
Ellie — OK, I... (come)!

B

Adam — Is Luca at home?
Ms Boateng — Sorry, Luca ... (ride) his bike in the park.

C

Ms Lee — What are you doing, Ellie?
Ellie — Sorry, Miss. I... (eat) a sweet.

D

Ms Lee — Is Ellie OK?
Berry — She... (feel) tired.

E

Adam — Are they looking at me?
Luca — No, they... (look) at me!

F

Adam — Who... (sit) here?
Luca — Ellie. Look, she's there.

4 What's Cyril doing? ▸ Unit 5, p. 97

a) What's Cyril doing now? Write the numbers 1–5. Then listen and write what you think.
Example: *1 Cyril is ..., 2 ...*

Unit 5

More practice 4 An email to Adam ▸ Unit 5, p. 99

Write an email to Adam about the story. Here are some ideas.

I think	the girls and boys on the bus were ... you were ... Josie was ... your rap is ... PMZ is ... your parents are ...

bad • boring • bossy • cool • different • friendly • fun • great • good • happy • important • interesting • mean • nervous • nice • stupid • terrible • ...

Dear Adam

I think the story about you at PMZ is ...

Best wishes
(Your name)

You can also tell Adam something about you:
– Do you like rap?
– Who's your favourite rapper?
– Can you rap?
– ...

More help 1 In the park ▸ Unit 5, p. 100

b) What are they doing? Make sentences.

On the left In the middle On the right	two dogs a boy three girls children a girl a baby two men	are working. are eating. is riding a bike. is sleeping are playing football. are talking and laughing. is reading a book.

More help 3 WRITING A text to Amanda ▸ Unit 5, p. 101

Write a text message to Amanda. Here are some ideas for your text.

- I'm sitting at home / ...
- I'm (not) working hard / ...
- I'm learning English / doing my homework / ...
- My friend / mum / brother / ... is here.
- He's / She's listening 2 music / ...
- I'm feeling gr8 / happy / terrible / ...
- How R U?
- Yes, I can come 2 the party.
- Sorry. I can't come 2 the party.

Unit 5 Stop! Check! Go!

More help 1 REVISION Questions and answers ▸ Unit 5, p. 104

d) Make a quiz about another animal. Use these ideas:

- Do ... live in Germany?
- Do ... live in fields / on farms / in the sea / ...?
- Do ... live in cages / in zoos / ...?
- Do ... eat fruit / nuts / special food / other animals / ...?
- Do ... like people?
- Do ... walk fast?

More help 8 READING and WRITING On Saturday morning ▸ Unit 5, p. 107

b) Here are some ideas for another picture for the story.

I'm hungry. • A big chicken sandwich, please. • Can I help you? • Anything else? • ...

Hi, Dad. • You're early. • That's great. • This is a surprise. • I'm really happy. • How's it going? • How are you? • ...

Unit 6

More help 1 Planning a trip ▸ Unit 6, p. 110

a) What things can you bring to the beach? Start a network like this. Then read the text for more ideas.

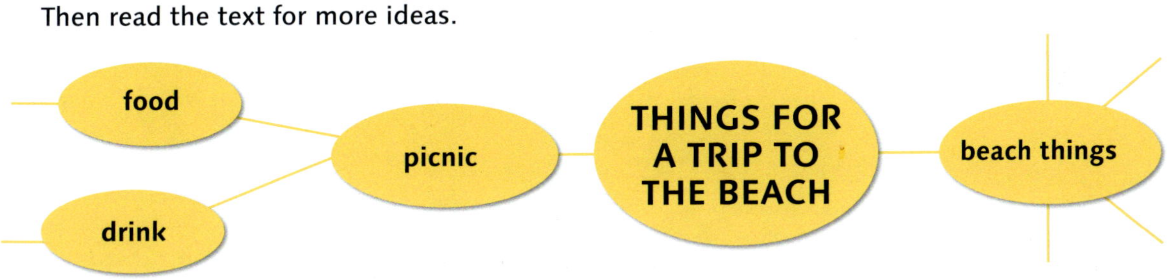

Unit 6

More help 2 You're going on a ferry trip! ► Unit 6, p. 112

b) Talk to a partner.

What's the ferry trip like? – It's fun / nice / ...
What do you see? – The harbour / ...
What do you hear? – The noisy ferry / ...
What do you feel? – The cool water / ...

the sea • seagulls • the harbour • buses • the cool water • the city • a beach • the noisy ferry • an old woman • a cafe • lots of kids • the swimming pool • cars • a village • nice houses • a man / ... • ...

//● 2 What are your summer plans? ► Unit 6, p. 116

Work with a partner. Talk about your summer plans.

A	B
Begrüße deinen Partner / deine Partnerin. Frage, wie es ihm / ihr geht.	Grüße zurück. Sage, wie es dir geht.
Frage, was er / sie im Sommer vorhat.	Sage, was du vorhast. (2 oder 3 Ideen)
Sage, wie du die Pläne deines Partners / deiner Partnerin findest.	Nun frage deinen Partner / deine Partnerin, was er / sie vorhat.
Sage, was <u>du</u> vorhast.	Sage, wie du die Pläne deines Partners / deiner Partnerin findest.

More help 2 People and places: A ferry trip to Cawsand ► Unit 6, p. 117

a) You're going on a ferry trip to Cawsand.
What do you think you can see?
Make a list.

buses • people • bags • food • shops • dogs • seagulls • bikes • cars • crabs • a ferry • boats • a harbour • houses • books • a beach • the sea • tents • picnics • smugglers • sunglasses • kids • tickets • a map • ...

TF 2

More practice **You stupid boy!** ▸ *Text file 2, p. 151*

Use your Cyril and Sandy puppets. Act a scene. The ideas in the boxes can help you.

- Thanks Sandy!
- Yes, we're good friends!
- Toby is a stupid boy.
- I'm OK.
- Is the picnic good?
- Oh, thanks, Johnsons!
- ...

- That's OK, Cyril.
- Are you OK now?
- We're friends.
- The Johnsons are stupid.
- This is good!
- Yeah, thanks, Toby!
- ...

2 **NOW YOU** ▸ *Unit 5, p. 100*

Partner A

a) Describe *picture 1* to your partner. Say what you can see, where the things and people are, and what they're doing:

On the left / In the middle / On the right I can see ...
There's a ... next to / in front of ...
He's / She's playing ...

Your partner listens and looks at his / her picture. Some things are different in your picture. He / She must find five differences.

b) Then listen to your partner. He / She is talking about *picture 2*. There are five differences in your picture. When you hear a difference, tell your partner.

In my picture there's a seagull on the ...
In my picture the boy is ...

1

2

Lösung:

Unit 1

1 **The unit quiz** ▸ *Unit 1, p. 22*

Check your anwers:

1 Plymouth
2 Ellie and Berry
3 Luca
4 Luca and Jack
5 Harry / Berry's pet
6 Ms Lee
7 Berry
8 Ellie, Berry, Luca, Adam
9 Grace / Luca's sister
10 Ellie
11 PE
12 (your name)

TF 1 Puppets[1] for your classroom[2]

Make crab and seagull puppets for your classroom.

[1] puppet ['pʌpɪt] *Handpuppe* [2] classroom ['klɑːsruːm] *Klassenzimmer*

You need[1] ...

two cards

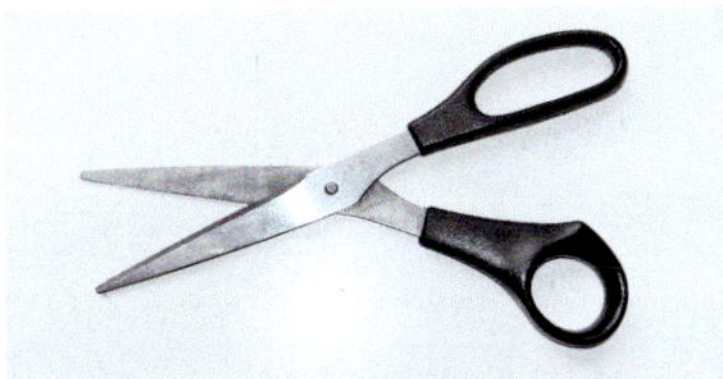

scissors

felt tips or crayons[1)]

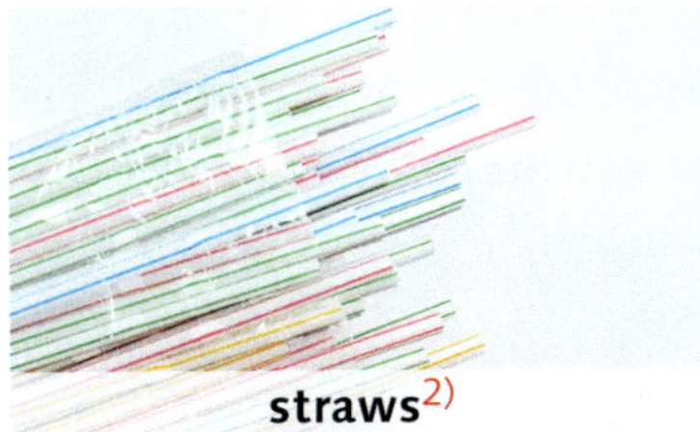

straws[2)]

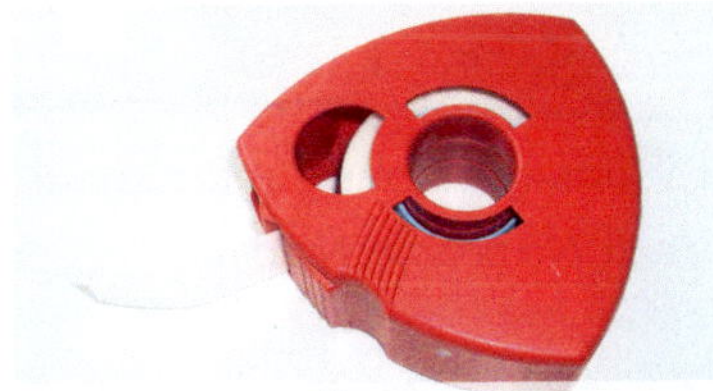

cellotape

STEP 1: Copy or draw a puppet on the card.

STEP 2: Cut out the puppet.
Put the straw on your puppet.

STEP 3: Make a 'beach' for your puppets.

STEP 4: Make dialogues with your puppets.

[1] need [niːd] *brauchen*

1 [ˈkreɪənz] 2 [strɔːz]

TF 2 You stupid boy!

It's Sunday morning at Kingsand. Cyril is on the beach. No people. No children. Cyril is happy!

Sandy is near the beach. No people. No children. No lunch for Sandy! She isn't very happy!

Look! It's Mr Johnson, Mrs Johnson and Toby Johnson! They're very happy – a nice day on the beach!

Look! Sandy is on the beach now. She's with Cyril. Cyril isn't happy now.

Can Toby Johnson see Cyril? Can he see Benny and Babe?

Toby can see Cyril!

Go, Cyril, go!

Toby has Cyril!

Cyril isn't very happy. But Toby is happy!

Benny and Babe are Cyril's friends. They're next!

Toby isn't very happy now!

Where's Toby?

Cyril is OK now!

Mrs Johnson can't[1] see Toby.

Toby is wet[2]. He's cold. He isn't happy.

The nice day on the beach is over – for the Johnsons.

More practice p. 147

[1] can't [kɑːnt] *kann nicht* [2] wet [wet] *nass*

3.11–3.13

TF 3 The best Christmas present[1]

24th December: Christmas Eve[2]

It's Christmas Eve and there are lots of people in Plymouth. They all need things for Christmas. Ellie and her mum are in Plymouth too. First they go to the big supermarket. It's very busy. They need icing[3] for the Christmas cake[4]. Then they go to *Whoopee*, a nice toy[5] shop. Ellie buys a present for Finn – a small red crab.
Now Ellie and her mum are at home. Pete and Conor are there too. But Zoe isn't at home. She's with her boyfriend, Alan.

There are lots of jobs for Christmas Day[6]. Ellie helps her mum with the Christmas cake.

The living room is very nice. There are lots of Christmas cards and decorations. Conor and Ellie put[7] decorations on the Christmas tree.
"It's great!" Pete says.
"It's really nice!" mum says.

"Ding-dong." Carol singers are at the door.

"We wish you a Merry Christmas,
We wish you a Merry Christmas,
We wish you a Merry Christmas
And a Happy New Year."

"Ding-dong." Now Zoe is at the door too. But she isn't happy.
"Hi, Zoe," mum says. "What's the problem?"
"I think it's over with Alan and me," Zoe says and she goes to her room.

[1] Christmas present ['krɪsməs preznt] *Weihnachtsgeschenk* [2] Christmas Eve [krɪsməs 'iːv] *Heiligabend* [3] icing ['aɪsɪŋ] *Zuckerguss* [4] cake [keɪk] *Kuchen* [5] toy [tɔɪ] *Spielzeug* [6] Christmas Day [krɪsməs 'deɪ] *1. Weihnachtsfeiertag* [7] put [pʊt] *hängen*

25th December: Christmas Day

It's Christmas morning – 6 o'clock. Ellie is in bed.
"Zoe! Zoe!" she says.
"What?" Zoe says.

"Our Christmas stockings[1] are here!" Ellie says.
She looks into her stocking.
"Oh, look Zoe. A computer game – *Let's Dance!* Great!"
"Ellie, please be quiet," Zoe says.
"And a book ... and a new hoodie ... and chocolate ... Thank you, Father Christmas," Ellie says and she laughs[2].
Ellie is happy. But Zoe isn't very happy.

Later the family has a big Christmas breakfast. Then they go to the living room. It's present time.
"Here's a present for you, Conor. It's from Pete," mum says.

"Thanks dad," Conor says. "Oh, speakers – great!"
"And here's a present for you Zoe – from Alan," mum says.
"I don't want it![3]" Zoe says and she goes to her room. She isn't very happy.

It's time for Christmas lunch. There are lots of nice things – a big turkey[4], potatoes[5], vegetables[6]. And then there's Christmas pudding. And they all have Christmas crackers.
"Conor, pull[7] a cracker with me," Ellie says.

BANG! In the cracker there's a small present – a pen. There's a paper hat[8] and a joke[9] too.
"Why[10] is it always cold at Christmas?" Ellie reads.
"Er ... no idea! What's the answer?" Pete says.
"Because it's Decemberrrrrrrrr!" Ellie says and they all laugh.
"Zoe, pull a cracker with me," Pete says.
"No, thanks," Zoe says.

Christmas dinner

Christmas pudding

[1] stocking ['stɒkɪŋ] *(langer) Strumpf* [2] laugh [lɑːf] *lachen* [3] I don't want it! [dəʊnt 'wɒnt] *Ich will es nicht!*
[4] turkey ['tɜːki] *Truthahn* [5] potatoes [pə'teɪtəʊz] *Kartoffeln* [6] vegetable ['vedʒtəbl] *Gemüse* [7] pull [pʊl] *ziehen*
[8] hat [hæt] *Hut* [9] joke [dʒəʊk] *Witz* [10] why [waɪ] *warum*

Later on Christmas Day

"Ellie, it's your dad," Conor says. "He's at the door."
"Happy Christmas, dad," Ellie says.
"Happy Christmas, Ellie. Let's go to our flat, to Finn and Alisha," her dad says.
It's Finn's first Christmas.
He's very happy.
And his present from Ellie is great.

The Queen's Christmas Message[2]

At 3 o'clock the Queen[1] is on TV. She's always on TV on Christmas Day.
"At Christmas, family and friends are very important ...," the Queen says.
Ellie has an idea. She writes a text message on her mobile phone to Alan, Zoe's boyfriend:

Later Ellie is in the kitchen with her dad, Finn and Alisha. It's time for tea and Christmas cake. Ellie has a text message from Zoe:

1 Christmas in Britain

What are the Christmas things (1–5) in the photo?

a paper hat • a turkey • a Christmas cracker • a Christmas tree • a Christmas card

2 Be a Christmas detective: Right or wrong?

1 On Christmas Eve lots of people go shopping.
2 In Britain people get presents on Christmas Eve.
3 Carol singers go from door to door and sing Christmas songs.
4 The presents in the Christmas stockings are from Father Christmas.
5 There are no presents under[3] the Christmas tree.
6 There's fish for lunch on Christmas Day.
7 There's a small present, a paper hat and a joke in a Christmas cracker.
8 The Queen is on TV on Christmas Eve.

[1] queen [kwi:n] *Königin* [2] Christmas Message ['krɪsməs mesɪdʒ] *Weihnachtsansprache* [3] under ['ʌndə] *unter*

TF 4 What's bicycle[1] motocross?

Bicycle motocross (BMX) is a popular bicycle sport.

The equipment[2]

Where you can ride

On a track[5] – You can ride your bike on a special BMX track. BMX is a new Olympic sport. It's very fast[6].

In a special park – You can do tricks on your bike in BMX parks or skateboard parks. There are special jumps[7].

In the street – You can ride in the street or in a sports hall. You can do tricks there too. You don't need jumps.

THE PLYMOUTH NEWS

A world champion

This is Shanaze Reade. She's from England. Her dad is from Jamaica. Her mum is from Ireland.
Shanaze rides on BMX tracks all around the world for the British national team. She's the world champion of 2008. She got[8] her first BMX bike when she was 10. It was £1!

Shanaze Reade

Find a picture of your bike or your dream bike. Make labels for the bike.

1 bicycle ['baɪsɪkl] *Fahrrad* 2 equipment [ɪ'kwɪpmənt] *Ausrüstung* 3 low [ləʊ] *niedrig* 4 gears (pl) [gɪəz] *Gänge; Gangschaltung* 5 track [træk] *Piste* 6 fast [fɑːst] *schnell* 7 jump [dʒʌmp] *Schanze, Rampe (zum Springen)* 8 got [gɒt] *bekam*

TF 5 The greatest show on earth[1]

3.14–3.16

It's 9 o'clock on Friday morning. The classroom is noisy because the teacher isn't there. All the students are happy. They like Fridays. Then Ms Lee comes in – with a boy. "Good morning," she says. "We have a new student." All the students look at the new boy.
"This is Ben", Ms Lee says.
"Hello," Ben says. He's very quiet and doesn't look happy.
"Ben is from Russell's Circus," Ms Lee says.
"Wow – a circus!" Luca says.
"Do you live in Plymouth?" Ellie asks.
"No. We're here for two weeks," Ben says. "We go to different towns and I go to different schools."
"Cool," Berry says.

1 How does Ben feel at 9 o'clock?

It's 1 o'clock, time for lunch, Ellie, Adam, Luca and Berry are in the canteen. They see Ben.
"Hi, Ben. Do you want to sit with us?" Berry asks.
"Sure, thanks," Ben says.

"I bet[2] life in a circus is fun," Adam says.
"Yeah, it's OK," Ben says.
"Where do you live?" Ellie asks.
"In a caravan. We're in Central Park now," Ben says.
"Cool – it's like camping!" Luca says.
"And what animals do you have?" Adam asks.
"We don't have animals in our circus," Ben says.
Luca is surprised. "No animals? Why?"
"Because it isn't good for animals to live in a circus," Ben says.
"But a circus with no animals – that isn't a real circus," Adam says.
"You can visit our circus and see a real circus – with no animals," Ben says.
"Great. When can we come?" Berry asks.
"Tomorrow is Saturday. Come tomorrow morning," Ben says.
"OK. See you tomorrow morning."

2 How does Ben feel at lunch time?
3 What's special about[3] Ben's circus?

[1] The greatest show on earth ['greɪtɪst ʃəʊ ɒn 'ɜːθ] *Die großartigste Show der Welt* [2] bet [bet] *wetten*
[3] special about ['speʃl əbaʊt] *besonders in*

It's Saturday morning and Ellie, Luca, Adam and Berry are in Central Park, at Russell's Circus. Ben sees his new friends.
"Hi. Welcome to my home," he says.
Ben brings the four kids to his caravan first.
"This is cool," Ellie says. "And so big!"
"This isn't like camping!" Luca says. "It's like a normal house."
"Where do you sleep?" Adam asks.
The friends visit Ben's room. It's very nice. They meet Ben's mum. She works in the ticket office[1]. And they meet Ben's dad. He's a clown.

4 What is Ben's caravan like?

It's time for a tour of the circus. There are lots of people in the big tent[2].
"This is Maria. And this is Darek. They're from Poland. And they're trapeze artists," Ben says.
"Do you like your work?" Berry asks.
"Yes, we love it," Maria says.
"Is it dangerous?" Luca asks.
"Yes, it is. But we're careful[3]," Darek answers.

Then they talk to Raymond. He's from France and he's a juggler[4].
"Do you want to try?" he asks Ellie.
"OK," she says. But she's terrible. The other kids laugh.

"Come here," Ben's dad says. He's with two other clowns. He's on their shoulders, but then they all fall down. The friends laugh.

They have lunch in Ben's caravan.
"Do you want to see the show today?" Ben's mum asks. "It's at 3 o'clock."
"Wow. Yes please. That's great!" the kids say.
"Can we help you?" Berry asks.
"That's a good idea," Ben's father says. "You can see what life in the circus is really like."

5 What circus people do the kids meet?

[1] ticket office ['tɪkɪt ɒfɪs] *Schalter* [2] tent [tent] *Zelt* [3] careful ['keəfl] *vorsichtig* [4] juggler ['dʒʌglə] *Jongleur/in*

It's 2.30 on Saturday afternoon. Lots of people are at Russell's Circus. Berry is in the ticket office with Ben's mum.

"Do you want a circus brochure?" Berry asks. Then she sees her parents. They're at the circus too.

"Hi mum, hi dad! This is great fun," she says.

Luca is in the big tent. His job is to bring people to their seats[1].

"Hello, Mr and Mrs Donovan," he says. "Let me look at your tickets. Yes, here are your seats."

It's 3 o'clock, time for the circus. First there's music. Then the ringmaster[2] speaks to the people. "Welcome to Russell's Circus – the greatest show on earth! And here are my two helpers – Ben and Ellie!"

The first act is the clowns. It's Ben's dad and the two other clowns. Today there's a fourth clown – it's Adam!

6 **Who has the best job at the circus – Adam, Berry, Ellie or Luca? What do you think?**

Two weeks later the four friends are at Russell's Circus again. But today things are different. The big tent isn't there. The circus people are in their cars and trucks. The circus is over. It's time to go to the next town.

"Bye, Ben. Thanks for a great day at the circus. It really is the greatest show on earth!" Berry says.

"You're welcome. See you next year!" Ben says.

7 **Is Ben happy or unhappy in the end? What do you think?**

[1] seat [siːt] *Sitzplatz* [2] ringmaster [ˈrɪŋmɑːstə] *Zirkusdirektor/in*

TF 6 Hip-hop workout[1]

3.17

1 Listen and look at the instructions

A Step[2]-touch[3]

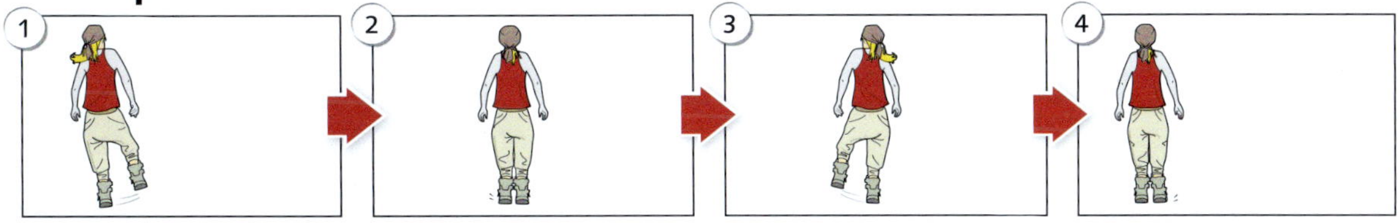

Step to the right[4]. | Left foot[5] – touch. | Step to the left. | Right foot – touch.

B Two step-touch

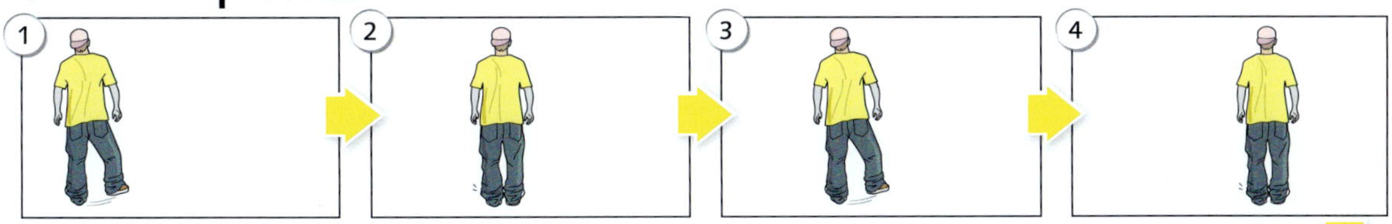

Step to the right. | Left foot – touch. | Step to the right again. | And left foot – touch.

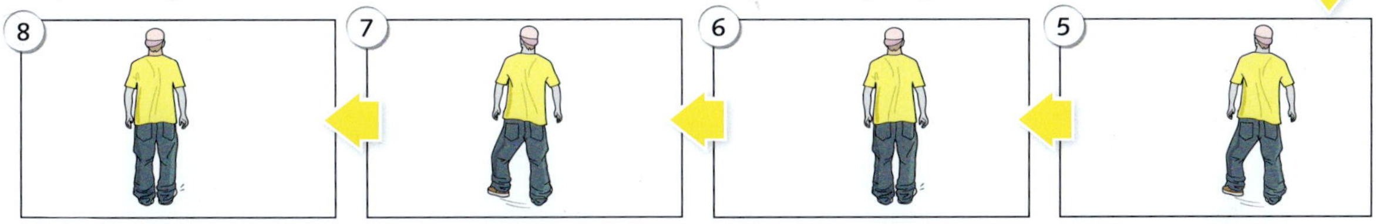

And right foot – touch. | Step to the left again. | Right foot – touch. | Step to the left.

C Grapevine[6]

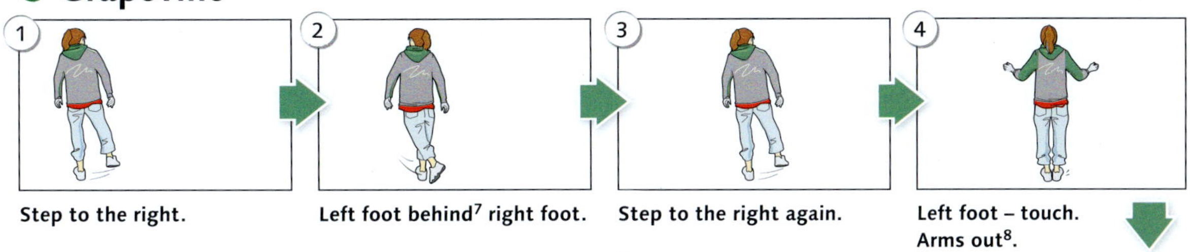

Step to the right. | Left foot behind[7] right foot. | Step to the right again. | Left foot – touch. Arms out[8].

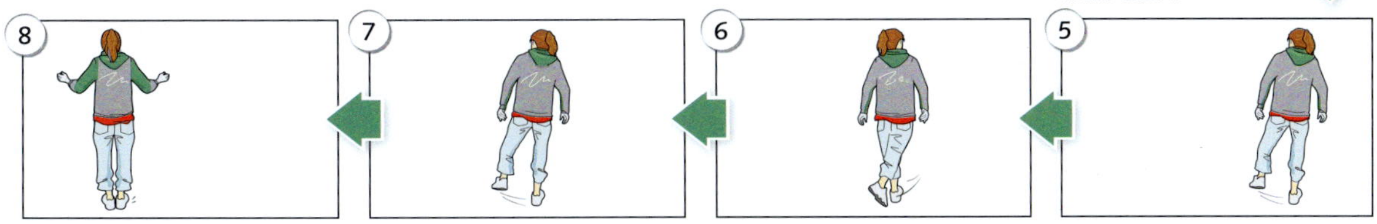

Right foot – touch. Arms out. | Step to the left again. | Right foot behind left foot. | Step to the left.

2 Practise the workouts with your class. One student can say the instructions. Play the CD and do the hip-hop workout. Have fun!

[1] workout ['wɜːkaʊt] *Fitnesstraining* [2] step [step] *einen Schritt machen* [3] touch [tʌtʃ] *berühren*
[4] to the right [raɪt] *nach rechts* [5] foot [fʊt] *Fuß* [6] grapevine ['greɪpvaɪn] *Kreuzschritt* [7] behind [bɪ'haɪnd] *hinter*
[8] arms out [ɑːmz 'aʊt] *Arme ausstrecken*

SF 1 Learning words – Vokabellernen leicht gemacht ▸ Unit 1, p. 27

Woran muss ich **immer** denken?

- Lerne nur 5 bis 10 Vokabeln auf einmal.
- Lerne und wiederhole regelmäßig. Zehn Minuten am Tag sind sinnvoller als einmal zwei Stunden pro Woche. Wiederhole direkt am nächsten Tag.
- Lerne mit jemandem zusammen. Es macht mehr Spaß und ihr könnt euch gegenseitig abfragen.
- Beim Wiederholen solltest du die Vokabeln abwechselnd lesen, laut aussprechen und vor allem auch schreiben. Beginne mal mit dem deutschen Wort und mal mit dem englischen Wort.

1 Vokabeln lernen mit dem *Vocabulary*

Vokabellernen beginnt mit dem *Vocabulary* in deinem Englischbuch (S. 179–207). Auf S. 179 kannst du sehen, wie es aufgebaut ist.
- Lies das englische Wort laut.
- Lies dann die deutsche Übersetzung und den Beispielsatz.

hoffen	I **hope** you like my school uniform.	
glücklich, froh	She's **happy**.	He isn't **happy**.
bitte	Can you help me, **please**?	

Wenn du testen möchtest, ob du die Wörter weißt, gehe eine Seite Zeile für Zeile durch:
- Decke die beiden rechten Spalten ab und sage die deutsche Übersetzung/den Beispielsatz.

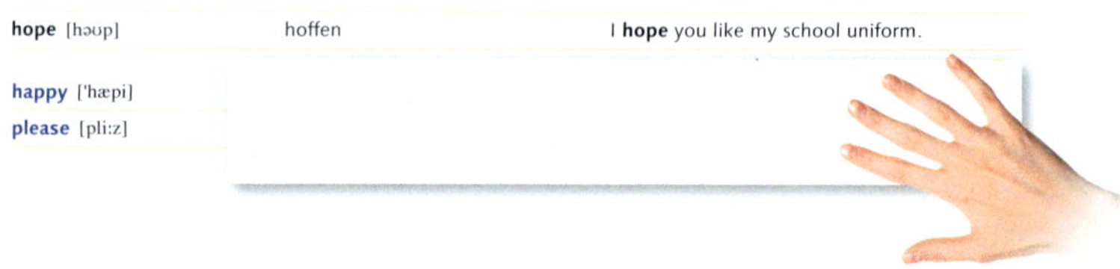

- Gehe die Seite erneut durch und decke mit zwei Blatt Papier die linke Spalte und die rechte Spalte ab und sage die englischen Wörter.

Schreibe Vokabeln, mit denen du Probleme hast, auf selbstklebende Zettel. Die klebst du dann zu Hause an Gegenstände im Zimmer, die du immer wieder ansiehst.

2 Vokabelheft

- Du kannst neue Wörter in ein Vokabelheft oder -ringbuch schreiben. Benutze ein **dreispaltiges** Vokabelverzeichnis.
- Trage in die linke Spalte das englische Wort ein und daneben die deutsche Übersetzung.
- In die rechte Spalte kannst du ein Bild einfügen oder einen Beispielsatz schreiben. Manchmal findest du gute Beispiele im *Vocabulary* deines Buches.
- Lies die geschriebenen englischen Wörter dabei immer laut vor.

3 Sammeln und ordnen – Make networks

Du behältst neue Vokabeln leichter, wenn du sie beim Aufschreiben in Gruppen ordnest, z.B. in einem Wörternetz.

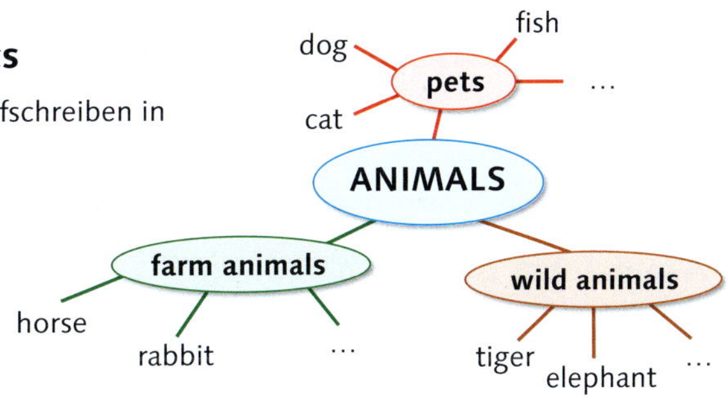

4 Vokabeln lernen mit Karteikarten

1. Du kannst neue Vokabeln auch auf Karteikarten schreiben.
   Dazu benötigst du:
   - viele kleine Kärtchen (oder gleich große Zettel)
   - einen passenden Kasten (oder einfach zwei Gummibänder)
   - eine **OK**- und eine **?**-Karte.
2. Auf die Vorderseite der Kärtchen schreibst du die englischen Wörter mit einem Beispielsatz und, wenn du magst, einem Bild. Auf die Rückseite schreibst du das deutsche Wort.
   Dann sortierst du die Kärtchen. Wie? Wie du willst!
   Am Anfang stehen alle Kärtchen im **?**-Fach.
3. Schau dir die Rückseite jeder Karte an:
   Du weißt das englische Wort?
   ▸ Die Karte wandert in das **OK**-Fach (oder auf den **OK**-Stapel).

   Du weißt es nicht?
   ▸ Die Karte kommt zurück in das **?**-Fach (oder auf den **?**-Stapel).

   Beim nächsten Mal beginnst du mit diesen Karten.

Wiederhole auch regelmäßig die Vokabeln aus dem **OK**-Fach. Wenn du sie nach zwei bis drei Wochen noch weißt, kannst du sie aussortieren.

5 Vokabellernen am Computer

Vielleicht fällt dir das Vokabellernen auch leichter, wenn du am Computer übst – mit dem e-Workbook oder mit der elektronischen Vokabelkartei.

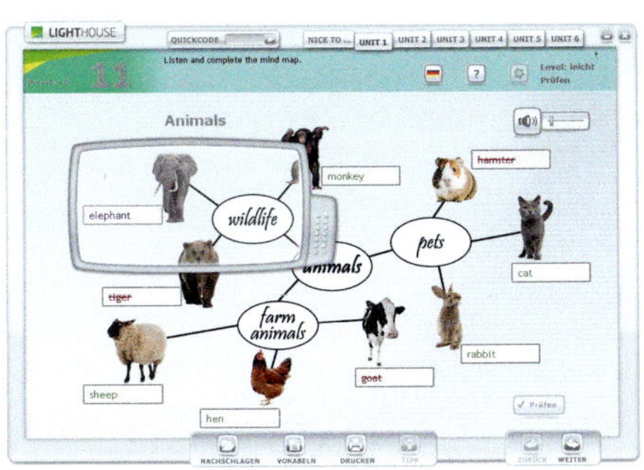

SF 2 Mindmaps ▸ Unit 2, p. 44

Wozu sind Mindmaps gut?

Mindmaps helfen beim Sammeln und Ordnen von Ideen, z.B. bevor du einen Text schreibst oder etwas vorträgst.

Wie machst du eine Mindmap?

Stell dir vor, du sollst einen Text über deine Familie schreiben. Dazu fertigst du zunächst eine Mindmap an.

Was benötigst du?

- ein leeres, unliniertes Blatt Papier im Querformat
- Stifte in verschiedenen Farben

Wie erstellst du eine Mindmap?

1. Schreibe in die **Mitte** des Blattes das **Thema** und male z.B. einen **Kreis** oder eine **Wolke** darum.

2. Überlege, über welche Hauptthemen du schreiben oder sprechen willst. Zeichne für jedes Hauptthema einen **Hauptast** in unterschiedlichen Farben und schreibe das Thema darauf. Verwende nur Schlüsselwörter.

3. Wenn dir zu den Hauptthemen noch Unterthemen einfallen, dann ergänze Nebenäste in der gleichen Farbe. Schreibe die Unterthemen auf die Nebenäste. Verwende auch hier nur Schlüsselwörter.

   An die Nebenäste kannst du noch mehr Ideen „anhängen".

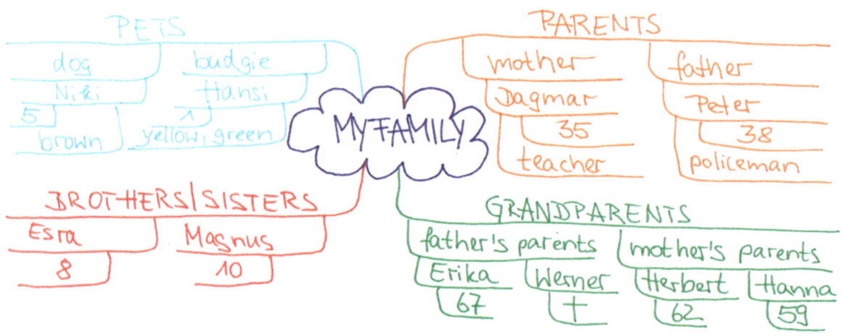

4. Du kannst statt Wörtern auch **Zahlen, Bilder oder Symbole** verwenden.

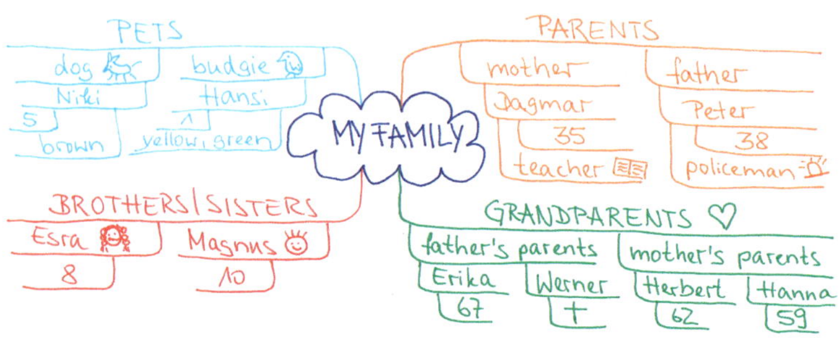

Es gibt auch Computerprogramme, mit denen du Mindmaps erstellen kannst.

SF 3 Unbekannte Wörter verstehen? – Kein Problem!

▸ Unit 3, p. 64

Englische Texte enthalten oft Wörter, die du noch nicht kennst oder gelernt hast. Aber du kannst viele Texte verstehen, wenn du folgende Dinge beachtest.

Was hilft dir, unbekannte Wörter zu verstehen?

1 Schau auf die Bilder

Häufig gibt es zu Texten auch Bilder. Sie zeigen oft die Dinge, die du im Text nicht verstehst.

Was bedeuten *forefinger* und *wrist* im folgenden Text?

How to check your pulse:

Put your forefinger and your middle finger on your wrist.
Count your pulse for 60 seconds.

2 Denke an ähnliche Wörter im Deutschen

Viele englische Wörter werden ähnlich wie im Deutschen geschrieben oder klingen ähnlich wie deutsche Wörter, z.B. in dem kleinen Text oben:

– *pulse* hat Ähnlichkeit mit dem deutschen Wort "Puls"

– *middle finger* ist natürlich im Deutschen der "Mittelfinger"

Was bedeuten wohl die folgenden Wörter auf Deutsch?

brilliant • camera • cost • Danish • fresh • half • price • hang • loudspeaker • nervous • ocean • penguin • plan • round • study • suncream • tomato sauce

3 Schau auf die Wörter vor und nach dem unbekannten Wort

Häufig kannst du ein unbekanntes Wort aus dem Satzzusammenhang erschließen. Dabei helfen dir die Wörter, die vor oder nach dem unbekannten Wort stehen.

Was könnten *building* und *stay* bedeuten?

1. Our school is new. It's a very nice building with lots of big classrooms.
2. You can't see your friend this afternoon. Stay at home and do your homework!

SF 4 Im Wörterbuch nachschlagen

▸ Unit 4, p. 84

Wenn du in einem englischen Text ein Wort noch nicht kennst oder vergessen hast (z.B. *donkey*), dann hilft dir das *English-German Dictionary* weiter (S. 208–218). Dort kannst du Wörter nachschlagen.

Uncle Ernie's farm

Uncle Ernie has a farm near Plymouth. On his farm there are lots of animals. He has 20 pigs and 85 cows. But his favourite animal is his donkey.

Wie kannst du englische Wörter im *Dictionary* finden?

1. Die **blau** und **fett** gedruckten Stichwörter (z.B. **family**, **farm**, **fast**) sind alphabetisch angeordnet, also **f** vor **g**, **fa** vor **fe**, **fam** vor **far**.

   Ordne die folgenden *farm animals* alphabetisch:

   horse • cat • bull • donkey • chicken • pig • duck • sheep • dog • rabbit

   Wo findest du ***donkey*** im *Dictionary*? Zwischen *dinner* und *dog* oder zwischen *do* und *door*?
   Überprüfe dich selbst (*Dictionary* S. 210)!

Welche Informationen liefert dir das *Dictionary*?

2. Beachte die Wörter und Wendungen, die **schwarz** und **fett** gedruckt sind. Es sind
   – zusammengesetzte Wörter, z.B. **family name**
   – Redewendungen oder längere Ausdrücke, z.B. **I'm fine, thanks** oder **in the field**.
3. Zusammengesetzte Wörter und längere Ausdrücke findest du oft unter mehr als einem Stichwort, z.B. **feel fed up** unter **fed** und **feel** oder **in the field** unter **in** und **field**.
4. In den eckigen Klammern hinter den Stichwörtern steht, wie das Wort ausgesprochen und betont wird.
   (Lautschriftzeichen → S. 178; Betonungszeichen → S. 193).

   Wie wird das ‚a' in *family* und *father* ausgesprochen?
   Wie das ‚o' in *donkey* oder in *home*?

5. Die Ziffern **1.**, **2.** usw. zeigen, dass das englische Wort mehrere unterschiedliche Bedeutungen hat. Welche Bedeutung die richtige ist, kannst du meist aus dem Satzzusammenhang erkennen.

   Welche Mehrfachbedeutungen kannst du für folgende Wörter finden?

   text • before • phone • too • right • drink

F

face [feɪs] Gesicht 5 (98)
fall [fɔːl] fallen; hinfallen 3 (61)
family [ˈfæməli] Familie 2 (36)
family name Familienname, Nachname 3 (52) **family tree** (Familien-)Stammbaum 2 (37)
farm [fɑːm] Bauernhof, Farm 4 (70)
fast [fɑːst] schnell 3 (61)
father [ˈfɑːðə] Vater 2 (34)
favourite [ˈfeɪvərɪt] Lieblings- (10)
favourite colour Lieblingsfarbe (10)
February [ˈfebruəri] Februar 3 (56)
fed up [fed ˈʌp]**: feel fed up** genervt sein, sauer sein; die Nase voll haben 4 (74)
feed [fiːd] füttern 4 (72)
feel [fiːl] sich fühlen; fühlen 4 (74)
feel fed up genervt sein, sauer sein; die Nase voll haben 4 (74)
feeling [ˈfiːlɪŋ] Gefühl 4 (74)
ferry [ˈferi] Fähre 5 (91)
field [fiːld] Feld; Weide 4 (70)
in the field auf dem Feld 4 (70)
fill sth. in [fɪl ˈɪn] etwas ausfüllen
film [fɪlm] Film 3 (64)
find [faɪnd] finden 4 (79)
°find out herausfinden
fine [faɪn] gut; in Ordnung 1 (17)
I'm fine, thanks. Danke, (es geht mir) gut. 1 (17)
finish [ˈfɪnɪʃ] beenden
fire station [ˈfaɪə steɪʃn] Feuerwache 3 (52)
first [fɜːst]**:**
1. erste(r, s) 1 (17)
2. zuerst, als Erstes 3 (54)
the first morning der erste Morgen 1 (17)
fish [fɪʃ] Fisch; Fische (12)
fisherman, *pl* **-men** [ˈfɪʃəmən] Fischer/in, Angler/in
five [faɪv] fünf (8)
flat [flæt] Wohnung 2 (34)

SF 5 Über Bilder und Fotos sprechen ▸ Unit 5, p. 100

Häufig ist es notwendig, jemandem ein Bild oder ein Foto genau zu beschreiben. Das geht besonders gut, wenn du die folgenden Schritte beachtest.

1 Beginne allgemein

Sage zunächst, was du allgemein im Bild oder Foto siehst.
Welcher Ort, welcher Gegenstand oder welche Personen sind zu sehen?

In the picture I can see a classroom with a teacher and his students.

2 Gehe in einer bestimmten Reihenfolge vor

Sage dann, **wen** oder **was** du siehst und wo sich die Personen oder Gegenstände im Bild oder Foto befinden.
Gehe dabei in einer bestimmten **Reihenfolge** vor: Sage z.B. zunächst, was du links siehst, gehe dann zur Mitte und zum Schluss beschreibst du, was du rechts im Bild oder Foto siehst.
Benutze dabei **allgemeine Ortsangaben** wie:

On the left I can see …
In the middle there are …
On the right there's …

3 Beschreibe alle Teile genauer

Beschreibe genauer, **wo** sich eine Person oder ein Gegenstand befindet:

There's a student under the table.
A student with a green T-shirt is behind the teacher.
There's a girl with a mobile phone next to the boy.
The teacher is in front of the class.

4 Beschreibe, was die Personen machen

Wenn du sagen willst, was gerade im Bild oder Foto passiert oder **was die Personen gerade tun**, benutze das ***present progressive***.

On the right there's a girl in a red T-shirt.
She's eating an apple.
A girl in a red T-shirt is sitting next to her.
She's reading a comic.

▸ Language file 10, p. 171

LF 1 Personalpronomen (Personal pronouns)

▸ Unit 1, pp. 22–23

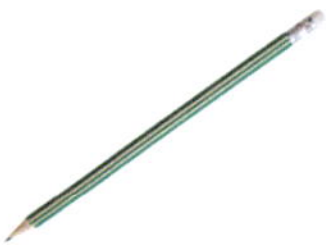

It is new.
Er ist neu.

It is new.
Sie ist neu.

It is new.
Es ist neu.

Du bist nett. **Ihr** seid nett. **Sie** sind nett, Frau Lee.

Das Pronomen ***it*** steht für alle Dinge:

it → **er**, **sie**, **es**

Das Pronomen ***you*** steht für Personen:

you → **du**, **ihr**, **sie**

Über Haustiere, die einen Namen haben, sprichst du mit **he** oder **she**, nicht mit **it**.

LF 2 'm – 's – 're: das Verb be („sein") in der Gegenwart

a) Aussagen (Statements)

▸ Unit 1, p. 22

Das Verb *be* hat in der Gegenwart *(present)* drei Formen: *'m*, *'s* und *'re*. Das sind die Kurzformen. Es gibt auch Langformen, das sind: ***am***, ***is*** und ***are***.

Bejahte Aussagen (Yes)

I'm (= I am) You're (= You are) He's (= He is) She's (= She is) It's (= It is) We're (= We are) You're (= You are) They're (= They are)	new.

Kurzformen sind sehr häufig.
Sie werden besonders in der gesprochenen Sprache verwendet.

Ellie / Luca / The bike The teachers / The books	**is** **are**	new.

Die Langformen benutzt du meistens nach Eigennamen *(Ellie, Luca)* oder Nomen *(bike, teachers)*.

Verneinte Aussagen (No)

I'm not (= I am not) You aren't (= You are not) He isn't (= He is not) She isn't (= She is not) It isn't (= It is not) We aren't (= We are not) You aren't (= You are not) They aren't (= They are not)	from Plymouth.

Bei der Verneinung werden fast immer die Kurzformen benutzt.

LF 3 b) Fragen und Kurzantworten (Questions and short answers)

► Unit 2, p. 40

Fragen

Am I ...?
Is he/she/it ...?

Are we ...?
Are you ...?
Are they ...?

What's this?
Who are they?
Where are your books?

Du kannst Fragen stellen
- **ohne Fragewort** *(Are you ...?)*, auf die du Antworten mit Ja oder Nein bekommst, oder
- **mit Fragewort** *(Who ...?/Where ...?)*. Nach einem Fragewort kannst du ***is*** verkürzen:
  What's *your name?*
  Where's *your tie, Ellie?*

Kurzantworten

Yes	No
Yes, I am. Yes, he/she/it is. Yes, you/we/they are.	No, I'm not. No, he/she/it isn't. No, you/we/they aren't.

Eine kurze Antwort nur mit ***yes*** oder ***no*** kann unhöflich klingen. Antworte besser: *Yes, I am./No, she isn't./...*

LF 4 There's … / There are …

► Unit 2, p. 39

Mit ***There's … / There are …*** drückst du aus, dass irgendwo etwas vorhanden ist:

– In meinem Zimmer steht ein Tisch. → **There's** a table in my room.
– Auf dem Tisch liegen Bücher. → **There are** books on the table.
– Es gibt/sind drei Stühle in … → **There are** three chairs in …

Nie: It ~~gives~~ …, sondern immer: ***There's … / There are …***

Im Deutschen beginnst du oft mit einer Ortsangabe:
In meinem Zimmer **steht ein Tisch**.

Im Englischen steht die Ortsangabe meist am Ende und die Sätze beginnen mit ***There's … / There are …***
There's a table in my room.

In Fragen stehen ***is*** und ***are*** vor dem ***there***:

– Gibt es auch einen Kleiderschrank? → **Is there** a wardrobe too?
– Sind Jungen in deiner Klasse? → **Are there** boys in your class?

LF 5 Der Plural der Nomen (The plural of nouns)

► Unit 3, p. 62

		Singular (Einzahl) a/one **crab**	**Plural** (Mehrzahl) two/three/lots of **crabs**
1	+ -s	a pet one snake a crab one seagull	two pets [-s] three snakes [-s] lots of crabs [-z] four seagulls [-z]
2	+ -es	a bus one beach	two buses [-ɪz] two beaches [-ɪz]
3	-y → -ies	a story one pony **Aber:** a boy one day	lots of stories [-ɪz] five ponies [-ɪz] two boys [-z] three days [-z]
4	keine Regel	a man one child a fish	lots of men two children five fish

1 Die meisten Nomen (Hauptwörter) haben im Plural die Endung ***-s***. Beachte die unterschiedliche Aussprache!

2 Nach ***-s***, ***-x***, ***-sh*** oder ***-ch*** wird ***-es*** angehängt.

3 Nach einem Konsonanten (Mitlaut) **+*y*** (z. B. ***-ry***, ***-ny***, ***-ly***, ***-ty***) wird ***-y*** zu ***-ies***.

4 Ein paar Nomen haben unregelmäßige Pluralformen. Diese musst du auswendig lernen.

LF 6 Die einfache Form der Gegenwart (The simple present)

a) Bejahte Aussagen (Positive statements)

▸ Unit 3, p. 58

Mit dem **simple present** sprichst du darüber, was **wiederholt** (oder auch **nie**) passiert, oft mit *always* (immer), *sometimes* (manchmal), *often* (oft), *never* (niemals), in the *morning/afternoon* (vormittags/nachmittags).

Yes

I	like	
You	like	
He	likes	
She	likes	the beach.
It	likes	
We	like	
You	like	
They	like	

He, she, it – ein *-s* muss mit!

Das **simple present** hat zwei Formen:
1 *I/you/we/they* + verb
2 *he/she/it* + verb + ***s***

Wenn das Verb auf ***-ss***, ***-x***, ***-sh***, ***-ch*** (z. B. *watch*) oder auf ***-o*** (z. B. *go*) endet, fügst du bei *he/she/it* ***-es*** hinzu:

- *watch:* *he/she/it watches* [-ɪz]
- *go:* *he/she/it goes* [gəʊz]
- *do:* *he/she/it does* [dʌz]

(siehe auch LF 5: Plural der Nomen)

LF 7 b) Verneinte Aussagen (Negative statements)

▸ Unit 4, p. 76

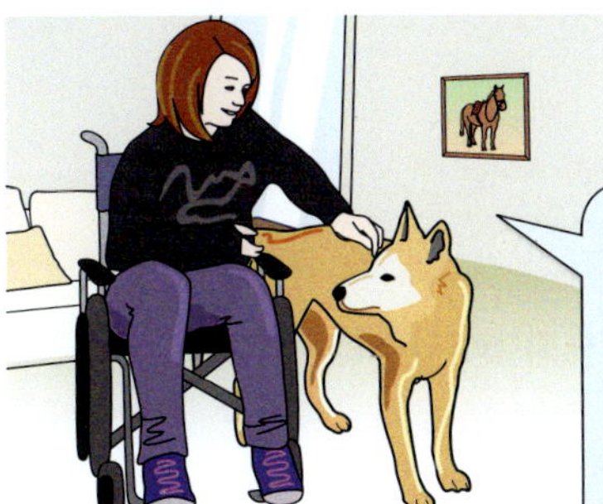

Das **simple present** verneinst du mit ***don't*** oder ***doesn't*** + verb:

- *I/you/we/they* *don't* + verb
- *he/she/it* *doesn't* + verb

Die Langformen sind: ***do not*** und ***does not***.

No

I don't like	
You don't like	dogs.
He/She/It doesn't like	
We/You/They don't like	

LF 8 Fragen mit do / does und Kurzantworten
(*Do-* / *Does*-questions and short answers)

▸ Unit 4, p. 78

a) Fragen

Do I like ...? Do you like ...? Does he/she/it like ...?	Do we like ...? Do you like ...? Do they like ...?

Wenn du im **simple present** auf eine Frage die Antwort „Ja" oder „Nein" erwartest, fängst du die Frage mit ***Do*** oder ***Does*** an:

- ***Do*** + *I / you / we / they* + verb ?
  Do *you* ***have*** *ponies?*
- ***Does*** + *he / she / it* + *verb ?*
  Does *the farm* ***have*** *a shop?*

b) Kurzantworten

Yes	No
Yes, I do. Yes, he/she/it does. Yes, you/we/they do.	No, I don't. No, he/she/it doesn't. No, you/we/they don't.

Es ist oft unhöflich, nur mit *Yes* oder *No* zu antworten. Besser ist eine Kurzantwort:

- nach *Yes* mit *do* oder *does*, z. B.
  Yes, I do. / Yes, she does.
- nach *No* mit *don't* oder *doesn't*, z. B.
  No, I don't. / No, he doesn't.

LF 9 Fragen mit Fragewörtern (Questions with question words)

▸ Unit 4, p. 78

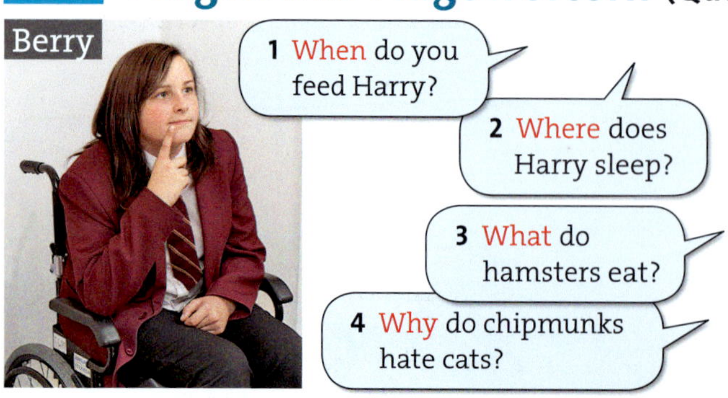

1 Wann fütterst du Harry?
2 Wo schläft Harry?
3 Was fressen Hamster?
4 Warum hassen Streifenhörnchen Katzen?

Wenn du eine Frage mit Fragewort *(When, Where, What, Why, How)* bilden willst, setzt du das Fragewort vor *do* bzw. *does*:

Do *you* ***like*** *rabbits?*
Why ***do*** *you* ***like*** *rabbits?*

Does *Berry* ***feed*** *the donkeys?*
When ***does*** *she* ***feed*** *the donkeys?*

LF 10 Die Verlaufsform der Gegenwart (The present progressive)

▸ Unit 5, p. 96

In the photo mum and I are working in the cafe.
I'm setting the tables and mum is talking to a customer.
We aren't making sandwiches.

Im Gegensatz zum Deutschen gibt es im Englischen zwei Formen der Gegenwart: die einfache Form und die Verlaufsform.

Mit der einfachen Form **(simple present)** sprichst du über Dinge, die wiederholt passieren (siehe LF 6, S. 169).

Wenn du aber über etwas sprichst, das **gerade jetzt** passiert, benutzt du die Verlaufsform der Gegenwart **(present progressive)**, oft mit *now* (jetzt) oder *at the moment* (im Moment).

Diese Form benutzt du auch, um Bilder zu beschreiben.

Im Deutschen gibt es keine Verlaufsform.

Adam is setting the tables.

– Adam deckt gerade die Tische.
– Adam ist gerade dabei, die Tische zu decken.

Yes

I'm helping. You're helping. He's/She's/It's helping.	We're helping. You're helping. They're helping.

Du bildest das **present progressive** mit
'm/'re/'s* + *verb* + *-ing
z. B. *she's* + ***talking***

No

I'm not helping. You aren't helping. He/She/It isn't helping.	We aren't helping. You aren't helping They aren't helping.

Achtung Schreibung:
– ein nicht mitgesprochenes ***e*** fällt weg:
make → making *write → writing*
– nach einem Vokal (a, e, i, o, u) wird der Konsonant (meist p, b, m, n, d, t) verdoppelt:
rap + -ing → rapping
swim + -ing → swimming
set + -ing → setting

?

Am I helping? Are you helping? Is he/she/it helping?	Are we helping? Are you helping? Are they helping?
What are you doing? Are you helping?	– Yes, I am./ No, I'm not.
What's Adam doing? Is he making sandwiches?	– Yes, he is./ No, he isn't.

Die Kurzantworten sind wie beim Verb *be* (siehe LF 3, S. 167).
Nach einem Fragewort kannst du ***is*** verkürzen: ***What's ... / When's ...***

Grammatische Fachbegriffe (Grammatical terms)

answer	['ɑːnsə]	Antwort(satz)
negative statement	[negətɪv 'steɪtmənt]	verneinte Aussage
noun	[naʊn]	Nomen, Hauptwort, Substantiv
persononal pronoun	[pɜːsənl 'prəʊnaʊn]	Personalpronomen (persönliches Fürwort)
plural	['plʊərəl]	Plural, Mehrzahl
positive statement	[pɒzətɪv 'steɪtmənt]	bejahte Aussage
present	['preznt]	Gegenwart
present progressive	[preznt prə'gresɪv]	Verlaufsform der Gegenwart
pronoun	['prəʊnaʊn]	Pronomen, Fürwort
question	['kwestʃən]	Frage(satz)
question word	['kwestʃən wɜːd]	Fragewort
short answer	[ʃɔːt 'ɑːnsə]	Kurzantwort
simple present	[sɪmpl 'preznt]	einfache Form der Gegenwart
singular	['sɪŋgjələ]	Singular, Einzahl
statement	['steɪtmənt]	Aussage(satz)
verb	[vɜːb]	Verb

Wordbank 1: Sports and hobbies ▸ Nice to meet you!, p. 11

I like	dancing. football. playing games. reading books. riding. skateboarding. swimming. watching TV.

basketball

boxing

canoeing

climbing

collecting stamps

cycling

doing athletics

drawing

ice hockey

ice skating

inline-skating

listening to music

making models

skiing

snowboarding

surfing the internet

table tennis

taking photos

Wordbank 2: My favourite thing

► Nice to meet you!, p. 13

bag

book

DVD player

football

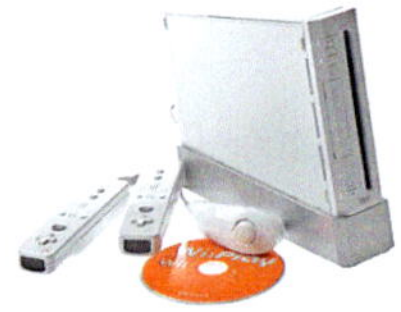
game console

guitar

laptop

mobile phone

remote-control car

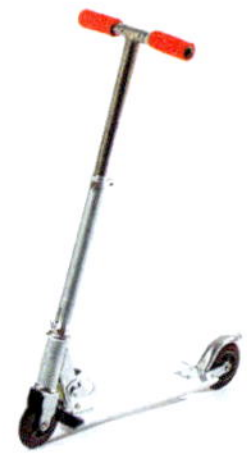
scooter

TV

watch

game console ['geɪm kɒnsəʊl] *Spielkonsole* remote-control car [rɪ'məʊt kəntrəʊl 'kɑː] *ferngesteuertes Auto*
scooter ['skuːtə] *Roller*

Wordbank 3: Timetable

► Unit 1, p. 33

I have art, drama, English, French, geography, German, history, ICT, maths, music, PE, science, technology, ...

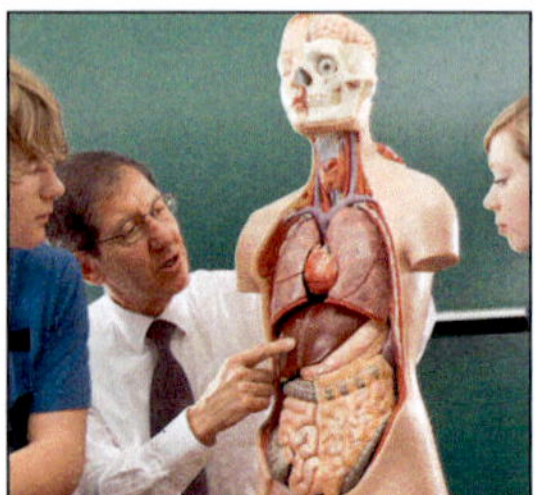
biology

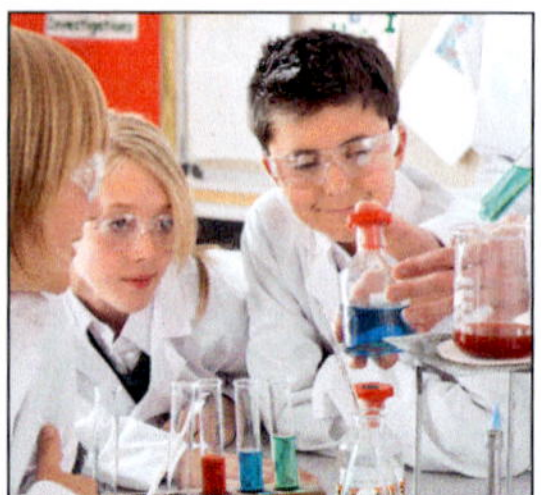
chemistry

class assembly

ethics

home economics

physics

projects

RE

social studies

Spanish

special needs training

woodwork

class assembly *Klassenlehrerstunde* RE = religious education *Religionslehre* social studies *Gesellschaftslehre*
special needs training *Förderunterricht*

Wordbank 4: My family

▸ Unit 2, p. 37

nephew ['nefjuː] *Neffe* niece [niːs] *Nichte* grandson *Enkel* granddaughter *Enkelin* husband *Ehemann*
wife [waɪf] *Ehefrau* single *alleinstehend* married to *verheiratet mit* divorced *geschieden* dead *tot*

Wordbank 5: My house

▸ Unit 2, p. 44

Wordbank 6: My town

► Unit 3, p. 52

my town

In my town we have …

a church

a bus station

a fire station

a train station

a police station

a mosque

a library

an airport

a school

a cinema

a hospital

a market

a museum

My favourite places are …

the fast food restaurant

the swimming pool

the park

the video shop

the zoo

the football stadium

the sports club

the shopping centre

the department store

the youth centre

the skate park

department store [dɪ'pɑːtmənt stɔː] *Kaufhaus* library ['laɪbrəri] *Bücherei, Bibliothek* mosque [mɒsk] *Moschee*

Wordbank 7: Talking about pets

▸ Unit 4, p. 78

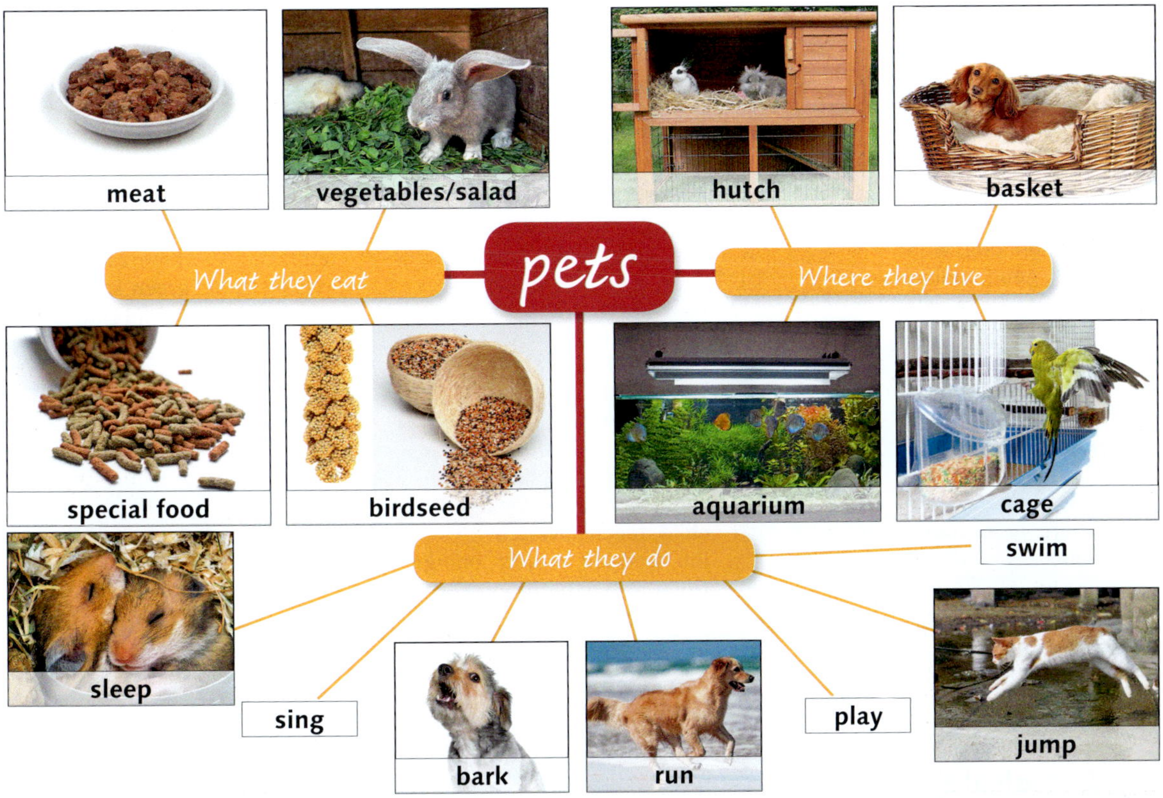

bark [bɑːk] bellen *birdseed* [ˈbɜːdsiːd] *Körnerfutter, Vogelfutter* hutch [hʌtʃ] *Hütte, kleiner Stall*
jump [dʒʌmp] *springen* meat [miːt] *Fleisch* run [rʌn] *rennen*

Wordbank 8: Instruments

▸ Unit 5, p. 95

I play the drums, the guitar, the piano, the ... **I don't play an instrument. I like the ...**

flute [fluːt] *(Quer-)Flöte* violin [vaɪəˈlɪn] *Violine, Geige*

English sounds

[iː]	green, he, sea
[ɑː]	ask, class, car, park
[ɔː]	or, ball, door, four, morning
[uː]	ruler, blue, too, two, you
[ɜː]	early, her, girl, work, T-shirt
[ɪ]	in, big, expensive
[e]	yes, bed, again, breakfast
[æ]	animal, apple, black, cat
[ʌ]	mum, bus, colour
[ɒ]	song, on, dog, what
[ʊ]	book, good, pullover
[ə]	again, today, a sister
[i]	happy, monkey
[eɪ]	name, eight, play, great
[aɪ]	I, time, right, my
[ɔɪ]	boy, toilet, noise
[əʊ]	old, no, road, yellow
[aʊ]	now, house
[eə]	where, pair, share, their
[ʊə]	tour

[b]	bike, table, verb
[p]	pen, paper, shop
[d]	day, window, good
[t]	ten, letter, at
[g]	go, again, bag
[k]	kitchen, car, back
[m]	man, remember, mum
[n]	no, one, ten
[ŋ]	wrong, young, uncle, thanks
[l]	like, old, small
[r]	ruler, friend, sorry
[w]	we, where, one
[j]	yes, you, uniform
[f]	family, after, laugh
[v]	very, seven, have
[s]	six, poster, yes
[z]	zoo, quiz, his, music, please
[ʃ]	she, station, English
[ʒ]	ususally, revision, garage
[tʃ]	child, teacher, watch
[dʒ]	job, German, project, orange
[θ]	thing, three, bathroom, both
[ð]	the, father, with
[h]	house, who, behind

Am besten kannst du dir die Aussprache der einzelnen Lautzeichen einprägen, wenn du dir zu jedem Zeichen ein einfaches Wort merkst – das [iː] ist der **green**-Laut, das [eɪ] ist der **name**-Laut usw.

The English alphabet

a [eɪ]	**h** [eɪtʃ]	**o** [əʊ]	**v** [viː]
b [biː]	**i** [aɪ]	**p** [piː]	**w** [ˈdʌbljuː]
c [siː]	**j** [dʒeɪ]	**q** [kjuː]	**x** [eks]
d [diː]	**k** [keɪ]	**r** [ɑː]	**y** [waɪ]
e [iː]	**l** [el]	**s** [es]	**z** [zed]
f [ef]	**m** [em]	**t** [tiː]	
g [dʒiː]	**n** [en]	**u** [juː]	

Das **Vocabulary** (S. 179–207) enthält alle neuen Wörter und Wendungen des Buches, die du **lernen** musst. Sie stehen in der Reihenfolge, in der sie im Buch zum ersten Mal vorkommen.

Hier siehst du, wie das **Vocabulary** aufgebaut ist:

Diese Zahl gibt die **Seite** an, auf der die Wörter zum ersten Mal vorkommen. p. 13 = Seite 13

Die **Lautschrift** zeigt dir, wie ein Wort ausgesprochen wird. Eine Übersicht über die **Lautschriftzeichen** findest du auf S. 178.

p. 13	**park** [pɑːk]	Park	
	on [ɒn]	auf	
	bike [baɪk]	Fahrrad	
	great [ɡreɪt]	großartig, prima	
	it's fun [fʌn]	es macht Spaß	

a girl on a bike a boy on a pony

	small [smɔːl]	klein	[s] ist ein scharfes „s" wie in „lassen".
	big [bɪɡ]	groß	big ◄► small
	old [əʊld]	alt	
	new [njuː]	neu	new ◄► old
	cool [kuːl]	cool	
p. 14	**the last day** [lɑːst ˈdeɪ]	der letzte Tag	
	holidays [ˈhɒlədeɪz]	Ferien	
	the last day **of** the holidays [ɒv], [əv]	der letzte Tag der Ferien	**of** • the colour **of** my bike (die Farbe meines Rades) • the last day **of** the holidays (der letzte Tag der Ferien)
	story [ˈstɔːri]	Geschichte, Erzählung	! one **story** – two, three, four **stories**
	Hello. [həˈləʊ]	Hallo. / Guten Tag.	
	It's me, Sandy. [miː]	Ich bin es, Sandy.	**„ich": me statt I** • Hello, Ellie. It's **me**, Luca. (Hallo, Ellie. Ich bin's, Luca.) • I'm twelve. – **Me** too. (Ich bi…

Blau gedruckte Wörter kennst du wahrscheinlich schon aus dem Englischunterricht in der Grundschule.

Dies ist das „Gegenteil"-Zeichen. **big ◄► small** bedeutet: „**big** ist das Gegenteil von **small**".

Das **rote Ausrufezeichen** bedeutet: Vorsicht, hier macht man leicht Fehler!

Der **blaue Pfeil** heißt: Zu diesem Eintrag gibt es in der rechten Spalte einen blauen Kasten.

Die **blauen Kästen** solltest du dir immer besonders gut ansehen. Dort stehen wichtige Hinweise zu den neuen Wörtern.

Tipps zum Wörterlernen findest du im **Skills file** auf den Seiten 160 und 161.

Im **Vocabulary** werden folgende **Abkürzungen und Symbole** verwendet:

p. = page (Seite)
sth. = something (etwas)
pl = *plural* (Mehrzahl)
infml = *informal* (umgangssprachlich)

Wenn du **nachschlagen** möchtest, was ein englisches Wort bedeutet oder wie man es ausspricht, dann solltest du das **Dictionary English – German** auf den Seiten 208–218 verwenden.

Und wenn du vergessen hast, wie etwas auf Englisch heißt, dann kann dir das **Dictionary German – English** auf den Seiten 219–227 eine erste Hilfe sein.

Nice to meet you!

p. 8	**Nice to meet you!**	Freut mich, dich/euch kennenzulernen.	
	nice [naɪs]	nett, schön	
	meet [miːt]	kennenlernen; treffen	
	you [ju], [juː]	du; dich; dir ihr; euch	
	Hi. [haɪ]	Hallo.	

	I'm Cyril. [aɪm] (= **I am** Cyril.)	Ich bin Cyril. / Ich heiße Cyril.	! „I" wird immer großgeschrieben – auch wenn es nicht am Satzanfang steht.
	the crab [ðə 'kræb]	der Krebs	→ **the** **the** computer – **der** Computer **the** show – **die** Show **the** baby – **das** Baby
	What's your name?	Wie heißt du? (*wörtlich:* Was ist dein Name?)	
	what? [wɒt]	was?	Der Laut [ɒ] klingt wie das „o" in „d**o**ch".
	your [jɔː], [jə]	dein/e; euer/eure	[ɔː] ist der „o"-Laut aus dem englischen Wort „Baseb**a**ll".
	name [neɪm]	Name	

1 one [wʌn]	**5 five** [faɪv]	**9 nine** [naɪn]	**13 thirteen** [θɜː'tiːn]
2 two [tuː]	**6 six** [sɪks]	**10 ten** [ten]	**14 fourteen** [fɔː'tiːn]
3 three [θriː]	**7 seven** ['sevn]	**11 eleven** [ɪ'levn]	
4 four [fɔː]	**8 eight** [eɪt]	**12 twelve** [twelv]	(► *Numbers*, p. 229)

	What about you?	Und du? / Und was ist mit dir?	→ **you**: du – ihr; dich – euch; dir – euch **your**: dein, deine; euer, eure
	I'm from Plymouth. [frɒm], [frəm]	Ich bin aus Plymouth. / Ich komme aus Plymouth.	
	in England [ɪn 'ɪŋglənd] **in Germany** [ɪn 'dʒɜːməni]	in England in Deutschland	! Ländernamen werden immer großgeschrieben: in **E**ngland; in **G**ermany
	class [klɑːs]	(Schul-)Klasse	[ɑː] ist ein langes „a" wie in „Kr**a**m".
p. 9	**I can see** Cyril. [siː]	Ich kann Cyril sehen.	
	can [kæn], [kən]	können	

	and [ænd], [ənd]	und	
	a beach [ə 'biːtʃ]	ein Strand	→ **a** **a** computer – **ein** Computer **a** show – **eine** Show **a** baby – **ein** Baby
	Cyril's song [sɒŋ]	Cyrils Lied, Cyrils Song	
p. 10	**my** [maɪ]	mein/e	**my** name (**mein** Name) **my** class (**meine** Klasse) [aɪ] klingt wie das „ei" in „Kl**ei**d".
	favourite colour ['feɪvərɪt]	Lieblingsfarbe	
	colour ['kʌlə]	Farbe	one **colour** – two, three, four **colours**
	Welcome to Plymouth. ['welkəm]	Willkommen in Plymouth.	[ə] ist ein „e" wie am Ende von „bitt**e**" oder „Aff**e**".

red [red]	rot	**brown** [braʊn]	braun	**purple** ['pɜːpl]	violett, lila
yellow ['jeləʊ]	gelb	**orange** ['ɒrɪndʒ]	orange	**white** [waɪt]	weiß
blue [bluː]	blau	**grey** [greɪ]	grau	**black** [blæk]	schwarz
green [griːn]	grün	**pink** [pɪŋk]	pink, rosa		

I like red. [laɪk]	Ich mag Rot.	
I don't like blue. ['dəʊnt laɪk]	Ich mag Blau nicht./ Ich mag kein Blau.	
like [laɪk]	mögen, gernhaben	
My favourite colour **is** … [ɪz]	Meine Lieblingsfarbe ist …	

student ['stjuːdənt]	Schüler/in; Student/in	→ **one** – **two/three/…** one **colour** – two/three **colours** **crab** – **crabs** **song** – **songs** **student** – **students**
p. 11 **sport** [spɔːt]	Sport; Sportart	
hobby ['hɒbi]	Hobby	! Englisch: one **hobby** – two, three **hobbies** Deutsch: ein **Hobby** – zwei, drei **Hobbys**
football ['fʊtbɔːl]	Fußball	
music ['mjuːzɪk]	Musik	[z] ist ein „s" wie in „Musik".
I like watching TV. ['wɒtʃɪŋ tiː'viː]	Ich sehe gern fern.	
watch TV [wɒtʃ tiː'viː]	fernsehen	[tʃ] klingt wie „tsch" in „Quatsch".
TV [tiː'viː]	Fernsehen, Fernsehgerät	[v] klingt wie „Vampir" – nicht wie „Vater"!
too [tuː]	auch	! I'm from Berlin. – I'm from Berlin **too**. – Ich bin **auch** aus Berlin.
dance [dɑːns]	tanzen	
play [pleɪ]	spielen	
game [geɪm]	Spiel	
read [riːd]	lesen	
book [bʊk]	Buch	
ride [raɪd]	reiten	
skateboard ['skeɪtbɔːd]	Skateboard fahren	

swim [swɪm]	schwimmen	
What are …? [ɑː]	Was sind …?	→ **What's …?** (= What is) • **What are …?** • **What's** your favourite song? (Was **ist** dein Lieblingslied?) • **What are** your hobbies? (Was **sind** deine Hobbys?)
our ['aʊə]	unser/e	**our** poster (**unser** Poster) **our** class (**unsere** Klasse)
p. 12 **animal** ['ænɪml]	Tier	
have [hæv], [həv]	haben	

pony ['pəʊni]	Pony	! Englisch: one **pony** – two, three **ponies** Deutsch: ein **Pony** – zwei, drei **Ponys**
love [lʌv]	lieben, sehr mögen	
cat [kæt]	Katze	
bear [beə]	Bär	
rat [ræt]	Ratte	
monkey ['mʌŋki]	Affe	
bird [bɜːd]	Vogel	
snake [sneɪk]	Schlange	
dog [dɒg]	Hund	
crocodile ['krɒkədaɪl]	Krokodil	
rabbit ['ræbɪt]	Kaninchen	
hamster ['hæmstə]	Hamster	
fish [fɪʃ]	Fisch; Fische	! one **fish** – two, three, four **fish**
tiger ['taɪgə]	Tiger	**a – an** **a** dog — **an** elephant **a** German name — **an** English name
an **elephant** [æn], [ən]	ein Elefant	→
Can you remember (the animals)? [rɪ'membə]	Kannst du dich (an die Tiere) erinnern?/Könnt ihr euch (an die Tiere) erinnern?	! Englisch: Can you **remember my name**? Deutsch: Kannst du **dich an meinen Namen erinnern**?
remember [rɪ'membə]	sich erinnern (an)	
pet [pet]	Haustier	
wild [waɪld]	wild; wild lebend	
pair [peə]	Paar	[eə] kennst du aus „fair".
p. 13 **thing** [θɪŋ]	Ding, Sache	 a **fish – it's** yellow (**er** ist gelb)
it's [ɪts] **(= it is)**	es ist *(bei Sachen und Tieren auch:* er ist; sie ist)	 a **snake – it's** brown (**sie** ist braun)  a **rabbit – it's** white (**es** ist weiß)
go [gəʊ]	gehen; fahren	
to [tu], [tə]	zu, nach	
park [pɑːk]	Park	
on [ɒn]	auf	 a girl on a bike — a boy on a pony
bike [baɪk]	Fahrrad	
great [greɪt]	großartig, prima	
it's fun [fʌn]	es macht Spaß	
small [smɔːl]	klein	[s] ist ein scharfes „s" wie in „lassen".
big [bɪg]	groß	**big** ◄► **small**
old [əʊld]	alt	

	new [njuː]	neu	**new ◄► old**
	cool [kuːl]	cool	
p. 14	**the last day** [lɑːst 'deɪ]	der letzte Tag	
	holidays ['hɒlədeɪz]	Ferien	
	the last day **of** the holidays [ɒv], [əv]	der letzte Tag der Ferien	→ **of** • the colour **of** my bike (die Farbe meines Rades) • the last day **of** the holidays (der letzte Tag der Ferien)
	story ['stɔːri]	Geschichte, Erzählung	! one **story** – two, three, four **stories**
	Hello. [hə'ləʊ]	Hallo. / Guten Tag.	
	It's me, Sandy. [miː]	Ich bin es, Sandy.	→ **„ich": me** statt **I** • Hello, Ellie. It's **me**, Luca. (Hallo, Ellie. Ich bin's, Luca.) • I'm twelve. – **Me** too. (Ich bin zwölf. – Ich auch.)
	no [nəʊ]	nein	
	away [ə'weɪ]	weg, fort	
	stupid ['stjuːpɪd]	dumm, blöd	
	seagull ['siːgʌl]	Möwe	
	This is ... ['ðɪs ɪz]	Dies ist ... / Das ist ...	
	Help! [help]	Hilfe!	

	help [help]	helfen	
	Goodbye. [gʊd'baɪ]	Auf Wiedersehen!	
p. 15	**chant** [tʃɑːnt]	Sprechgesang	

Unit 1: Welcome to our school

p. 16	**school** [skuːl]	Schule	
	sound [saʊnd]	Geräusch; Klang, Laut	[aʊ] klingt ähnlich wie das „au" in „bl**au**".
	boy [bɔɪ]	Junge	[ɔɪ] klingt ähnlich wie das „eu" in „tr**eu**".
	girl [gɜːl]	Mädchen	[ɜː] ist das Zeichen für den Laut in „T-Sh**ir**t".
	teacher ['tiːtʃə]	Lehrer/in	
	car [kɑː]	Auto	
	mobile (phone) ['məʊbaɪl 'fəʊn]	Mobiltelefon, Handy	! Deutsch: **Handy** Englisch: **mobile phone** oder **mobile**
p. 17	**the first morning** [fɜːst 'mɔːnɪŋ]	der erste Morgen	[ŋ] ist wie „ng" in „Di**ng**" oder „n" in „pi**n**k".
	How are you? [haʊ 'ɑː juː]	Wie geht's? / Wie geht es dir/euch?	
	I'm fine, thanks. [faɪn], [θæŋks]	Danke, (es geht mir) gut.	[θ] gibt es im Deutschen nicht. Der Laut klingt etwa so, als ob man das „s" in „be**ss**er" lispelt.

	I'm OK, thanks. [əʊ'keɪ]	Danke, (es geht mir) gut.	
	Bye. [baɪ]	Tschüs.	**Hello. ◄► Bye./Goodbye.**
	Have a good day.	Ich wünsch dir einen schönen Tag./Schönen Tag noch.	
	good [gʊd]	gut	a **good** school/teacher/story/...
	See you./ See you later. ['leɪtə]	Bis dann./ Bis später.	

Theme 1

p. 18	**Good morning.**	Guten Morgen.	
	Ms Lee [mɪz], [məz]	Frau Lee	
	English ['ɪŋglɪʃ]	Englisch; englisch	
	Who are you? [hu:]	Wer bist du?/Wer seid ihr? →	**what?** was? / **who?** wer? / **how?** wie?
	brother ['brʌðə]	Bruder	[ð] klingt wie ein gelispeltes „Wiese".
	sister ['sɪstə]	Schwester	
	we're ... [wɪə] (= **we are** [wi ɑ:])	wir sind ...	
	my **best** friends [best]	meine besten Freunde/ Freundinnen	
	friend [frend]	Freund/in	
	they're ... [ðeə] (= **they are** [ðeɪ ɑ:])	sie sind ... →	**'re (are)** you**'re** (you are) – du **bist**; ihr **seid** we**'re** (we are) – wir **sind** they**'re** (they are) – sie **sind**
	at this school [æt], [ət]	auf/an dieser Schule	
	they aren't ... [ɑ:nt]	sie sind nicht ...; sie sind keine ...	They **aren't** in the park. They **aren't** brothers. Sie sind **nicht** im Park. Sie sind **keine** Brüder.
	I'm not ... [nɒt]	ich bin nicht ...; ich bin kein/e ...	I'm **not** ten. And I'm **not** a boy. Ich bin **nicht** zehn. Und ich bin **kein** Junge.
	he's ... [hi:z] (= **he is**)	er ist ... →	**'s (is)** he**'s** (he is) – He**'s** my brother. she**'s** (she is) – She**'s** my sister. it**'s** (it is) – It**'s** fun. what**'s** (what is) – What**'s** your name? who**'s** (who is) – Who**'s** in class 7Y?
	she's ... [ʃi:z] (= **she is**)	sie ist ... →	
	he/she/it isn't ... ['ɪznt]	er/sie/es ist nicht ...; er/sie/es ist kein/e ... →	**n't** **isn't** (is not) **aren't** (are not)
	ride a bike [raɪd]	Rad fahren	
	village ['vɪlɪdʒ]	Dorf	
	near [nɪə]	in der Nähe von, nahe (bei)	Woolwell is **near** Plymouth.
	no [nəʊ]	kein, keine	We have **no** car. 
	age [eɪdʒ]	Alter	
p. 19	Hendrik **has ...** [hæz], [həz]	Hendrik hat ... →	I **have** / you **have** / we **have** / they **have** he **has** / she **has** / it **has**

about me/you/... [ə'baʊt]	über mich/dich/...	
me [mi:]	mich; mir	→ **me** Meet **me** in the park. **mich** Help **me**. **mir**
Mrs Schmidt ['mɪsɪz]	Frau Schmidt	! **Ms** = *allgemeine Anrede für Frauen* **Mrs** = *Anrede für verheiratete Frauen*
Mr Jahn ['mɪstə]	Herr Jahn	

Theme 2

p. 20	**at school**	in der Schule	! Englisch: they're **at school** Deutsch: sie sind **in der Schule**
	a **tour of** the school [tʊə]	ein Rundgang durch die Schule	
	room [ru:m], [rʊm]	Raum, Zimmer	
	canteen [kæn'ti:n]	Kantine, (Schul-)Mensa	
	art [ɑ:t]	Kunst	
	science ['saɪəns]	Naturwissenschaft	
	lab [læb]	Labor	
	sports hall ['spɔ:ts hɔ:l]	Sporthalle	
	PE [pi: 'i:] (physical education)	(Schul-)Sport	
	lesson ['lesn]	(Unterrichts-)Stunde	
	now [naʊ]	nun, jetzt	
	where? [weə]	wo?/wohin?	! Nicht verwechseln: **who?** wer? **where?** wo?
	here [hɪə]	hier; hierher	
	ICT [aɪ si: 'ti:] (information and communication technology)	Informations- und Kommunikationstechnologie	
	I'm not lost. [lɒst]	Ich habe mich nicht verlaufen/verirrt.	
p. 21	**timetable** ['taɪmteɪbl]	Stundenplan	
	time [taɪm]	Zeit; Uhrzeit	

Monday ['mʌndeɪ], ['mʌndi]	Montag	**Thursday** ['θɜ:zdeɪ], ['θɜ:zdi]	Donnerstag
Tuesday ['tju:zdeɪ], ['tju:zdi]	Dienstag	**Friday** ['fraɪdeɪ], ['fraɪdi]	Freitag
Wednesday ['wenzdeɪ], ['wenzdi]	Mittwoch		

! Die Wochentage werden immer großgeschrieben.

assembly [ə'sembli]	Schulversammlung, Morgenappell
technology [tek'nɒlədʒi]	Technik, Technologie
geography [dʒi'ɒgrəfi]	Geografie, Erdkunde

maths [mæθs]	Mathematik	
history ['hɪstri]	Geschichte	
French [frentʃ]	Französisch; französisch	
break [breɪk]	Pause	
lunch [lʌntʃ]	Mittagessen	[ʌ] klingt ähnlich wie das kurze „a" in „Kamm".
drama ['drɑːmə]	Schauspiel, darstellende Kunst	
every day/room/... ['evri]	jeder Tag/jedes Zimmer/...	We go to school **every** morning.
on Monday/Tuesday/...	am Montag/Dienstag/...	What's lesson one **on** Monday?
right [raɪt]	richtig	
wrong [rɒŋ]	falsch	**right** ◄► **wrong**

Focus on language

p. 22	**city** ['sɪti]	(Groß-)Stadt	! one **city** – two, three, four **cities**
	it starts	er/sie/es beginnt; er/sie/es fängt an	
	start [stɑːt]	anfangen, beginnen	
	with [wɪð]	mit	
	classroom ['klɑːsruːm]	Klassenzimmer	
	yes [jes]	ja	**yes** ◄► **no**
p. 23	**Look at** our new books. [lʊk]	Sieh/Schau dir unsere neuen Bücher an.	

15 fifteen [fɪf'tiːn]	**20 twenty** ['twenti]	**30 thirty** ['θɜːti]
16 sixteen [sɪks'tiːn]	**21 twenty-one** [twenti'wʌn]	**31 thirty-one** [θɜːti'wʌn]
17 seventeen [sevn'tiːn]	**22 twenty-two** [twenti'tuː]	**32 thirty-two** [θɜːti'tuː]
18 eighteen [eɪ'tiːn]	...	...
19 nineteen [naɪn'tiːn]		

(► *Numbers*, p. 229)

but [bʌt], [bət]	aber	Luca is ten, **but** Jack is fourteen.
all (the) [ɔːl]	alle	We're **all** friends here at our school. **All the** students in class 7Y are nice.
people ['piːpl]	Leute, Menschen	The **people** in Plymouth are nice.
place [pleɪs]	Ort, Platz, Stelle	Plymouth is a great **place**.
make [meɪk]	machen, herstellen	
for [fɔː], [fə]	für	

Story

p. 24	**before** you read [bɪ'fɔː]	bevor du liest	
	blazer ['bleɪzə]	Blazer *(Jackett, oft Teil der Schuluniform)*	
	pullover ['pʊləʊvə]	Pullover	
	shirt [ʃɜːt]	Hemd	
	shoe [ʃuː]	Schuh	
	skirt [skɜːt]	Rock	
	sock [sɒk]	Socke, Strumpf	
	tie [taɪ]	Krawatte	
	tights *(pl)* [taɪts]	Strumpfhose	→ **tights** und **trousers** sind immer Plural: • My **tights are** blue. **They're** new. (Meine **Stumpfhose** **ist** blau. **Sie ist** neu.) • **Are** your **trousers** new? **They're** cool. (**Ist** deine **Hose** neu? **Sie ist** cool.)
	trousers *(pl)* ['traʊzəz]	Hose	→
	uniform ['juːnɪfɔːm]	(Schul-)Uniform	
	important [ɪm'pɔːtnt]	wichtig	
	Miss Borowski [mɪs]	Frau Borowski	! **Miss** = *Anrede für unverheiratete Frauen*
	principal ['prɪnsəpl]	Rektor/in, Schulleiter/in	
	hope [həʊp]	hoffen	I **hope** you like my school uniform.
	happy ['hæpi]	glücklich, froh	She's **happy**. He isn't **happy**.
	please [pliːz]	bitte	Can you help me, **please**?
	Please remember ... [rɪ'membə]	Bitte denk dran .../ Bitte merk dir ...	
	be over ['əʊvə]	vorbei sein, zu Ende sein	Olivia isn't at school. School **is over**.
	Sorry./I'm sorry. ['sɒri]	Tut mir leid./Entschuldigung.	
	at home	daheim, zu Hause	Luca is at school. Grace is **at home**.
	home [həʊm]	Heim, Zuhause	
	That isn't good. [ðæt]	Das ist nicht gut.	**That** isn't right. **That**'s wrong.
	homework ['həʊmwɜːk]	Hausaufgabe(n)	→ **homework** hat keinen Plural: **Homework is** important. **Hausaufgaben sind** wichtig.
	write [raɪt]	schreiben	
	know [nəʊ]	wissen; kennen	
p. 25	**Look**, Adam.	Sieh mal, Adam./ Schau mal, Adam.	
	bad [bæd]	schlecht; schlimm	**good** ◂▸ **bad**
	idea [aɪ'dɪə]	Idee	[ɪə] klingt wie das „ier" in „hier".
	need [niːd]	brauchen, benötigen	
	paper ['peɪpə]	Papier	
	scissors *(pl)* ['sɪzəz]	Schere	→ **scissors** ist immer Plural: Where **are** my **scissors**? Wo **ist** meine **Schere**? 
	guys [gaɪz]	Leute *(als Anrede verwendet)*	

	very nice ['veri]	sehr nett, sehr schön	
	say [seɪ]	sagen	! Aussprache: I/you/we/they **say** [seɪ] – he/she **says** [sez]
	What do you think?	Was meinst du?/ Was denkst du?	Are uniforms a good idea? **What do you think?**
	think [θɪŋk]	denken, meinen, glauben	I **think** uniforms are cool.
	theatre ['θɪətə]	Theater	

Skills training

p. 26	**brochure** ['brəʊʃə]	Broschüre, Prospekt	[ʃ] klingt wie das „sch" in „**sch**ön".
	back [bæk]	zurück	
	pound (£) [paʊnd]	Pfund *(britische Währung)*	! you write: **£**5 – you say: five **pounds**
	pencil sharpener ['pensl ʃɑːpnə]	Bleistiftanspitzer	
	rubber ['rʌbə]	Radiergummi	
	ruler ['ruːlə]	Lineal	
	pen [pen]	Kugelschreiber, Stift, Füller	
	pencil ['pensl]	Bleistift	
	pencil case ['pensl keɪs]	Federmäppchen	
	calculator ['kælkjuleɪtə]	Taschenrechner	
	exercise book	Schulheft, Übungsheft	
	exercise ['eksəsaɪz]	Übung, Aufgabe	
	diary ['daɪəri]	Tagebuch; Kalender	
	hole punch ['həʊl pʌntʃ]	Locher	
	buy [baɪ]	kaufen	
	at MARTINS	bei MARTINS	

	child, *pl* **children** [tʃaɪld], ['tʃɪldrən]	Kind, Kinder	! one **child** – two, three, four **children**
	Africa ['æfrɪkə]	Afrika	
p. 27	**network** ['netwɜːk]	Netz; Wortnetz	
	Saturday ['sætədeɪ], ['sætədi]	Samstag, Sonnabend	
	Sunday ['sʌndeɪ], ['sʌndi]	Sonntag	
	weekend [wiːk'end]	Wochenende	
	school bag ['skuːl bæg]	Schultasche	
	phrase [freɪz]	Ausdruck, (Rede-)Wendung	
	card [kɑːd]	Karte	
	box [bɒks]	Kasten, Kiste, Kästchen	
	in English	auf Englisch	What's 'Schultasche' **in English**, please?

p. 28	**talk (to)** [tɔ:k]	sprechen, reden (mit)	**Talk to** your friends about your favourite songs.
	borrow ['bɒrəʊ]	(aus)leihen, sich borgen	Can I **borrow** your calculator, please?
	next [nekst]	nächste(r, s)	→ **last** weekend – letztes Wochenende **this** weekend – dieses Wochenende **next** weekend – nächstes Wochenende
	sure [ʃʊə], [ʃɔ:]	sicher	The next lesson is art. – Are you **sure**? Can you help me? – **Sure**. (Sicher!/Na klar!)
	Here you are.	Bitte schön./Hier, bitte.	
	German ['dʒɜ:mən]	Deutsch; deutsch	

Unit 2: At home with Ellie

p. 34	**with** Ellie [wɪð]	bei Ellie	Where's Cyril? – He's **with** Sandy.
	road [rəʊd]	Straße *(Landstraße zwischen Orten; Straße in Orten)*	→ **in Hill Road** – in der Hill Road **in Park Street** – in der Park Street
	street [stri:t]	Straße *(in Orten)*	
	in the photo ['fəʊtəʊ]	auf dem Foto	
	house [haʊs]	Haus	
	flat [flæt]	Wohnung	
	kitchen ['kɪtʃɪn]	Küche	
	bedroom ['bedru:m]	Schlafzimmer	
	garden ['gɑ:dn]	Garten	
	living room ['lɪvɪŋ ru:m]	Wohnzimmer	
	mum [mʌm]	Mama, Mutti	
	mother ['mʌðə]	Mutter	
	dad [dæd]	Papa, Vati	
	father ['fɑ:ðə]	Vater	
	live [lɪv]	leben; wohnen	Ellie **lives** in Plymouth.
	her dad [hɜ:], [hə]	ihr Vater	**Her** friends live in Plymouth too.
p. 35	**hall** [hɔ:l]	Flur, Diele	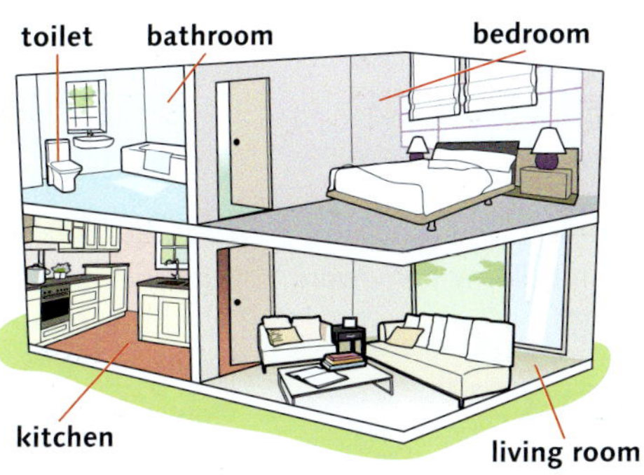
	toilet ['tɔɪlət]	Toilette	
	bathroom ['bɑ:θru:m]	Badezimmer, Bad	
	garage ['gærɑ:ʒ]	Garage	
	dream [dri:m]	Traum	

Theme 1

p.36	**family** ['fæməli]	Familie
	upstairs [ʌp'steəz]	oben; nach oben
	downstairs [daʊn'steəz]	unten; nach unten
	always ['ɔːlweɪz]	immer
	there's … [ðeəz] **there are …** ['ðeər ɑː]	es ist … / es gibt … es sind … / es gibt …
	space [speɪs]	Platz
	into the living room ['ɪntʊ]	in das Wohnzimmer (hinein)
	stepdad ['stepdæd]	Stiefvater →
	miss [mɪs]	vermissen
	real [rɪəl]	echt, wirklich
	his partner [hɪz]	sein Partner, seine Partnerin →
	cute [kjuːt]	niedlich, süß
	you're lucky ['lʌki]	du hast Glück
	at Ellie's house	bei Ellie daheim, bei Ellie zu Hause
p.37	**family tree**	(Familien-)Stammbaum
	tree [triː]	Baum
	together [tə'geðə]	zusammen
	cousin ['kʌzn]	Cousin, Cousine
	aunt [ɑːnt]	Tante
	uncle ['ʌŋkl]	Onkel
	parents ['peərənts]	Eltern
	grandparents ['grænpeərənts]	Großeltern →

! one **family** – two, three, four **families**

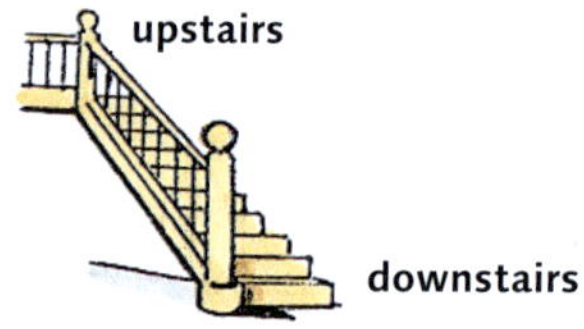

There's a ruler in the pencil case, but **there are** no pencils.

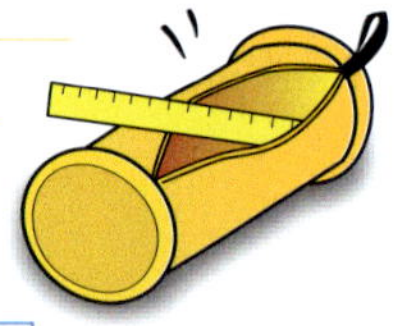

step- („Stief-")
stepdad, stepfather
stepmum, stepmother
stepsister
stepbrother

my	mein/e	**his**	sein/e
your	dein/e, euer/eure	**her**	ihr/e

grand- („Groß-")
grandparents
grandfather
grandmother

Theme 2

p.38	**problem** ['prɒbləm]	Problem
	share a room with … [ʃeə]	sich ein Zimmer mit … teilen
	yours [jɔːz]	deiner, deine, deins
	messy ['mesi]	unordentlich
	bossy ['bɒsi]	herrisch; rechthaberisch
	I **can't** do my homework. [kɑːnt]	Ich kann meine Hausaufgaben nicht machen. →
	do [duː]	machen, tun

can – can't
I/you/he/she/it/we/you/they **can** sing
I/you/he/she/it/we/you/they **can't** dance

	too old/big/… [tuː]	zu alt/groß/…	This shirt is **too** big.
	The kitchen is too **busy**. ['bɪzi]	In der Küche ist zu viel los.	
	noisy ['nɔɪzi]	laut, voller Lärm	
p. 39	**rug** [rʌg]	Teppich, Läufer	
	chair [tʃeə]	Stuhl	
	desk [desk]	Schreibtisch	
	shelf, *pl* **shelves** [ʃelf], [ʃelvz]	Regal, Regale	! one **shelf** – two, three, four **shelves**
	lamp [læmp]	Lampe	
	table ['teɪbl]	Tisch	

a table

a desk

	bed [bed]	Bett	
	cushion ['kʊʃn]	Kissen	
	mirror ['mɪrə]	Spiegel	
	wardrobe ['wɔːdrəʊb]	Kleiderschrank	

	different ['dɪfrənt]	verschieden; anders	You can buy the shirt in three **different** colours. That's a **different** photo.

Focus on language

p. 40	**surprise** [sə'praɪz]	Überraschung	
	tired ['taɪəd]	müde	
	really ['rɪəli]	wirklich	Our English teacher is **really** nice.
	strict [strɪkt]	streng	But our maths teacher is too **strict**.
	mean [miːn]	gemein, fies	
	listen ['lɪsn]	zuhören	→ **Listen**, please. (Hört zu, bitte.) **Listen to** Ellie. (Hört Ellie zu.) **Listen to** the song. (Hört euch das Lied an.)
	question ['kwestʃn]	Frage	
	answer ['ɑːnsə]	Antwort	
p. 41	**easy** ['iːzi]	einfach, leicht	
	difficult ['dɪfɪkəlt]	schwierig, schwer	

Story

p. 42	**example** [ɪg'zɑːmpl]	Beispiel	
	in the picture ['pɪktʃə]	auf dem Bild	

the best of both worlds [bəʊθ], [wɜːldz]	das Beste von beidem	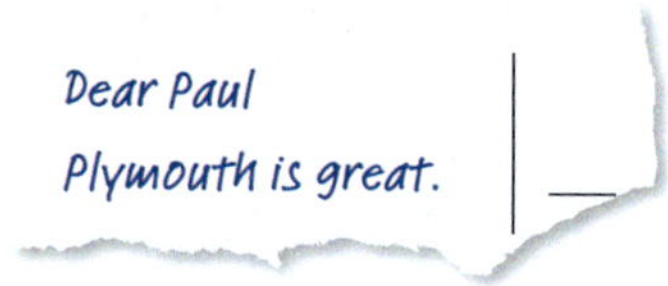
Dear ... [dɪə]	Liebe .../Lieber ...	
news [njuːz]	Nachrichten	! Englisch: That'**s** good **news**. Deutsch: Das **sind** gute **Nachrichten**.
at the cinema ['sɪnəmə]	im Kino	
watch [wɒtʃ]	*sich etwas* anschauen; beobachten	→ **look • see • watch** • **Look**! There's Cyril. • I can **see** Sandy. • I always **watch** the news on TV. Can we **watch** the monkeys?
programme ['prəʊgræm]	(Fernseh-)Sendung	
at work [wɜːk]	bei der Arbeit, am Arbeitsplatz	
soon [suːn]	bald	
at a restaurant ['restrɒnt]	in einem Restaurant	→ **at** **at** the cinema – **im** Kino **at** a restaurant – **in** einem Restaurant **at** school – **in** der Schule **at** work – **bei** der Arbeit **at** Ellie's house – **bei** Ellie daheim
It's her birthday. ['bɜːθdeɪ]	Sie hat Geburtstag.	
again [ə'gen]	wieder; noch einmal	Look, there's Sandy **again**. Can you say that **again**, please?
Be quiet. ['kwaɪət]	Sei still./Sei leise./Sei ruhig.	
p. 43 **in town** [taʊn]	in der Stadt	
lonely ['ləʊnli]	einsam	
text [tekst]	SMS; Text	
a text **from** mum	eine SMS von Mama	
from Monday **to** Friday	von Montag bis Freitag	
week [wiːk]	Woche	
lots of ... ['lɒts əv]	viel ..., viele ...	There are **lots of** books on the desk.
because [bɪ'kɒz]	weil	Ellie is lonely **because** she misses her mum.

Skills training

p. 44 **on the beach**	am Strand	
sea [siː]	Meer	
What's it like?	Wie ist es?/Wie sieht es aus?	Our house is near Plymouth. – **What's it like?** – It's small and blue and very nice.
p. 45 **go with**	gehören zu, passen zu	Picture 4 **goes with** text 2.
It's your turn. [tɜːn]	Du bist dran./Du bist an der Reihe.	
work [wɜːk]	arbeiten	
close [kləʊz]	schließen, zumachen	
door [dɔː]	Tür	Can you close the **door**, please?

	What's for homework?	Was haben wir als Hausaufgabe auf?	
	What page is it?	Auf welcher Seite sind wir?/ Auf welcher Seite steht das?	
	page [peɪdʒ]	Seite	
	I forgot my homework. [fə'gɒt]	Ich habe meine Hausaufgaben vergessen.	
p. 46	**alphabet** ['ælfəbet]	Alphabet	

Betonung
['] ist das **Betonungszeichen**. Es steht immer vor der betonten Silbe.

Beispiel: Im Deutschen heißt es *Alpha**bet*** – die dritte Silbe wird betont.
Im Englischen betont man die erste Silbe: ***al**phabet* ['ælfəbet].

Die richtige Betonung kannst du an der Position des Betonungszeichens ['] erkennen.

	address [ə'dres]	Adresse, Anschrift	What's your **address**? – 11 Greatfield Street.
	phone number ['fəʊn nʌmbə]	Telefonnummer	
	spell [spel]	buchstabieren	

Unit 3: My Plymouth

p. 52	**often** ['ɒfn], ['ɒftən]	oft	I **often** ride my bike to school.
	to the cinema	ins Kino	→ go **to** the cinema – **ins** Kino gehen go **to** the beach – **an** den Strand gehen go **to** school – **zur** Schule gehen go **to** work – **zur** Arbeit gehen go **to** bed – **ins** Bett gehen
	summer ['sʌmə]	Sommer	
	fire station ['faɪə steɪʃn]	Feuerwache	Luca's dad works at a **fire station**.
	family name	Familienname, Nachname	
	never ['nevə]	nie, niemals	I **never** ride my bike on the beach. **always** ◄► **never**
p. 53	**aquarium** [ə'kweəriəm]	Aquarium	
	market ['mɑːkɪt]	Markt	at a **market**
	shopping centre ['sentə]	Einkaufszentrum	

Theme 1

p. 54	**stay** [steɪ]	bleiben	Can't we **stay** at home? Can't I **stay** in bed?
	breakfast ['brekfəst]	Frühstück	our **breakfast**
	everybody ['evribɒdi]	jeder; alle	**Everybody** likes the beach.
	in the morning	am Morgen, morgens	I'm always tired **in the morning**.
	go shopping ['ʃɒpɪŋ]	einkaufen gehen	On Saturdays we **go shopping** at the market.

first [fɜːst]	zuerst, als Erstes	**First** we go shopping , …
then [ðen]	dann, danach	… **then** we play games.
vegetables *(pl)* ['vedʒtəblz]	Gemüse	! Englisch: **Vegetables are** good for you. Deutsch: **Gemüse <u>ist</u>** gut für dich.
boring ['bɔːrɪŋ]	langweilig	
like	wie	The English word 'supermarket' is **like** the German word 'Supermarkt'.
sweets *(pl)* [swiːts]	Süßigkeiten	
afternoon [ɑːftə'nuːn]	Nachmittag	
usually ['juːʒuəli]	meistens, normalerweise	
there [ðeə]	da, dort; dahin, dorthin	I often go to the park. I usually meet my friends **there**.
evening ['iːvnɪŋ]	Abend	

• **in** the morning	morgens, am Morgen	• **on** Monday	am Montag
in the afternoon	nachmittags, am Nachmittag	**on** Tuesdays	dienstags, an Dienstagen
in the evening	abends, am Abend	**on** Friday morning	freitagmorgens, am Freitagmorgen

sometimes ['sʌmtaɪmz]	manchmal	→ **always** / **usually** / **often** / **sometimes** / **never**
come [kʌm]	kommen	
p. 55 **have breakfast; have lunch**	frühstücken; (zu) Mittag essen	
present ['preznt]	Geschenk	a **present**
want to do sth. [wɒnt]	etwas tun wollen	! Englisch: We **want <u>to</u> buy** a present. Deutsch: Wir **wollen** ein Geschenk **kaufen.**
today [tə'deɪ]	heute	
trainers *(pl)* ['treɪnəz]	Turnschuhe	
expensive [ɪk'spensɪv]	teuer	
hoodie ['hʊdi]	Kapuzenpullover, -jacke	

The red **trainers** are great,
but the **hoodie** is too **expensive**.

40 forty ['fɔːti]	**80 eighty** ['eɪti]	**101 a/one hundred and one**
50 fifty ['fɪfti]	**90 ninety** ['naɪnti]	**102 a/one hundred and two**
60 sixty ['sɪksti]	**100 a hundred/one hundred** [ə'hʌndrəd], ['wʌn'hʌndrəd]	**103 a/one hundred and three**
70 seventy ['sevnti]		**…**

(► *Numbers*, p. 229)

hate [heɪt]	hassen, gar nicht mögen	**love** ◄► **hate**
terrible ['terəbl]	schrecklich, fürchterlich	Dad thinks dogs are **terrible** – he hates dogs.

Theme 2

p. 56	**on my birthday**	an meinem Geburtstag
	have a party	eine Party feiern

Einzahl (Singular)	**Mehrzahl** (Plural)	**Einzahl** (Singular)	**Mehrzahl** (Plural)
baby	**babies**	**hobby**	**hobbies**
city	**cities**	**party**	**parties**
diary	**diaries**	**pony**	**ponies**
family	**families**	**story**	**stories**

! Aber:

day	**days**
boy	**boys**
monkey	**monkeys**

The months [mʌnθs] (Die Monate)

1 **January** ['dʒænjuəri] Januar
2 **February** ['februəri] Februar
3 **March** [mɑːtʃ] März
4 **April** ['eɪprəl] April
5 **May** [meɪ] Mai
6 **June** [dʒuːn] Juni
7 **July** [dʒu'laɪ] Juli
8 **August** ['ɔːgəst] August
9 **September** [sep'tembə] September
10 **October** [ɒk'təʊbə] Oktober
11 **November** [nəʊ'vembə] November
12 **December** [dɪ'sembə] Dezember

! Monatsnamen werden immer großgeschrieben.

	go swimming	schwimmen gehen	
	get [get]	bekommen	I usually **get** nice presents on my birthday.
	visit ['vɪzɪt]	besuchen	Can we **visit** Sophie on Sunday?
p. 57	**date** [deɪt]	Datum	
	when? [wen]	wann?	→

what?	was?	**where?**	wo(hin)?
who?	wer?	**when?**	wann?
how?	wie?		

When's your birthday?	Wann hast du Geburtstag?	! Englisch: **When is** your birthday? Deutsch: **Wann hast** du Geburtstag?
on 5th May	am 5. Mai	! • you write: **on 5th May** – you say: **on the fifth of May** • mit Datum: My birthday is **on 5th May**. ohne Datum: My birthday is **in May**.
second ['sekənd]	zweite(r, s)	→
third [θɜːd]	dritte(r, s)	→

1	**one**	eins	1st	**first**	erste(r, s)
2	**two**	zwei	2nd	**second**	zweite(r, s)
3	**three**	drei	3rd	**third**	dritte(r, s)
4	**four**	vier	4th	**fourth**	vierte(r, s)
5	**five**	fünf	5th	**fifth**	fünfte(r, s)

(► *Numbers*, p. 229)

at 1 o'clock [ə'klɒk]	um 1 Uhr/um 13 Uhr	It's **1 o'clock** now.

free [friː]	frei	Can we meet at 1 o'clock? Are you **free**?

Focus on language

p. 58	**get up** [get 'ʌp]	aufstehen	My sister **gets up** at 6 o'clock every morning.
	early ['ɜːli]	früh	I get up **early** too.
	lazy ['leɪzi]	faul	My brother is **lazy** – he often stays in bed.
	late [leɪt]	spät	**early ◂▸ late**
	at night [ət 'naɪt]	nachts, in der Nacht	→ **in** the morning **in** the afternoon **in** the evening **! at** night
	come home; **go home**	nach Hause kommen; nach Hause gehen	
	after dinner [ɑːftə 'dɪnə]	nach dem Abendessen	**After dinner** we sometimes watch TV.
	us [ʌs], [əs]	uns	We're here. Can you see **us**?
	go by bus [baɪ 'bʌs]	mit dem Bus fahren	I usually **go** to school **by bus**. My brother always **goes by bike**.
	walk [wɔːk]	(zu Fuß) gehen	My sister often **walks** to school.

Story

p. 60	**unhappy** [ʌn'hæpi]	unglücklich	**happy ◂▸ unhappy**
	Happy birthday!	Herzlichen Glückwunsch zum Geburtstag!	
	Let's ... [lets]	Lass uns .../Lasst uns ...	It's late. **Let's** go home.
	plan [plæn]	planen	
	something ['sʌmθɪŋ]	etwas	Can I ask you **something**?
	Shut up! [ʃʌt 'ʌp] *(infml)*	Halt den Mund!	**!** Vorsicht! Viele Erwachsene finden **Shut up!** sehr unhöflich.
	concert ['kɒnsət]	Konzert	
	zoo [zuː]	Zoo	**!** Aussprache: **zoo** [zuː] – Der Anfangslaut ist wie im deutschen Namen „**S**usie".
	excited [ɪk'saɪtɪd]	aufgeregt, gespannt	
	their bikes [ðeə]	ihre Fahrräder	→ **I** – **my** bike **you** – **your** bike **he** – **his** bike **she** – **her** bike **we** – **our** bikes **you** – **your** bikes **they** – **their** bikes
p. 61	**hill** [hɪl]	Hügel	
	down this hill [daʊn]	diesen Hügel hinunter	**!** Englisch: **down this hill** Deutsch: **diesen Hügel hinunter**
	fast [fɑːst]	schnell	They always go down the hill very **fast**. 
	Come on, Luca!	Na los, Luca!/Komm, Luca!	
	leg [leg]	Bein	

	fall [fɔːl]	fallen; hinfallen	
	hospital ['hɒspɪtl]	Krankenhaus	
	I **have a sore leg**. [sɔː]	Mein Bein tut weh.	Luca can't walk. He **has a sore leg**.
	or [ɔː]	oder	Are you a boy **or** a girl?
	want sth. [wɒnt]	etwas (haben) wollen	**!** • **want sth.** etwas (haben) wollen — I **want** a new bike. • **want <u>to do</u> sth.** etwas tun wollen — I **want to buy** it now.
	end [end]	Ende, Schluss	

Skills training

p. 62	**sale** [seɪl]	Verkauf; Schlussverkauf	
	The calculator **is** £1.	Der Taschenrechner kostet 1 Pfund.	
	The mobiles **are** £10.	Die Handys kosten 10 Pfund.	
	How much is ...?/ How much are ...? [mʌtʃ]	Was (Wie viel) kostet ...?/ Was (Wie viel) kosten ...?	**How much is** the football? And **how much are** the books?
	50p [fɪfti 'piː]	50 Pence	
	British ['brɪtɪʃ]	britisch	
	money ['mʌni]	Geld	
p. 63	It **looks** nice.	Es sieht schön aus.	→ **look** • **Look at** the pictures. (Sieh dir die Bilder an.) • **Look**, Adam. There's a crab. (Schau mal, Adam. Da ist ein Krebs.) • My new bike **looks** great. (Mein neues Rad sieht toll aus.)
	Excuse me, ... [ɪk'skjuːz miː]	Entschuldigung, .../ Entschuldigen Sie, ...	**Excuse me,** please. How much is this mobile?
	man, *pl* **men** [mæn], [men]	Mann, Männer	**!** one **man** – two, three, four **men**
	special offer [speʃl 'ɒfə]	Sonderangebot	
	special ['speʃl]	besondere(r, s)	
	It's **good value.** ['væljuː]	Es ist sein Geld wert.	
	the same [seɪm]	derselbe/dieselbe/dasselbe; dieselben	Luca and his brother Jack are at **the same** school.
	try [traɪ]	probieren, ausprobieren	
	I'll take it. [aɪl 'teɪk ɪt]	Ich nehme es (ihn, sie). *(beim Einkaufen)*	How much is the football? – £12. – OK, **I'll take it**.
	That's £159.	Das macht 159 Pfund.	
	helmet ['helmɪt]	Helm	**helmets** 
p. 64	**advert** ['ædvɜːt]	Anzeige, Werbung	
	guess [ges]	raten, erraten	**Guess** how old I am. – 15? – No, I'm 14.

Unit 4: Berry's world

pp. 70/71	**world** [wɜːld]	Welt	
	visitor ['vɪzɪtə]	Besucher/in; Gast	
	barn [bɑːn]	Scheune, Stall	
	stroke [strəʊk]	streicheln	
	donkey ['dɒŋki]	Esel	
	duck [dʌk]	Ente	
	pond [pɒnd]	Teich	
	field [fiːld]	Feld; Weide	! Englisch: the ponies **in the field** Deutsch: die Ponys **auf der Weide**
	cow [kaʊ]	Kuh	
	pig [pɪg]	Schwein	
	sheep, *pl* **sheep** [ʃiːp]	Schaf, Schafe	! one **sheep** – two, three, four **sheep**
	chicken ['tʃɪkɪn]	Huhn; (Brat-)Hähnchen	

Theme 1

p. 72	**life**, *pl* **lives** [laɪf], [laɪvz]	*(das)* Leben, *(die)* Leben	! one **life** – two, three, four **lives**
	she doesn't have a … ['dʌznt]	sie hat kein/keine/keinen …	→ Berry **doesn't** have a cat. She has a dog.
	alarm clock [ə'lɑːm klɒk]	Wecker	
	wake [weɪk]	wecken	
	other ['ʌðə]	andere(r, s)	The dog is in the garden. Where are the **other** animals?
	outside [aʊt'saɪd]	draußen; nach draußen	The other animals are **outside**, in the field. Let's go **outside** and play.
	inside [ɪn'saɪd]	drinnen; nach drinnen	Berry isn't in the garden. She's **inside**. Let's go **inside** too.
	before breakfast [bɪ'fɔː]	vor dem Frühstück	**before breakfast** ◄► **after breakfast**
	feed [fiːd]	füttern	Can I **feed** the rabbits?
	get ready (for) ['redi]	sich fertig machen (für), sich vorbereiten (auf)	First I have breakfast, then I **get ready for** school.
	all day/summer/…	den ganzen Tag/Sommer/… (lang)	
	eat [iːt]	essen; fressen	
	about [ə'baʊt]	ungefähr	We get up at **about** 8.30 on Sundays.
	look after [lʊk 'ɑːftə]	sich kümmern um; aufpassen auf	On Saturday mornings I always **look after** my baby sister.
	do sport	Sport treiben	And on Saturday afternoons I **do sport**.

I	**don't have**	he	**doesn't have**
you	**don't have**	she	**doesn't have**
we	**don't have**	it	**doesn't have**
they	**don't have**		

	nothing ['nʌθɪŋ]	(gar) nichts	
p.73	**sit** [sɪt]	sitzen; sich setzen	
	year [jɪə]	Jahr	Our dog is two **years** old.
	dialogue ['daɪəlɒg]	Dialog	
	What's the time?	Wie spät ist es?	
	You're welcome.	Bitte, gern geschehen./ Nichts zu danken.	

„bitte"

- in Aufforderungen und Bitten: **please** — Close the door, **please**./What's the time, **please**? (Schließ die Tür, bitte./Wie spät ist es, bitte?)
- wenn sich jemand bedankt hat: **You're welcome.** — It's 9.30. – Thank you. – **You're welcome.** (9 Uhr 30. – Danke. – Bitte, gern geschehen.)
- wenn du jemandem etwas gibst: **Here you are.** — Can I borrow your pen, please? – **Here you are.** (Kann ich deinen Stift leihen? – Hier, bitte.)

Theme 2

p.74	**feeling** ['fiːlɪŋ]	Gefühl	
	discussion [dɪ'skʌʃn]	Diskussion	
	feel [fiːl]	sich fühlen; fühlen	
	feel fed up [fed 'ʌp]	genervt sein, sauer sein; die Nase voll haben	
	when [wen]	wenn	I always feel happy **when** I listen to this song. ! **when** = **1. wann**: **When**'s your birthday? **2. wenn**: I feel great **when** I do sport.
	work [wɜːk]	funktionieren	I need your help. My computer doesn't **work**.
	text a friend [tekst]	einem Freund/einer Freundin eine SMS schicken	**Text** me when you're back from London, OK?
	Not me!	Ich nicht!	**Me too.** (Ich auch.) ◄► **Not me.** (Ich nicht.)
p.75	**a bit** [ə 'bɪt]	ein bisschen	5 o'clock in the morning? That's **a bit** early for me.
	the only student ['əʊnli]	der einzige Schüler/ die einzige Schülerin	Lily is **the only** English student at our school.
	wheelchair ['wiːltʃeə]	Rollstuhl	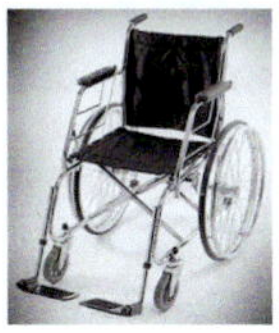 a **wheelchair**
	normal ['nɔːml]	normal, gewöhnlich	
	win [wɪn]	gewinnen	I feel good when my football team **wins**.
	ask [ɑːsk]	fragen	Can I feed the pigs? – **Ask** my dad, please. ! Englisch: Can I **ask** you a **question**? Deutsch: Kann ich dir eine **Frage stellen**?
	drink [drɪŋk]	Getränk	
	drink [drɪŋk]	trinken	
	understand [ʌndə'stænd]	verstehen	In English, please. I don't **understand** German.
	speak [spiːk]	sprechen	Can you **speak** French?

	for myself [maɪ'self]	für mich selbst	
	work/speak/… **well** [wel]	gut funktionieren/sprechen/…	My computer doesn't work very **well**. My parents speak English very **well**.
	mouth [maʊθ]	Mund	

Focus on language

p.76	**furry** ['fɜːri]	flauschig; pelzig	
p.77	**interesting** ['ɪntrəstɪŋ]	interessant	This book is great. It's very **interesting**.
	It doesn't like **to** be lonely.	Es mag es nicht, allein zu sein. →	**to** („zu") I don't like **to** be lonely. allein **zu** sein It's time **to** go now. Zeit **zu** gehen Here's something **to** eat. etwas **zu** essen
	cage [keɪdʒ]	Käfig	
p.78	**why?** [waɪ]	warum? →	**what?** was? **where?** wo(hin)? **who?** wer? **when?** wann? **why?** warum? **how?** wie?
	friendly ['frendli]	freundlich	
	shoulder ['ʃəʊldə]	Schulter	
	fruit [fruːt]	Obst	
	nut [nʌt]	Nuss	

fruit and nuts

	sleep [sliːp]	schlafen	
p.79	**find** [faɪnd]	finden	
	Find a person who … ['pɜːsn]	Finde eine Person, die …	

Story

p.80	**on the bus**	im Bus	! Englisch: **on the bus** Deutsch: **im Bus**
	nervous ['nɜːvəs]	nervös, aufgeregt	
	adventure [əd'ventʃə]	Abenteuer	
	country ['kʌntri]	Land	! Englisch: **in the country** Deutsch: **auf dem Land** ! one **country** – two, three, four **countries**
	scene [siːn]	Szene	
	invite (to) [ɪn'vaɪt]	einladen (zu, nach)	Can I **invite** all my friends to my party?
	sleepover ['sliːpəʊvə]	Schlafparty	
	bring [brɪŋ]	bringen, mitbringen	

	sleeping bag ['sli:pɪŋ bæg]	Schlafsack	
	Don't worry. [dəʊnt 'wʌri]	Mach dir keine Sorgen.	→
	worry (about) ['wʌri]	sich Sorgen machen (wegen, um)	Mum always **worries about** me when I come home late.
	her [hɜ:]	sie; ihr	→
	wet [wet]	nass	
	laugh [lɑ:f]	lachen	
p. 81	**through** [θru:]	durch	
	that field [ðæt], [ðət]	das Feld (dort), jenes Feld	

Don't …
Don't go now. – Geh jetzt (noch) nicht.
Don't ask. – Frag nicht.
Don't be stupid. – Sei nicht dumm.
Don't watch TV. – Sieh nicht fern.

her
- *(wessen?)* **ihr, ihre**
  her birthday; **her** children
- *(wen?)* **sie**
  Sally? We can meet **her** in the park.
- *(wem?)* **ihr**
  There's Sophie. Let's help **her**.

this – that
- Wenn etwas **näher beim Sprecher** ist, verwendet man eher **this** („dies hier").
- Wenn etwas **weiter entfernt** ist, verwendet man eher **that** („das dort").

	be hungry ['hʌŋgri]	hungrig sein, Hunger haben	**!** Englisch: **We're hungry.** Deutsch: **Wir haben Hunger.**
	be in trouble ['trʌbl]	in Schwierigkeiten sein; Ärger kriegen	My friends always help me when **I'm in trouble**.
	dangerous ['deɪndʒərəs]	gefährlich	a **dangerous** snake
	noise [nɔɪz]	Geräusch; Lärm	Listen! What's that **noise** in the garden? What's that **noise**? I can't do my homework.
	only ['əʊnli]	nur, bloß	
	Go to sleep!	Schlaf jetzt!	Be quiet now and **go to sleep**.

Skills training

p. 82	**sign** [saɪn]	Schild; Zeichen	
	left [left]	links; nach links	
	right [raɪt]	rechts; nach rechts	

p. 83	**invitation (to)** [ɪnvɪ'teɪʃn]	Einladung (zu, nach)
	picnic ['pɪknɪk]	Picknick
	5 **pm** [pi:'em]	5 Uhr nachmittags/abends; 17 Uhr
	9 **am** [eɪ'em]	9 Uhr morgens/vormittags
	I'd love to come. (= I would love to …) [wʊd]	Ich komme sehr gern. / Ich würde sehr gern kommen.
	Best wishes ['wɪʃɪz]	Viele Grüße, … *(Briefschluss)*

p. 84	**use** [juːz]	benutzen, verwenden	→ ! Aussprache: **use** he/she **use**s ['juːzɪz] **close** he/she **close**s ['kləʊzɪz] **dance** he/she **dance**s ['dɑːnsɪz] **guess** he/she **guess**es ['gesɪz] **watch** he/she **watch**es ['wɒtʃɪz]
	dictionary ['dɪkʃənri]	Wörterbuch, *(alphabetisches)* Wörterverzeichnis	! one **dictionary** – two, three, four **dictionar**ies
	poem ['pəʊɪm]	Gedicht	

Unit 5: All about Adam

p. 90	**harbour** ['hɑːbə]	Hafen
	on the left	links, auf der linken Seite
	on the right	rechts, auf der rechten Seite
	in the middle ['mɪdl]	in der Mitte

Lily is on the left, Ben is in the middle, Ava is on the right.

p. 91	**Where is Adam going?**	Wohin geht Adam (gerade)?
	cafe ['kæfeɪ]	Café
	ferry ['feri]	Fähre

Theme 1

p. 92	**chips** *(pl)* [tʃɪps]	Pommes frites
	salad ['sæləd]	Salat *(als Gericht oder Beilage)*
	soup [suːp]	Suppe
	a **bottle of ...** ['bɒtl]	eine Flasche ...
	water ['wɔːtə]	Wasser
	a **cup of ...** [kʌp]	eine Tasse ...
	coffee ['kɒfi]	Kaffee
	tea [tiː]	Tee
	scone [skɒn]	*kleines rundes Milchbrötchen, leicht süß, oft mit Rosinen*
	Anything else? ['eniθɪŋ 'els]	Sonst noch etwas?

two bottles of juice **a bottle of water** **a cup of coffee**

	How's it going?	Wie geht's?/Wie läuft's?
	ring [rɪŋ]	läuten, klingeln
	job [dʒɒb]	Job, (Arbeits-)Stelle

Adam's mobile is **ringing**.

	be busy ['bɪzi]	beschäftigt sein; viel zu tun haben	
	cook [kʊk]	kochen, *(Essen)* zubereiten	What are you **cooking**, Mum? – Omelettes.
	wash up [wɒʃ 'ʌp]	abwaschen	
	must [mʌst]	müssen	
	work **hard** [hɑːd]	hart arbeiten	We must work **hard** at school.
	I must go.	*(am Telefon)* Ich muss Schluss machen.	
	Say hi to everybody.	Grüß alle.	
p. 93	**letter** ['letə]	Brief	
	be worried (about) ['wʌrid]	beunruhigt sein, besorgt sein (wegen)	Ms Lee **is worried about** Adam because he's often tired at school.
	at the moment ['məʊmənt]	im Moment, gerade	
	phone [fəʊn]	anrufen	
	happen ['hæpən]	geschehen, passieren	Say what's **happening** in the pictures.

Theme 2

p. 94	**so** boring/tired/... [səʊ]	so langweilig/müde/...	
	dive [daɪv]	einen Kopfsprung machen	
	hide [haɪd]	verstecken; sich verstecken	→ Let's **hide** in the wardrobe. **!** Schreibung: **come** – **coming**, **dive** – **diving**, **have** – **having**, **hide** – **hiding**, **make** – **making**, **phone** – **phoning**, **ride** – **riding**, **write** – **writing**
	send [send]	schicken, senden	
p. 95	**guitar** [gɪ'tɑː]	Gitarre	
	learn [lɜːn]	lernen	
	drums [drʌmz]	Schlagzeug; Trommeln	**!** Englisch: **play the guitar/the drums** Deutsch: **Gitarre/Schlagzeug spielen**
	group [gruːp]	Gruppe	
	instrument ['ɪnstrəmənt]	Instrument	
	young [jʌŋ]	jung	**young** ◄► **old**
	musician [mju'zɪʃn]	Musiker/in	
	singer ['sɪŋə]	Sänger/in	
	sing [sɪŋ]	singen	
	piano [pi'ænəʊ]	Klavier, Piano	**!** Englisch: **play the piano** Deutsch: **Klavier spielen** 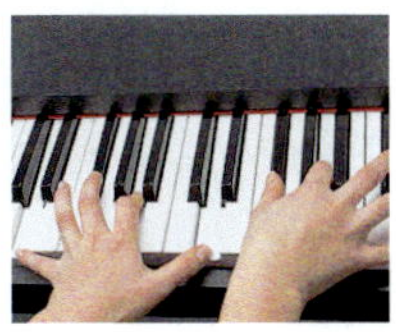
	join a club [dʒɔɪn]	sich einem Klub anschließen; in einen Klub eintreten	I want to **join** the guitar club. What about you?
	price [praɪs]	(Kauf-)Preis	

Focus on language

p. 96	**set the table** [set]	den Tisch decken →	**!** Schreibung: **get** **getting**, **rap** **rapping**, **set** **setting**, **sit** **sitting**, **swim** **swimming**
	clean [kliːn]	sauber machen, putzen	
	little ['lɪtl]	klein	On Saturday mornings I always look after my **little** sister.
	maybe ['meɪbi]	vielleicht	
	cook [kʊk]	Koch, Köchin	**two cooks** 
	Well, … [wel]	Nun, … / Also, … / Na ja, …	
	form [fɔːm]	Form	'am', 'is' and 'are' are **forms** of 'be'.
p. 97	**food** [fuːd]	Essen; Lebensmittel; Futter	
	him [hɪm]	ihn; ihm	Look, there's Zack. Can you see **him**? Let's help **him**.
	them [ðem], [ðəm]	sie; ihnen	Look, there are the boys. Can you see **them**? Let's help **them**.

I (ich) – **me**	Can you see **me**? (mich)	Help **me**. (mir)
you (du; Sie) – **you**	Can I phone **you**? (dich; Sie)	Can I help **you**? (dir; Ihnen)
he (er) – **him**	Can you see **him**? (ihn)	Help **him**. (ihm)
she (sie) – **her**	Can you see **her**? (sie)	Help **her**. (ihr)
it (es) – **it**	Can you see **it**? (es)	Help **it**. (ihm)
we (wir) – **us**	Can you see **us**? (uns)	Help **us**. (uns)
you (ihr; Sie) – **you**	Can I phone **you**? (euch; Sie)	Can I help **you**? (euch; Ihnen)
they (sie) – **them**	Can you see **them**? (sie)	Help **them**. (ihnen)

window ['wɪndəʊ]	Fenster	
hear [hɪə]	hören	**!** **hear** = hören (können) **listen (to)** = zuhören, horchen **Listen**! Can you **hear** that noise?

Story

p. 98	**difference** ['dɪfrəns]	Unterschied	
	it **was** Friday [wɒz], [wəz]	es war Freitag →	• **I am** (ich bin) – **I was** (ich war) • **he/she/it is** (er/sie/es ist) – **he/she/it was** (er/sie/es war)
	on the way to … [weɪ]	auf dem Weg zu/nach …	
	some [sʌm], [səm]	einige, ein paar; etwas	There are **some** sandwiches for you on the table. And there's **some** juice too.

they **were** on the bus [wɜː], [wə]	sie waren im Bus	→
he **said** [sed]	er sagte; er hat gesagt	
seat [siːt]	(Sitz-)Platz	

• **we are** (wir sind)	**we were** (wir waren)
• **you are** (du bist; ihr seid)	**you were** (du warst; ihr wart)
• **they are** (sie sind)	**they were** (sie waren)

they **laughed** [lɑːft]	sie lachten; sie haben gelacht	
face [feɪs]	Gesicht	
she **asked** [ɑːskt]	sie fragte; sie hat gefragt	
I **had** [hæd], [həd]	ich hatte; ich habe gehabt	
girlfriend ['gɜːlfrend]	(feste) Freundin	
boyfriend ['bɔɪfrend]	(fester) Freund	
Any ideas? ['eni]	Irgendwelche Ideen?	I need help with my text. **Any** ideas?
hard [hɑːd]	schwer, schwierig; hart	This exercise isn't **hard**. You can do it. It's **hard** work to write a rap.

p. 99	**Well done.** [wel 'dʌn]	Gut gemacht!
	proud (of) [praʊd]	stolz (auf)
	true [truː]	wahr
	false [fɔːls]	falsch
	he **wasn't** there ['wɒznt]	er war nicht da

Skills training

p. 100	**describe** [dɪ'skraɪb]	beschreiben	**!** Englisch: **Describe** the picture **to** **him/her**. Deutsch: **Beschreibe** **ihm/ihr** das Bild.
	next to	neben	
	between [bɪ'twiːn]	zwischen	
	behind [bɪ'haɪnd]	hinter	
	under ['ʌndə]	unter	
	in front of [ɪn 'frʌnt əv]	vor	

	apple ['æpl]	Apfel
p. 101	**text message** ['tekst mesɪdʒ]	SMS
p. 102	**recipe** ['resəpi]	(Koch-)Rezept
	jam [dʒæm]	Marmelade
	cream [kriːm]	Sahne

°Unit 6: School is out – for summer

Die Unit 6 ist keine Pflichtunit.
Aber wenn ihr die Unit im Unterricht behandelt, solltest du die neuen Wörter aus Unit 6 lernen. Dann kennst du sie schon, wenn sie im nächsten Band als Lernwortschatz im *Vocabulary* auftreten.

p. 108	**°school is out** [aʊt]	die Schule ist aus/vorbei
	°I'd prefer … [prɪ'fɜː]	ich würde … vorziehen
	°canoe [kə'nuː]	Kanu, Paddelboot
	°theme park ['θiːm pɑːk]	Themenpark *(Freizeitpark mit Attraktionen zu einem bestimmten Thema)*

Theme

p. 110	**°swimsuit** ['swɪmsuːt]	Badeanzug
	°swimming trunks *(pl)* ['swɪmɪŋ trʌŋks]	Badehose →
	°towel ['taʊəl]	Handtuch
	°sunglasses *(pl)* ['sʌnglɑːsɪz]	Sonnenbrille →
	°hat [hæt]	Hut
	°That's a pity. ['pɪti]	Das ist schade!
	°crisps *(pl)* [krɪsps]	(Kartoffel-)Chips
	°sausage ['sɒsɪdʒ]	(Brat-, Bock-)Würstchen, Wurst
	°cake [keɪk]	Kuchen, Torte
	°orange ['ɒrɪndʒ]	Orange, Apfelsine
	°chocolate ['tʃɒklət]	Schokolade
	°biscuit ['bɪskɪt]	Keks, Plätzchen
p. 111	**°speaker** ['spiːkə]	Lautsprecher
	°tube [tjuːb]	Schwimmreifen
	°umbrella [ʌm'brelə]	(Regen-)Schirm
	°suncream ['sʌnkriːm]	Sonnencreme, Sonnenschutzmittel
	°bodyboard ['bɒdɪbɔːd]	*kurzes Surfbrett, mit dem man auf dem Bauch liegend surft*
	°blanket ['blæŋkɪt]	Decke *(zum Zudecken u.Ä.)*
	°forget [fə'get]	vergessen
	°chain [tʃeɪn]	Kette

swimming trunks und **sunglasses** sind immer Plural:
Your **swimming trunks/sunglasses are** great. **Are they** new?
(Deine **Badehose/Sonnenbrille ist** toll. **Ist sie** neu?)

! Englisch: **crisps** = Deutsch: **Chips**
Englisch: **chips** = Deutsch: **Pommes frites**

a chocolate cake

! Englisch: **biscuit** = Deutsch: **Keks**
Englisch: **cake** = Deutsch: **Kuchen, Torte**

Story

p. 113	°**aboard** [ə'bɔːd]	an Bord	
	°**message in a bottle** ['mesɪdʒ]	Flaschenpost	 a message in a bottle
	°**woman,** *pl* **women** ['wʊmən], ['wɪmɪn]	Frau, Frauen	**!** one **woman** – two, three, four **women**
	°**smuggler** ['smʌɡlə]	Schmuggler/in	
	°**put** [pʊt]	*(etwas wohin)* tun, legen, stellen, stecken	
	°**better** ['betə]	besser	**good – better – best**
	°**the sea's coming in**	die Flut kommt; das Wasser steigt	
	°**minute** ['mɪnɪt]	Minute	
	°**hurry** ['hʌri]	sich beeilen	
	°**square** [skweə]	Platz *(in der Stadt)*	 maps
	°**map** [mæp]	Landkarte, Stadtplan	
	°**another** [ə'nʌðə]	noch ein(e)	
	°**follow** ['fɒləʊ]	folgen; verfolgen	
p. 114	°**push** [pʊʃ]	schieben	
	°**clock** [klɒk]	(Wand-, Stand-, Turm-)Uhr	
	°**quick** [kwɪk]	schnell	
	°**slow** [sləʊ]	langsam	
	°**look for** sth.	etwas suchen; nach etwas Ausschau halten	
	°**hot** [hɒt]	heiß	
	°**ice cream** [aɪs 'kriːm]	(Speise-)Eis	
p. 115	°**wait (for)** [weɪt]	warten (auf)	
	°**daughter** ['dɔːtə]	Tochter	
	°**get out** [get 'aʊt]	herauskommen	
	°**out of ...** ['aʊt əv]	aus ... (heraus/hinaus)	
	°**scary** ['skeəri]	unheimlich	
	°**over there** [əʊvə 'ðeə]	da drüben, dort drüben	

Skills training

p. 116	°**fly** [flaɪ]	fliegen	

Das **DICTIONARY** besteht aus **zwei alphabetischen Wörterlisten**:
English – German (S. 208–218) und **German – English** (S. 219–227)

Im **English – German dictionary** kannst du nachschlagen, wenn du wissen möchtest, was ein englisches Wort bedeutet, wie man es ausspricht oder wie es geschrieben wird.

Im **Dictionary** werden folgende **Abkürzungen und Symbole** verwendet:

sth. = something (etwas) *pl* = *plural* (Mehrzahl) *infml* = *informal* (umgangssprachlich)

° Mit diesem Kringel sind Wörter markiert, die nicht zum Lernwortschatz gehören.

Die **Fundstellenangaben** zeigen, wo ein Wort zum ersten Mal in *Lighthouse 1* vorkommt.
Die Ziffern in Klammern bezeichnen Seitenzahlen:

(8) = Seite 8
1 (19) = Unit 1, Seite 19

Tipps zur Arbeit mit einem Wörterbuch findest du im Skills file auf Seite 164.

A

a [ə] ein, eine (9)
a bit [ə 'bɪt] ein bisschen 4 (75)
°**aboard** [ə'bɔːd] an Bord
about [ə'baʊt]:
1. über 1 (19)
2. ungefähr 4 (72)
about me/you/... über mich/dich/... 1 (19) **What about ...?** Wie wär's mit ...? 3 (55)
What about you? Und du?/Und was ist mit dir? (8)
°**act** [ækt] (vor)spielen, aufführen
°**activity** [æk'tɪvəti] Aktivität
°**add** [æd] hinzufügen
address [ə'dres] Adresse, Anschrift 2 (46)
adventure [əd'ventʃə] Abenteuer 4 (80)
advert ['ædvɜːt] Anzeige, Werbung 3 (64)
Africa ['æfrɪkə] Afrika 1 (26)
after ['ɑːftə] nach 3 (58) **after dinner** nach dem Abendessen 3 (58) **look after** sich kümmern um; aufpassen auf 4 (72)
afternoon [ɑːftə'nuːn] Nachmittag 3 (54) **in the afternoon** nachmittags, am Nachmittag 3 (54) **on Friday afternoon** freitagnachmittags, am Freitagnachmittag 3 (54)
again [ə'gen] wieder; noch einmal 2 (42)
age [eɪdʒ] Alter 1 (18)
°**agree on sth.** [ə'griː] sich auf etwas einigen
alarm clock [ə'lɑːm klɒk] Wecker 4 (72)
all (the) [ɔːl] alle 1 (23) **all day/summer/...** den ganzen Tag/Sommer/... (lang) 4 (72)
°**all around me** ganz um mich herum
°**alone** [ə'ləʊn] allein
°**along** [ə'lɒŋ]: **sing along** mitsingen
°**aloud** [ə'laʊd]: **read sth. aloud** etwas laut (vor)lesen
alphabet ['ælfəbet] Alphabet 2 (46)
°**alphabetical order** [ælfə'betɪkl 'ɔːdə] alphabetische Reihenfolge
always ['ɔːlweɪz] immer 2 (36)
am [eɪ'em]: **9 am** 9 Uhr morgens/vormittags 4 (83)
an [ən] ein, eine (12)
and [ænd, ənd] und (9)
animal ['ænɪml] Tier (12)
°**another** [ə'nʌðə] noch ein(e)
answer ['ɑːnsə]:
1. Antwort 2 (40)
°**2.** (be)antworten
Any ideas? ['eni] Irgendwelche Ideen? 5 (98)
Anything else? ['eniθɪŋ 'els] Sonst noch etwas? 5 (92)
apple ['æpl] Apfel 5 (100)
°**appointment** [ə'pɔɪntmənt] Verabredung, Termin
April ['eɪprəl] April 3 (56)
aquarium [ə'kweəriəm] Aquarium 3 (53)
are [ɑː] bist; sind; seid 1 (18)
Here you are. Bitte schön./Hier, bitte. 1 (28) **How are you?** Wie geht's?/Wie geht es dir/euch? 1 (17) **The mobiles are £ 10.** Die Handys kosten 10 Pfund. 3 (62)
°**around** [ə'raʊnd]: **all around me** ganz um mich herum **Walk around.** Geh umher.
art [ɑːt] Kunst 1 (20)
°**as many sentences/questions as you can** [æz, əz] so viele Sätze/Fragen wie du kannst
ask [ɑːsk] fragen 4 (75) **ask questions** Fragen stellen 4 (75)
she asked [ɑːskt] sie fragte; sie hat gefragt 5 (98) °**ask for sth.** um etwas bitten
assembly [ə'sembli] Schulversammlung, Morgenappell 1 (21)
at [æt, ət]:
at 1 o'clock um 1 Uhr/um 13 Uhr 3 (57) **at a restaurant** in einem Restaurant 2 (42)
at Ellie's house bei Ellie daheim, bei Ellie zu Hause 2 (36)
at home daheim, zu Hause 1 (24)
at MARTINS bei MARTINS 1 (26)
at night nachts, in der Nacht 3 (58) **at school** in der Schule 1 (20) **at the cinema** im Kino 2 (42) **at the market** auf dem Markt 3 (53) **at the moment** im Moment, gerade 5 (93) **at the weekend** am Wochenende 4 (73) **at this school** auf/an dieser Schule 1 (18) **at work** bei der Arbeit, am Arbeitsplatz 2 (42)
August ['ɔːgəst] August 3 (56)
aunt [ɑːnt] Tante 2 (37)
away [ə'weɪ] weg, fort (14)

B

baby ['beɪbi] Baby 2 (36)
babysitter ['beɪbisɪtə] Babysitter 5 (91)
back [bæk]:
1. zurück 1 (26)
°2. Rückseite
bad [bæd] schlecht; schlimm 1 (25)
°**badminton** ['bædmɪntən] Badminton, Federball
bag [bæg] Tasche, Beutel 1 (27)
°**baking powder** ['beɪkɪŋ paʊdə] Backpulver
°**balcony** ['bælkəni] Balkon
ball [bɔːl] Ball 5 (100)
°**banana skin** [bə'nɑːnə skɪn] Bananenschale
band [bænd] Band, (Musik-) Gruppe 5 (95)
barn [bɑːn] Scheune, Stall 4 (71)
basketball ['bɑːskɪtbɔːl] Basketball 4 (75)
bathroom ['bɑːθruːm] Badezimmer, Bad 2 (35)
°**battle** ['bætl] Kampf, Schlacht
be [biː] sein 1 (24) **Be quiet.** Sei still./Sei leise. 2 (42)
beach [biːtʃ] Strand (9) **on the beach** am Strand 2 (44)
bear [beə] Bär (12)
°**beats per minute** ['biːts pɜː 'mɪnɪt] *(Musik)* Schläge pro Minute
because [bɪ'kɒz] weil 2 (43)
bed [bed] Bett 2 (39)
bedroom ['bedruːm] Schlafzimmer 2 (34)
before [bɪ'fɔː]:
1. vor 4 (72) **before breakfast** vor dem Frühstück 4 (72)
2. bevor 1 (24) **before you read** bevor du liest 1 (24)
behind [bɪ'haɪnd] hinter 5 (100)
°**belong** [bɪ'lɒŋ] (hin)gehören
best [best]:
my best friends meine besten Freunde/Freundinnen 1 (18) **the best of both worlds** das Beste von beidem 2 (42) **Best wishes** Viele Grüße, ... *(Briefschluss)* 4 (83)
°**better** ['betə] besser
between [bɪ'twiːn] zwischen 5 (100)
big [bɪg] groß (13)
bike [baɪk] Fahrrad (13)
by bike mit dem Rad 3 (58)
go by bike mit dem Rad fahren 3 (58) **ride a bike** Rad fahren 1 (18)
bird [bɜːd] Vogel (12)
birthday ['bɜːθdeɪ] Geburtstag 2 (42) **It's her birthday.** Sie hat Geburtstag. 2 (42) **My birthday is on 5th May.** Ich habe am 5. Mai Geburtstag. 3 (57) **on my birthday** an meinem Geburtstag 3 (56) **When's your birthday?** Wann hast du Geburtstag? 3 (57)
°**biscuit** ['bɪskɪt] Keks, Plätzchen
bit [bɪt]: **a bit** ein bisschen 4 (75)
black [blæk] schwarz (10)
°**blanket** ['blæŋkɪt] Decke *(zum Zudecken u.Ä.)*
blazer ['bleɪzə] Blazer *(Jackett, oft Teil der Schuluniform)* 1 (24)
blue [bluː] blau (10)
BMX [biː em 'eks] BMX-Rad 1 (18)
°**board** [bɔːd] Tafel
°**bodyboard** ['bɒdɪbɔːd] *kurzes Surfbrett, mit dem man auf dem Bauch liegend surft*
book [bʊk] Buch (11)
°**bored** [bɔːd]: **I'm bored** ich langweile mich
boring ['bɔːrɪŋ] langweilig 3 (54)
borrow ['bɒrəʊ] (aus)leihen, sich borgen 1 (28)
bossy ['bɒsi] herrisch; rechthaberisch 2 (38)
both [bəʊθ]: **the best of both worlds** das Beste von beidem 2 (42)
bottle ['bɒtl]: **a bottle of ...** eine Flasche ... 5 (92) °**message in a bottle** Flaschenpost
°**bowl** [bəʊl] Schüssel, Schale
box [bɒks] Kasten, Kiste, Kästchen 1 (27)
boy [bɔɪ] Junge 1 (16)
boyfriend ['bɔɪfrend] (fester) Freund 5 (98)
°**bracket** ['brækɪt] Klammer
break [breɪk] Pause 1 (21)
breakfast ['brekfəst] Frühstück 3 (54) **have breakfast** frühstücken 3 (55)
bring [brɪŋ] bringen, mitbringen 4 (80)
British ['brɪtɪʃ] britisch 3 (62)
brochure ['brəʊʃə] Broschüre, Prospekt 1 (26)
brother ['brʌðə] Bruder 1 (18)
brown [braʊn] braun (10)
°**budgie** ['bʌdʒi] Wellensittich
°**bull** [bʊl] Stier, Bulle
bus [bʌs] Bus 3 (58) **by bus** mit dem Bus 3 (58) **go by bus** mit dem Bus fahren 3 (58) **on the bus** im Bus 4 (80)
busy ['bɪzi]: **be busy** beschäftigt sein; viel zu tun haben 5 (92) **The kitchen is too busy.** In der Küche ist zu viel los. 2 (38)
but [bʌt, bət] aber 1 (23)
°**butter** ['bʌtə] Butter
buy [baɪ] kaufen 1 (26)
by bus/bike/car/... [baɪ] mit dem Bus/Rad/Auto/... 3 (58) **go by bus/bike/car/...** mit dem Bus/Rad/Auto/... fahren 3 (58)
Bye. [baɪ] Tschüs. 1 (17)

C

cafe ['kæfeɪ] Café 5 (91)
cage [keɪdʒ] Käfig 4 (77)
°**cake** [keɪk] Kuchen, Torte
calculator ['kælkjuleɪtə] Taschenrechner 1 (26)
°**calendar** ['kælɪndə] Kalender
can [kæn, kən] können (9) **Can you remember the animals?** Kannst du dich an die Tiere erinnern?/Könnt ihr euch an die Tiere erinnern? (12) **I can't do my homework.** [kɑːnt] Ich kann meine Hausaufgaben nicht machen. 2 (38)
°**canoe** [kə'nuː] Kanu, Paddelboot
canteen [kæn'tiːn] Kantine, (Schul-)Mensa 1 (20)
°**caption** ['kæpʃn] Bildunterschrift
car [kɑː] Auto 1 (16) **by car** mit dem Auto 3 (58) **go by car** mit dem Auto fahren 3 (58)
card [kɑːd] Karte 1 (27)
cat [kæt] Katze (12)
CD [siː'diː] CD 4 (83)
centre ['sentə] Zentrum, Center 3 (53)
°**chain** [tʃeɪn] Kette
chair [tʃeə] Stuhl 2 (39)
chant [tʃɑːnt] Sprechgesang (15)
°**character** ['kærəktə] Figur *(in Roman, Theaterstück u.Ä.)*
°**chat** [tʃæt] chatten, plaudern, sich unterhalten
°**check** [tʃek] (über)prüfen, kontrollieren
chicken ['tʃɪkɪn] Huhn; (Brat-) Hähnchen 4 (71)
child, *pl* **children** [tʃaɪld], ['tʃɪldrən] Kind, Kinder 1 (26)
°**chipmunk** ['tʃɪpmʌŋk] Streifenhörnchen

chips *(pl)* [tʃɪps] Pommes frites 5 (92)
°**chocolate** ['tʃɒklət] Schokolade
°**choose** [tʃuːz] (aus)wählen
°**chorus** ['kɔːrəs] Refrain
cinema ['sɪnəmə] Kino 2 (42)
°**circle** ['sɜːkl] Kreis
city ['sɪti] (Groß-)Stadt 1 (22)
class [klɑːs] (Schul-)Klasse (8)
classroom ['klɑːsruːm] Klassenzimmer 1 (22)
class teacher ['klɑːs tiːtʃə] Klassenlehrer/in 1 (19)
clean [kliːn] sauber machen, putzen 5 (96)
°**clock** [klɒk] (Wand-, Stand-, Turm-)Uhr
close [kləʊz] schließen, zumachen 2 (45)
°**clothes** *(pl)* [kləʊðz] Kleidung; Kleidungsstücke
club [klʌb] Klub 5 (95)
coffee ['kɒfi] Kaffee 5 (92)
°**cold** [kəʊld] kalt
°**collect** [kə'lekt] sammeln
colour ['kʌlə] Farbe (10)
°**column** ['kɒləm] Spalte
come [kʌm] kommen 3 (54) **come home** nach Hause kommen 3 (58) **Come on, Luca!** Na los, Luca! / Komm, Luca! 3 (61) °**the sea's coming in** die Flut kommt; das Wasser steigt
°**comment** ['kɒment] Kommentar
°**compare** [kəm'peə] vergleichen
°**complete** [kəm'pliːt] vervollständigen
computer [kəm'pjuːtə] Computer 1 (20)
concert ['kɒnsət] Konzert 3 (60)
cook [kʊk]:
1. kochen, *(Essen)* zubereiten 5 (92)
2. Koch, Köchin 5 (96)
cool [kuːl] cool (13)
°**copy** ['kɒpi] kopieren
°**correct** [kə'rekt]:
1. korrekt, richtig
2. korrigieren, verbessern
country ['kʌntri] Land 4 (80) **in the country** auf dem Land 4 (80)
cousin ['kʌzn] Cousin/e 2 (37)
cow [kaʊ] Kuh 4 (71)
crab [kræb] Krebs (8)
cream [kriːm] Sahne 5 (102)
°**crisps** *(pl)* [krɪsps] (Kartoffel-)Chips
crocodile ['krɒkədaɪl] Krokodil (12)
cup [kʌp]: **a cup of ...** eine Tasse ... 5 (92)
cushion ['kʊʃn] Kissen 2 (39)
°**customer** ['kʌstəmə] Kunde, Kundin
cute [kjuːt] niedlich, süß 2 (36)

D

dad [dæd] Papa, Vati 2 (34)
dance [dɑːns] tanzen (11)
dangerous ['deɪndʒərəs] gefährlich 4 (81)
date [deɪt] Datum 3 (57)
°**daughter** ['dɔːtə] Tochter
day [deɪ] Tag (14)
Dear ... [dɪə] Liebe ... / Lieber ... 2 (42)
December [dɪ'sembə] Dezember 3 (56)
°**degu** ['deɪguː, 'deguː] Degu *(Nagetierart)*
describe [dɪ'skraɪb] beschreiben 5 (100)
desk [desk] Schreibtisch 2 (39)
°**diagram** ['daɪəgræm] Diagramm
dialogue ['daɪəlɒg] Dialog 4 (73)
diary ['daɪəri] Tagebuch; Kalender 1 (26)
dictionary ['dɪkʃənri] Wörterbuch, *(alphabetisches)* Wörterverzeichnis (3)/4 (84)
difference ['dɪfrəns] Unterschied 5 (98)
different ['dɪfrənt] verschieden; anders 2 (39)
difficult ['dɪfɪkəlt] schwierig, schwer 2 (41)
°**digital clock** [dɪdʒɪtl 'klɒk] Digitaluhr
dinner ['dɪnə] Abendessen, Abendbrot 3 (58) **have dinner** Abendbrot essen, zu Abend essen 3 (58)
°**dirty** ['dɜːti] schmutzig
°**disabled** [dɪs'eɪbld] (körper)behindert
°**discuss sth.** [dɪ'skʌs] über etwas diskutieren, etwas besprechen
discussion [dɪ'skʌʃn] Diskussion 4 (74)
dive [daɪv] einen Kopfsprung machen 5 (94)
do [duː] machen, tun 2 (38) **do sport** Sport treiben 4 (72) **What do you think?** Was meinst du? / Was denkst du? 1 (25) **Don't worry.** [dəʊnt] Mach dir keine Sorgen. 4 (80) **I don't like blue.** Ich mag Blau nicht. / Ich mag kein Blau. (10) **she doesn't have a ...** ['dʌznt] sie hat kein/keine/keinen ... 4 (72)
dog [dɒg] Hund (12)
done: Well done. [wel 'dʌn] Gut gemacht! 5 (99) °**the holidays are done** *(infml)* die Ferien sind vorbei
donkey ['dɒŋki] Esel 4 (71)
door [dɔː] Tür 2 (45)
°**dossier** ['dɒsieɪ] Mappe
°**double circle** [dʌbl 'sɜːkl] Doppelkreis
down [daʊn]: **down this hill** diesen Hügel hinunter 3 (61) °**Turn the page upside down.** Dreh die Seite auf den Kopf.
downstairs [daʊn'steəz] unten; nach unten 2 (36)
drama ['drɑːmə] Schauspiel, darstellende Kunst 1 (21)
°**draw** [drɔː] zeichnen
dream [driːm] Traum 2 (35)
drink [drɪŋk]:
1. trinken 4 (75)
2. Getränk 4 (75)
drums *(pl)* [drʌmz] Schlagzeug; Trommeln 5 (95) **play the drums** Schlagzeug spielen 5 (95)
duck [dʌk] Ente 4 (70)
DVD [diːviː'diː] DVD 4 (83)

E

°**each** [iːtʃ]: **for each number/picture** für jede Nummer/jedes Bild
early ['ɜːli] früh 3 (58)
easy ['iːzi] einfach, leicht 2 (41)
eat [iːt] essen; fressen 4 (72)
°**egg** [eg] Ei
eight [eɪt] acht (8)
elephant ['elɪfənt] Elefant (12)
eleven [ɪ'levn] elf (8)
else: Anything else? ['eniθɪŋ 'els] Sonst noch etwas? 5 (92)
email ['iːmeɪl] E-Mail 4 (80)
end [end] Ende, Schluss 3 (61) °**in the end** schließlich; letzten Endes; am Ende
°**ending** ['endɪŋ] Ende, Abschluss
England ['ɪŋglənd] England (8)
English ['ɪŋglɪʃ] Englisch; englisch 1 (18)
°**enjoy** [ɪn'dʒɔɪ] genießen
°**e-pal** ['iːpæl] Brieffreund/in *(im Internet)*
evening ['iːvnɪŋ] Abend 3 (54) **in the evening** abends, am Abend 3 (54) **on Friday evening** freitagabends, am Freitagabend 3 (54)
every day/room/... ['evri] jeder Tag/jedes Zimmer/... 1 (21)

everybody ['evribɒdi] jeder; alle 3 (54)
°**everything** ['evriθɪŋ] alles
example [ɪg'zɑːmpl] Beispiel 2 (42)
°**for example** zum Beispiel
excited [ɪk'saɪtɪd] aufgeregt, gespannt 3 (60)
Excuse me, … [ɪk'skjuːz miː] Entschuldigung, … / Entschuldigen Sie, … 3 (63)
exercise ['eksəsaɪz] Übung, Aufgabe 1 (26)
exercise book ['eksəsaɪz bʊk] Schulheft, Übungsheft 1 (26)
expensive [ɪk'spensɪv] teuer 3 (55)
°**explain** [ɪk'spleɪn] erklären
°**eye** [aɪ] Auge

F

face [feɪs] Gesicht 5 (98)
fall [fɔːl] fallen; hinfallen 3 (61)
false [fɔːls] falsch 5 (99)
family ['fæməli] Familie 2 (36)
family name Familienname, Nachname 3 (52) **family tree** (Familien-)Stammbaum 2 (37)
farm [fɑːm] Bauernhof, Farm 4 (70)
fast [fɑːst] schnell 3 (61)
father ['fɑːðə] Vater 2 (34)
favourite ['feɪvərɪt] Lieblings- (10)
favourite colour Lieblingsfarbe (10)
February ['februəri] Februar 3 (56)
fed up [fed 'ʌp]: **feel fed up** genervt sein, sauer sein; die Nase voll haben 4 (74)
feed [fiːd] füttern 4 (72)
feel [fiːl] sich fühlen; fühlen 4 (74)
feel fed up genervt sein, sauer sein; die Nase voll haben 4 (74)
feeling ['fiːlɪŋ] Gefühl 4 (74)
ferry ['feri] Fähre 5 (91)
field [fiːld] Feld; Weide 4 (70)
in the field auf dem Feld 4 (70)
°**fill sth. in** [fɪl 'ɪn] etwas ausfüllen
film [fɪlm] Film 3 (64)
find [faɪnd] finden 4 (79)
°**find out** herausfinden
fine [faɪn] gut; in Ordnung 1 (17)
I'm fine, thanks. Danke, (es geht mir) gut. 1 (17)
°**finish** ['fɪnɪʃ] beenden
fire station ['faɪə steɪʃn] Feuerwache 3 (52)
first [fɜːst]:
1. erste(r, s) 1 (17)
2. zuerst, als Erstes 3 (54)
the first morning der erste Morgen 1 (17)
fish [fɪʃ] Fisch; Fische (12)
°**fisherman**, *pl* **-men** ['fɪʃəmən] Fischer/in, Angler/in
five [faɪv] fünf (8)
flat [flæt] Wohnung 2 (34)
°**flavour** ['fleɪvə] Geschmack(srichtung)
°**flour** [flaʊə] Mehl
°**fly** [flaɪ] fliegen
°**focus on language** ['fəʊkəs ɒn 'læŋgwɪdʒ] *etwa:* Blickpunkt „Sprache"
°**follow** ['fɒləʊ] folgen; verfolgen
food [fuːd] Essen; Lebensmittel; Futter 5 (97)
football ['fʊtbɔːl] Fußball (11)
for [fɔː, fə] für 1 (23) **for myself** für mich selbst 4 (75)
What's for homework? Was haben wir als Hausaufgabe auf? 2 (45) °**for example** zum Beispiel °**for free** kostenlos, umsonst
°**forget** [fə'get] vergessen
forgot [fə'gɒt]: **I forgot my homework.** Ich habe meine Hausaufgaben vergessen. 2 (45)
form [fɔːm] Form 5 (96)
four [fɔː] vier (8)
free [friː] frei 3 (57) °**for free** kostenlos, umsonst
French [frentʃ] Französisch; französisch 1 (21)
Friday ['fraɪdeɪ, 'fraɪdi] Freitag 1 (21)
friend [frend] Freund/in 1 (18)
friendly ['frendli] freundlich 4 (78)
from [frɒm, frəm] aus (8); von 2 (43) **I'm from Plymouth.** Ich bin/komme aus Plymouth. (8)
from Monday to Friday von Montag bis Freitag 2 (43) **a text from mum** eine SMS von Mama 2 (43)
front: in front of [ɪn 'frʌnt əv] vor 5 (100)
fruit [fruːt] Obst 4 (78)
fun [fʌn]: **it's fun** es macht Spaß (13)
furry ['fɜːri] flauschig; pelzig 4 (76)
°**fuss** [fʌs]: **I don't make a fuss** *(infml)* ich mache kein Theater

G

game [geɪm] Spiel (11)
garage ['gærɑːʒ] Garage 2 (35)
garden ['gɑːdn] Garten 2 (34)
geography [dʒi'ɒgrəfi] Geografie, Erdkunde 1 (21)
German ['dʒɜːmən] Deutsch; deutsch 1 (28)
Germany ['dʒɜːməni] Deutschland (8)
get [get] bekommen 3 (56)
get ready (for) sich fertig machen (für), sich vorbereiten (auf) 4 (72) **get up** aufstehen 3 (58) °**get out** herauskommen
°**gibbon** ['gɪbən] Gibbon
girl [gɜːl] Mädchen 1 (16)
girlfriend ['gɜːlfrend] (feste) Freundin 5 (98)
°**give** [gɪv] geben
°**glass** [glɑːs] Glas
go [gəʊ] gehen; fahren (13)
go by bus/bike/car/… mit dem Bus/Rad/Auto/… fahren 3 (58)
go home nach Hause gehen 3 (58) **go shopping** einkaufen gehen 3 (54) **go swimming** schwimmen gehen 3 (56)
go to bed ins Bett gehen 3 (52)
go to school zur Schule gehen 3 (52) **Go to sleep!** Schlaf jetzt! 4 (81) **go to work** zur Arbeit gehen 3 (52) **go with** gehören zu, passen zu 2 (45)
How's it going? Wie geht's? / Wie läuft's? 5 (92) **I must go.** *(am Telefon)* Ich muss Schluss machen. 5 (92)
°**goat** [gəʊt] Ziege
°**goldfish** ['gəʊldfɪʃ] Goldfisch
good [gʊd] gut 1 (17) **Good morning.** Guten Morgen. 1 (18)
°**be good at sth.** gut in etwas sein, etwas gut können
Goodbye. [gʊd'baɪ] Auf Wiedersehen! (14)
grandfather ['grænfɑːðə] Großvater 2 (37)
grandmother ['grænmʌðə] Großmutter 2 (37)
grandparents ['grænpeərənts] Großeltern 2 (37)
great [greɪt] großartig, prima (13)
green [griːn] grün (10)
grey [greɪ] grau (10)
°**groom** [gruːm] striegeln
group [gruːp] Gruppe 5 (95)
guess [ges] raten, erraten 3 (64)
°**guinea pig** ['gɪni pɪg] Meerschweinchen
guitar [gɪ'tɑː] Gitarre 5 (95)
play the guitar Gitarre spielen 5 (95)
guys [gaɪz] Leute *(als Anrede verwendet)* 1 (25)

H

had [hæd, həd]: **I had** ich hatte; ich habe gehabt 5 (98)
°**half past 2** [hɑːf pɑːst 'tuː] halb 3
°**half price** [hɑːf 'praɪs] zum halben Preis
hall [hɔːl] Flur, Diele 2 (35)
hamster ['hæmstə] Hamster (12)
°**hand** [hænd] Hand
°**handle sth.** ['hændl] mit etwas umgehen
happy ['hæpi] glücklich, froh 1 (24) **Happy birthday!** Herzlichen Glückwunsch zum Geburtstag! 3 (60)
happen ['hæpən] geschehen, passieren 5 (93)
harbour ['hɑːbə] Hafen 5 (90)
hard [hɑːd] schwer, schwierig; hart 5 (98) **work hard** hart arbeiten 5 (92)
has [hæz, həz]: **he has …** er hat … 1 (19)
°**hat** [hæt] Hut
hate [heɪt] hassen, gar nicht mögen 3 (55)
have [hæv, həv] haben (12) **Have a good day.** Ich wünsch dir einen schönen Tag. / Schönen Tag noch. 1 (17) **have a party** eine Party feiern 3 (56) **have breakfast** frühstücken 3 (55) **have dinner** Abendbrot essen, zu Abend essen 3 (58) **have lunch** (zu) Mittag essen 3 (55) **I have a sore leg.** Mein Bein tut weh. 3 (61) **I had** [hæd, həd] ich hatte; ich habe gehabt 5 (98)
he [hiː] er 1 (18) **he's …** [hiːz] (**= he is**) er ist … 1 (18)
°**heading** ['hedɪŋ] Überschrift
hear [hɪə] hören 5 (97)
Hello. [hə'ləʊ] Hallo. / Guten Tag. (14)
helmet ['helmɪt] Helm 3 (63)
help [help]:
1. helfen (14)
°**2.** Hilfe
her [hɜː, hə]:
1. sie; ihr 4 (80)
2. her dad ihr Vater 2 (34)
here [hɪə] hier; hierher 1 (20) **Here you are.** Bitte schön. / Hier, bitte. 1 (28)
Hi. [haɪ] Hallo. (8) **Say hi to everybody.** Grüß alle. 5 (92)
hide [haɪd] verstecken; sich verstecken 5 (94)
hill [hɪl] Hügel 3 (61)
him [hɪm] ihn; ihm 5 (97)
his [hɪz] sein/e 2 (36)
history ['hɪstri] Geschichte 1 (21)
hobby ['hɒbi] Hobby (11)
°**hockey** ['hɒki] Hockey
hole punch ['həʊl pʌntʃ] Locher 1 (26)
holidays ['hɒlədeɪz] Ferien (14)
home [həʊm] Heim, Zuhause 1 (24) **come home** nach Hause kommen 3 (58) **go home** nach Hause gehen 3 (58)
°**home-made** [həʊm'meɪd] hausgemacht, selbstgemacht
homework ['həʊmwɜːk] Hausaufgabe(n) 1 (24) **I forgot my homework.** Ich habe meine Hausaufgaben vergessen. 2 (45) **What's for homework?** Was haben wir als Hausaufgabe auf? 2 (45)
hoodie ['hʊdi] Kapuzenpullover, -jacke 3 (55)
hope [həʊp] hoffen 1 (24)
°**horse** [hɔːs] Pferd
hospital ['hɒspɪtl] Krankenhaus 3 (61)
°**hot** [hɒt] heiß
house [haʊs] Haus 2 (34)
how? [haʊ] wie? 1 (17) **How are you?** [haʊ 'ɑː juː] Wie geht's? / Wie geht es dir/euch? 1 (17) **How's it going?** Wie geht's? / Wie läuft's? 5 (92) **How much is …?** Was (Wie viel) kostet …? 3 (62) **How much are …?** Was (Wie viel) kosten …? 3 (62) °**How many …?** Wie viele …?
hundred ['hʌndrəd]: **a hundred, one hundred** (ein)hundert 3 (55)
hungry ['hʌŋgri]: **be hungry** hungrig sein, Hunger haben 4 (81)
°**hurry** ['hʌri] sich beeilen
°**hyena** [haɪ'iːnə] Hyäne

I

I [aɪ] ich (8) **I'm …** [aɪm] (**= I am**) ich bin … 1 (18)
°**ice cream** [aɪs 'kriːm] (Speise-)Eis
ICT [aɪ siː 'tiː] **(information and communication technology)** Informations- und Kommunikationstechnologie 1 (20)
idea [aɪ'dɪə] Idee 1 (25)
°**idiot** ['ɪdiət] Idiot/in
°**imagine sth.** [ɪ'mædʒɪn] sich etwas vorstellen
important [ɪm'pɔːtnt] wichtig 1 (24)
in [ɪn] in (8) **in England** in England (8) **in English** auf Englisch 1 (27) **in front of** vor 5 (100) **in the afternoon** nachmittags, am Nachmittag 3 (54) **in the country** auf dem Land 4 (80) **in the evening** abends, am Abend 3 (54) **in the field** auf dem Feld 4 (70) **in the middle** in der Mitte 5 (90) **in the morning** am Morgen, morgens 3 (54) **in the photo** auf dem Foto 2 (34) **in the picture** auf dem Bild 2 (42) **in town** in der Stadt 2 (43) °**in the end** schließlich; letzten Endes; am Ende
°**information** [ɪnfə'meɪʃn] Information(en)
°**inline-skating** ['ɪnlaɪn 'skeɪtɪŋ] Inlineskaten
inside [ɪn'saɪd] drinnen; nach drinnen 4 (72)
instrument ['ɪnstrəmənt] Instrument 5 (95)
interesting ['ɪntrəstɪŋ] interessant 4 (77)
interview ['ɪntəvjuː] Interview 1 (28)
into ['ɪntʊ] in (… hinein) 2 (36) **into the living room** in das Wohnzimmer (hinein) 2 (36)
invitation (to) [ɪnvɪ'teɪʃn] Einladung (zu, nach) 4 (83)
invite (to) [ɪn'vaɪt] einladen (zu, nach) 4 (80)
is [ɪz] *(er/sie/es)* ist (10) **The calculator is £ 1.** Der Taschenrechner kostet 1 Pfund. 3 (62)
it [ɪt] er/sie/es (13) **it's** [ɪts] (**= it is**) es ist; *(bei Sachen und Tieren auch:* er ist; sie ist*)* (13)

J

jam [dʒæm] Marmelade 5 (102)
January ['dʒænjuəri] Januar 3 (56)
job [dʒɒb] Job, (Arbeits-)Stelle 5 (92)
join a club [dʒɔɪn] sich einem Klub anschließen; in einen Klub eintreten 5 (95)
juice [dʒuːs] Saft 5 (92)
July [dʒu'laɪ] Juli 3 (56)
°**jump up** [dʒʌmp] aufspringen
June [dʒuːn] Juni 3 (56)
°**just** [dʒʌst] einfach (nur)

K

kid [kɪd] Kind; Jugendliche(r) 3 (59)
kitchen ['kɪtʃɪn] Küche 2 (34)
°**kitten** ['kɪtn] Kätzchen; junge Katze
know [nəʊ] wissen; kennen 1 (24)

L

lab [læb] Labor 1 (20)
°**label** ['leɪbl] Label, Etikett
lamp [læmp] Lampe 2 (39)
language ['læŋgwɪdʒ] Sprache (3)
°**large** [lɑːdʒ] groß
last [lɑːst] letzte(r, s) (14)
late [leɪt] spät 3 (58)
later ['leɪtə] später 1 (17)
laugh [lɑːf] lachen 4 (80) **they laughed** [lɑːft] sie lachten; sie haben gelacht 5 (98)
lazy ['leɪzi] faul 3 (58)
°**lead-in** ['liːd ɪn] *Einstieg in die neue Unit*
learn [lɜːn] lernen 5 (95)
°**learner log** ['lɜːnə lɒg] Lerner-Tagebuch
left [left] links; nach links 4 (82) **on the left** links, auf der linken Seite 5 (90)
leg [leg] Bein 3 (61)
lesson ['lesn] (Unterrichts-)Stunde 1 (20)
Let's … [lets] Lass uns …/Lasst uns … 3 (60)
letter ['letə] Brief 5 (93)
life, *pl* lives [laɪf], [laɪvz] *(das)* Leben, *(die)* Leben 4 (72)
°**lighthouse** ['laɪthaʊs] Leuchtturm
like [laɪk] wie 3 (54) **What's it like?** Wie ist es?/Wie sieht es aus? 2 (44) °**like this** so
like [laɪk] mögen, gernhaben (10) **I like red.** Ich mag Rot. (10) **I like watching TV.** Ich sehe gern fern. (11) **I don't like blue.** Ich mag Blau nicht./ Ich mag kein Blau. (10) **He doesn't like to be lonely.** Er mag es nicht, allein zu sein. 4 (77)
°**line** [laɪn] Zeile
°**list** [lɪst] Liste
listen ['lɪsn] zuhören 2 (40) **listen to** *jemandem* zuhören; sich *etwas* anhören 2 (40)
little ['lɪtl] klein 5 (96)
live [lɪv] leben; wohnen 2 (34)
lives [laɪvz] *Mehrzahl von* **life** 4 (72)
living room ['lɪvɪŋ ruːm] Wohnzimmer 2 (34)
°**llama** ['lɑːmə] Lama
lonely ['ləʊnli] einsam 2 (43)
look [lʊk]:
1. schauen, gucken 1 (25)
2. aussehen 3 (63)
Look, Adam. Sieh mal, Adam./ Schau mal, Adam. 1 (25) **look after** sich kümmern um; aufpassen auf 4 (72) **look at sth.** sich etwas anschauen 1 (23) **It looks nice.** Es sieht schön aus. 3 (63) °**look for sth.** etwas suchen; nach etwas Ausschau halten °**look up a word** ein Wort nachschlagen
lost [lɒst]: **I'm not lost.** Ich habe mich nicht verlaufen/verirrt. 1 (20)
lots of … ['lɒts əv] viel …, viele … 2 (43)
love [lʌv]:
1. lieben, sehr mögen (12) **I'd love to come. (= I would love to come.)** Ich komme sehr gern./ Ich würde sehr gern kommen. 4 (83)
°2. Liebe °**be in love** verliebt sein
lucky ['lʌki]: **you're lucky** du hast Glück 2 (36)
lunch [lʌntʃ] Mittagessen 1 (21) **have lunch** (zu) Mittag essen 3 (55)

M

°**madhouse** ['mædhaʊs] Irrenhaus, Tollhaus
make [meɪk] machen, herstellen 1 (23) °**make notes** (sich) Notizen machen
man, *pl* men [mæn], [men] Mann, Männer 3 (63)
°**many** ['meni]: **How many …?** Wie viele …?
°**map** [mæp] Landkarte, Stadtplan
March [mɑːtʃ] März 3 (56)
market ['mɑːkɪt] Markt 3 (53)
°**match** [mætʃ] zuordnen
maths [mæθs] Mathematik 1 (21)
May [meɪ] Mai 3 (56)
maybe ['meɪbi] vielleicht 5 (96)
me [miː] mich; mir 1 (19) **It's me, Sandy.** Ich bin es, Sandy. (14) **Me too.** Ich auch. 1 (14) **Not me!** Ich nicht! 4 (74)
mean [miːn] gemein, fies 2 (40)
°**mean** [miːn] bedeuten
°**mediation** [miːdi'eɪʃn] Vermittlung, Sprachmittlung, Mediation
meet [miːt] kennenlernen; treffen (8) **Nice to meet you!** Freut mich, dich/euch/Sie kennenzulernen. (8)
men [men] *Mehrzahl von* **man** 3 (63)
°**message** ['mesɪdʒ]: **message in a bottle** Flaschenpost
messy ['mesi] unordentlich 2 (38)
middle ['mɪdl] Mitte 5 (90) **in the middle** in der Mitte 5 (90)
°**milk** [mɪlk] Milch
°**mime** [maɪm] vorspielen, pantomimisch darstellen
°**mind map** ['maɪnd mæp] Mindmap
°**minute** ['mɪnɪt] Minute
mirror ['mɪrə] Spiegel 2 (39)
Miss Borowski [mɪs] Frau Borowski *(Anrede für unverheiratete Frauen)* 1 (24)
miss [mɪs] vermissen 2 (36)
°**missing** ['mɪsɪŋ] fehlend °**some are missing** einige fehlen
°**mistake** [mɪ'steɪk] Fehler
mobile phone ['məʊbaɪl 'fəʊn] *(kurz auch:* **mobile***)* Mobiltelefon, Handy 1 (16)
moment ['məʊmənt] Moment, Augenblick 5 (93) **at the moment** im Moment, gerade 5 (93)
Monday ['mʌndeɪ, 'mʌndi] Montag 1 (21)
money ['mʌni] Geld 3 (62)
monkey ['mʌŋki] Affe (12)
month [mʌnθ] Monat 3 (56)
°**more** [mɔː] mehr °**more than** mehr als °**no more work/ school/…** keine Arbeit/Schule/ … mehr
morning ['mɔːnɪŋ] Morgen 1 (17) **in the morning** am Morgen, morgens 3 (54) **on Friday morning** freitagmorgens, am Freitagmorgen 3 (54)
mother ['mʌðə] Mutter 2 (34)
mouth [maʊθ] Mund 4 (75)
Mr Jahn ['mɪstə] Herr Jahn 1 (19)
Mrs Schmidt ['mɪsɪz] Frau Schmidt *(Anrede für verheiratete Frauen)* 1 (19)
Ms Lee [mɪz, məz] Frau Lee *(allgemeine Anrede für Frauen)* 1 (18)
much [mʌtʃ]: **How much is …?** Was (Wie viel) kostet …? 3 (62) **How much are …?** Was (Wie viel) kosten …? 3 (62)
mum [mʌm] Mama, Mutti 2 (34)

music ['mju:zɪk] Musik (11)
musician [mju'zɪʃn] Musiker/in 5 (95)
must [mʌst] müssen 5 (92) **I must go.** *(am Telefon)* Ich muss Schluss machen. 5 (92)
my [maɪ] mein/e (10)
myself [maɪ'self]: **for myself** für mich selbst 4 (75)

N

name [neɪm]:
1. Name (8) **What's your name?** Wie heißt du? (8)
°2. benennen, nennen

°**narrator** [nə'reɪtə] Erzähler/in
near [nɪə] in der Nähe von, nahe (bei) 1 (18)
need [ni:d] brauchen, benötigen 1 (25)
nervous ['nɜ:vəs] nervös, aufgeregt 4 (80)
network ['netwɜ:k] Netz; Wortnetz 1 (27)
never ['nevə] nie, niemals 3 (52)
new [nju:] neu (13)
news [nju:z] Nachrichten 2 (42)
°**newspaper** ['nju:speɪpə] Zeitung
next [nekst] nächste(r, s) 1 (28)
next to ['nekst tʊ] neben 5 (100
nice [naɪs] nett, schön (8) **Nice to meet you!** Freut mich, dich/euch/Sie kennenzulernen. (8)
night [naɪt] Nacht 3 (58) **at night** nachts, in der Nacht 3 (58)
nine [naɪn] neun (8)
no [nəʊ] kein, keine 1 (18) °**no more work/school/...** keine Arbeit/Schule/... mehr
no [nəʊ] nein (14)
°**nobody** ['nəʊbədi] niemand
noise [nɔɪz] Geräusch; Lärm 4 (81)
noisy ['nɔɪzi] laut, voller Lärm 2 (38)
normal ['nɔ:ml] normal, gewöhnlich 4 (75)
not [nɒt]: **I'm not ten.** Ich bin nicht zehn. 1 (18) **I'm not a boy.** Ich bin kein Junge. 1 (18) **Not me!** Ich nicht! 4 (74)
°**note** [nəʊt] Notiz °**make notes** (sich) Notizen machen °**take notes** (sich) Notizen machen
nothing ['nʌθɪŋ] (gar) nichts 4 (72)
November [nəʊ'vembə] November 3 (56)
now [naʊ] nun, jetzt 1 (20)
number ['nʌmbə] Nummer 2 (46)
nut [nʌt] Nuss 4 (78)

O

o'clock: at 1 o'clock [ə'klɒk] um 1 Uhr/um 13 Uhr 3 (57)
October [ɒk'təʊbə] Oktober 3 (56)
°**odd** [ɒd]: **the odd word out** das Wort, das nicht passt
of [ɒv, əv]: **the last day of the holidays** der letzte Tag der Ferien (14) **the best of both worlds** das Beste von beidem 2 (42)
°**Off to bed.** [ɒf] Ab ins Bett.
often ['ɒfn, 'ɒftən] oft 3 (52)
OK [əʊ'keɪ] okay, gut, in Ordnung 1 (17) **I'm OK, thanks.** Danke, (es geht mir) gut. 1 (17) °**I'm OK at ...** ich bin ganz OK in ...
old [əʊld] alt (13)
omelette ['ɒmlət] Omelett 5 (92)
on [ɒn] auf (13) **on 5th May** am 5. Mai 3 (57) **on Friday morning** freitagmorgens, am Freitagmorgen 3 (54) **on Monday/Tuesday/...** am Montag/Dienstag/... 1 (21) **on my birthday** an meinem Geburtstag 3 (56) **on the beach** am Strand 2 (44) **on the bus** im Bus 4 (80) **on the left** links, auf der linken Seite 5 (90) **on the phone** am Telefon 5 (97) **on the right** rechts, auf der rechten Seite 5 (90) **on the way to ...** auf dem Weg zu/nach ... 5 (98)
one [wʌn] eins (8)
only ['əʊnli]:
1. nur, bloß 4 (81)
2. **the only student** der einzige Schüler/die einzige Schülerin 4 (75)

°**open** ['əʊpən] öffnen
or [ɔ:] oder 3 (61)
orange ['ɒrɪndʒ]:
1. orange (10)
°2. Orange, Apfelsine

°**order** ['ɔ:də] Reihenfolge
other ['ʌðə] andere(r, s) 4 (72)
our ['aʊə] unser/e (11)
°**out** [aʊt]: **school is out** die Schule ist aus/vorbei
°**out of ...** ['aʊt əv] aus ... (heraus/hinaus)
outside [aʊt'saɪd] draußen; nach draußen 4 (72)
°**oven** ['ʌvn] Backofen
over ['əʊvə]: **be over** vorbei sein, zu Ende sein 1 (24)
°**over there** [əʊvə 'ðeə] da drüben, dort drüben

°**owl** [aʊl] Eule
°**own** [əʊn]: **your own card/text/...** deine eigene Karte/dein eigener Text

P

p [pi:]: **50p** 50 Pence 3 (62)
page [peɪdʒ] Seite 2 (45) **What page is it?** Auf welcher Seite sind wir?/Auf welcher Seite steht das? 2 (45)
pair [peə] Paar (12)
paper ['peɪpə] Papier 1 (25)
parents ['peərənts] Eltern 2 (37)
park [pɑ:k] Park (13)
°**parrot** ['pærət] Papagei
°**part** [pɑ:t] Teil
partner ['pɑ:tnə] Partner/in 2 (36)
party ['pɑ:ti] Party 3 (56) **have a party** eine Party feiern 3 (56)
PE [pi: 'i:] **(physical education)** (Schul-)Sport 1 (20)
°**peahen** ['pi:hen] Pfauenhenne *(weiblicher Pfau)*
pen [pen] Kugelschreiber, Stift, Füller 1 (26)
pencil ['pensl] Bleistift 1 (26)
pencil case ['pensl keɪs] Federmäppchen 1 (26)
pencil sharpener ['pensl ʃɑ:pnə] Bleistiftanspitzer 1 (26)
°**penguin** ['peŋgwɪn] Pinguin
people ['pi:pl] Leute, Menschen 1 (23)
person ['pɜ:sn] Person 4 (79)
pet [pet] Haustier (12)
phone [fəʊn]:
1. anrufen 5 (93)
2. Telefon 2 (46)
on the phone am Telefon 5 (97)

phone number ['fəʊn nʌmbə] Telefonnummer 2 (46)
photo ['fəʊtəʊ] Foto 2 (34) **in the photo** auf dem Foto 2 (34)
phrase [freɪz] Ausdruck, (Rede-)Wendung 1 (27)
piano [pi'ænəʊ] Klavier, Piano 5 (95) **play the piano** Klavier spielen 5 (95)
°**pick** [pɪk] (aus)wählen °**Don't pick me up.** Heb mich nicht hoch.
picnic ['pɪknɪk] Picknick 4 (83)
picture ['pɪktʃə] Bild 2 (42) **in the picture** ['pɪktʃə] auf dem Bild 2 (42)
°**piece** [pi:s]: **a piece of paper** ein Stück Papier
pig [pɪg] Schwein 4 (71)

°**pinch** [pɪntʃ] zwicken, kneifen
pink [pɪŋk] pink, rosa (10)
°**pity** ['pɪti]: **That's a pity.** Das ist schade!
°**pizza** ['piːtsə] Pizza
place [pleɪs] Ort, Platz, Stelle 1 (23)
plan [plæn] planen 3 (60)
play [pleɪ] spielen (11) **play the guitar/the piano/the drums** Gitarre/Klavier/Schlagzeug spielen 5 (95)
please [pliːz] bitte 1 (24) **Please remember …** Bitte denk(t) dran … / Bitte merk dir/merkt euch … 1 (24)
pm [piː'em]: **5 pm** 5 Uhr nachmittags/abends; 17 Uhr 4 (83)
poem ['pəʊɪm] Gedicht 4 (84)
°**point at sth.** [pɔɪnt] auf etwas zeigen, auf etwas deuten
pond [pɒnd] Teich 4 (70)
pony ['pəʊni] Pony (12) **ride a pony** auf einem Pony reiten 4 (70)
poster ['pəʊstə] Poster (11)
pound (£) [paʊnd] Pfund *(britische Währung)* 1 (26) **That's £ 159.** Das macht 159 Pfund. 3 (63) **The calculator is £ 1.** Der Taschenrechner kostet 1 Pfund. 3 (62) **The mobiles are £ 10.** Die Handys kosten 10 Pfund. 3 (62)
°**practice** ['præktɪs] Übung(en)
°**practise** ['præktɪs] üben
°**prefer** [prɪ'fɜː]: **I'd prefer …** ich würde … vorziehen
present ['preznt] Geschenk 3 (55)
°**pretty** ['prɪti] hübsch
price [praɪs] (Kauf-)Preis 5 (95)
principal ['prɪnsəpl] Rektor/in, Schulleiter/in 1 (24)
problem ['prɒbləm] Problem 2 (38)
programme ['prəʊgræm] (Fernseh-)Sendung 2 (42)
°**progress** ['prəʊgres] Fortschritt
°**project** ['prɒdʒekt] Projekt
proud (of) [praʊd] stolz (auf) 5 (99)
pullover ['pʊləʊvə] Pullover 1 (24)
°**puppy** ['pʌpi] Welpe, junger Hund
purple ['pɜːpl] violett; lila (10)
°**push** [pʊʃ] schieben
°**put** [pʊt] *(etwas wohin)* tun, legen, stellen, stecken
°**put sth. in** etwas einsetzen
°**pyjamas** *(pl)* [pə'dʒɑːməz] Schlafanzug

Q

°**quarter past 2** ['kwɔːtə pɑːst 'tuː] Viertel nach 2 °**quarter to 2** Viertel vor 2
question ['kwestʃn] Frage 2 (40)
ask questions Fragen stellen 4 (75)
°**quick** [kwɪk] schnell
quiet ['kwaɪət] ruhig, still, leise 2 (42)
quiz [kwɪz] Quiz, Ratespiel 1 (22)

R

rabbit ['ræbɪt] Kaninchen (12)
rap [ræp]:
1. Rap *(rhythmischer Sprechgesang)* 1 (21)
2. rappen 5 (95)
rapper ['ræpə] Rapper/in 5 (95)
rat [ræt] Ratte (12)
read [riːd] lesen (11)
ready ['redi]: **get ready (for)** sich fertig machen (für), sich vorbereiten (auf) 4 (72)
real [rɪəl] echt, wirklich 2 (36)
really ['rɪəli] wirklich 2 (40)
recipe ['resəpi] (Koch-)Rezept 5 (102)
red [red] rot (10)
°**registration** [redʒɪ'streɪʃn] Anmeldung, Einschreibung, Registrierung
remember [rɪ'membə]:
1. sich erinnern (an) (12)
2. daran denken; sich merken 1 (24)
°**repeat** [rɪ'piːt] wiederholen
°**reporter** [rɪ'pɔːtə] Reporter/in
restaurant ['restrɒnt] Restaurant 2 (42)
°**revision** [rɪ'vɪʒn] Wiederholung *(von Lernstoff)*
ride [raɪd]:
1. reiten (11) **ride a bike** Rad fahren 1 (18) **ride a pony** auf einem Pony reiten 4 (70)
°2. Ritt, Ausritt
right [raɪt]:
1. richtig 1 (21) °**he is right** er hat Recht
2. rechts; nach rechts 4 (82)
on the right rechts, auf der rechten Seite 5 (90)
ring [rɪŋ] läuten, klingeln 5 (92)
road [rəʊd] Straße *(Landstraße zwischen Orten, aber auch Straße in Orten)* 2 (34)
°**role** [rəʊl] Rolle
°**role-play** ['rəʊlpleɪ] Rollenspiel
room [ruːm, rʊm] Raum, Zimmer 1 (20)
rubber ['rʌbə] Radiergummi 1 (26)
rug [rʌg] Teppich, Läufer 2 (39)
°**rule** [ruːl] Regel
ruler ['ruːlə] Lineal 1 (26)
°**run** [rʌn] rennen, laufen

S

said [sed]: **he said** er sagte; er hat gesagt 5 (98)
salad ['sæləd] Salat *(als Gericht oder Beilage)* 5 (92)
sale [seɪl] Verkauf; Schlussverkauf 3 (62)
°**salt** [sɔːlt] Salz
same [seɪm]: **the same** derselbe/dieselbe/dasselbe; dieselben 3 (63)
°**sand** [sænd] Sand
sandwich ['sænwɪtʃ, 'sænwɪdʒ] Sandwich 4 (80)
Saturday ['sætədeɪ, 'sætədi] Samstag, Sonnabend 1 (27)
°**sausage** ['sɒsɪdʒ] (Brat-, Bock-) Würstchen, Wurst
say [seɪ] sagen 1 (25) **Say hi to everybody.** Grüß alle. 5 (92)
he said [sed] er sagte; er hat gesagt 5 (98)
°**scary** ['skeəri] unheimlich
scene [siːn] Szene 4 (80)
school [skuːl] Schule 1 (16)
°**school is out** die Schule ist aus/vorbei
school bag ['skuːl bæg] Schultasche 1 (27)
science ['saɪəns] Naturwissenschaft 1 (20)
scissors *(pl)* ['sɪzəz] Schere 1 (25)
scone [skɒn] *kleines rundes Milchbrötchen, leicht süß, oft mit Rosinen* 5 (92)
sea [siː] Meer 2 (44)
seagull ['siːgʌl] Möwe (14)
seat [siːt] (Sitz-)Platz 5 (98)
second ['sekənd] zweite(r, s) 3 (57)
see [siː] sehen (9) **See you. / See you later.** Bis dann. / Bis später. 1 (17)
send [send] schicken, senden 5 (94)
°**sentence** ['sentəns] Satz
September [sep'tembə] September 3 (56)
set the table [set] den Tisch decken 5 (96)
seven ['sevn] sieben (8)

share a room with … [ʃeə] sich ein Zimmer mit … teilen 2 (38)
she [ʃiː] sie *(Singular)* 1 (18)
she's … [ʃiːz] **(= she is)** sie ist … 1 (18)
sheep, *pl* sheep [ʃiːp] Schaf, Schafe 4 (71)
shelf, *pl* shelves [ʃelf], [ʃelvz] Regal, Regale 2 (39)
shirt [ʃɜːt] Hemd 1 (24)
shoe [ʃuː] Schuh 1 (24)
shop [ʃɒp] Geschäft, Laden 1 (26)
shopping [ˈʃɒpɪŋ]: **go shopping** einkaufen gehen 3 (54)
shopping centre [ˈʃɒpɪŋ sentə] Einkaufszentrum 3 (53)
°**short** [ʃɔːt] kurz
shoulder [ˈʃəʊldə] Schulter 4 (78)
°**show** [ʃəʊ] zeigen
Shut up! [ʃʌt ˈʌp] *(infml)* Halt den Mund! 3 (60)
sign [saɪn] Schild; Zeichen 4 (82)
sing [sɪŋ] singen 5 (95) °**sing along** mitsingen
singer [ˈsɪŋə] Sänger/in 5 (95)
sister [ˈsɪstə] Schwester 1 (18)
sit [sɪt] sitzen; sich setzen 4 (73)
six [sɪks] sechs (8)
skateboard [ˈskeɪtbɔːd] Skateboard fahren (11)
°**skills training** [ˈskɪlz treɪnɪŋ] Training von (Lern- und Arbeits-) Techniken
skirt [skɜːt] Rock 1 (24)
sleep [sliːp] schlafen 4 (78)
Go to sleep! Schlaf jetzt! 4 (81)
sleeping bag [ˈsliːpɪŋ bæg] Schlafsack 4 (80)
sleepover [ˈsliːpəʊvə] Schlafparty 4 (80)
°**slow** [sləʊ] langsam
small [smɔːl] klein (13)
°**smuggler** [ˈsmʌglə] Schmuggler/in
snake [sneɪk] Schlange (12)
so boring/tired/… [səʊ] so langweilig/müde/… 5 (94)
sock [sɒk] Socke, Strumpf 1 (24)
some [sʌm, səm] einige, ein paar; etwas 5 (98)
something [ˈsʌmθɪŋ] etwas 3 (60)
sometimes [ˈsʌmtaɪmz] manchmal 3 (54)
song [sɒŋ] Lied, Song (9)
soon [suːn] bald 2 (42)
sore [sɔː]: **I have a sore leg.** Mein Bein tut weh. 3 (61)
Sorry. / I'm sorry [ˈsɒri] Tut mir leid. / Entschuldigung. 1 (24)

sound [saʊnd] Geräusch; Klang, Laut 1 (16)
soup [suːp] Suppe 5 (92)
space [speɪs] Platz 2 (36)
speak [spiːk] sprechen 4 (75)
°**speaker** [ˈspiːkə]:
1. Sprecher/in
2. Lautsprecher
special [ˈspeʃl] besondere(r, s) 3 (63)
special offer [speʃl ˈɒfə] Sonderangebot 3 (63)
°**speech bubble** [ˈspiːtʃ bʌbl] Sprechblase
spell [spel] buchstabieren 2 (46)
°**spelling** [ˈspelɪŋ] Schreibung, Rechtschreibung
sport [spɔːt] Sport; Sportart (11)
do sport Sport treiben 4 (72)
sports hall [ˈspɔːts hɔːl] Sporthalle 1 (20)
°**square** [skweə] Platz *(in der Stadt)*
start [stɑːt] anfangen, beginnen 1 (22)
stay [steɪ] bleiben 3 (54)
°**step** [step] Schritt
stepbrother [ˈstepbrʌðə] Stiefbruder 2 (36)
stepdad [ˈstepdæd] Stiefvater 2 (36)
stepfather [ˈstepfɑːðə] Stiefvater 2 (36)
stepmother [ˈstepmʌðə] Stiefmutter 2 (36)
stepmum [ˈstepmʌm] Stiefmutter 2 (36)
stepsister [ˈstepsɪstə] Stiefschwester 2 (36)
°**stick insect** [ˈstɪk ɪnsekt] Stabheuschrecke
°**stoat** [stəʊt] Hermelin
°**stop** [stɒp] anhalten; aufhören
story [ˈstɔːri] Geschichte, Erzählung (3)/(14)
street [striːt] Straße *(in Orten)* 2 (34)
strict [strɪkt] streng 2 (40)
stroke [strəʊk] streicheln 4 (71)
student [ˈstjuːdənt] Schüler/in; Student/in (10)
studio [ˈstjuːdiəʊ] Studio 5 (95)
stupid [ˈstjuːpɪd] dumm, blöd (14)
°**sugar** [ˈʃʊgə] Zucker
summer [ˈsʌmə] Sommer 3 (52)
°**sun** [sʌn] Sonne
°**suncream** [ˈsʌnkriːm] Sonnencreme, Sonnenschutzmittel

Sunday [ˈsʌndeɪ, ˈsʌndi] Sonntag 1 (27)
°**sunglasses** *(pl)* [ˈsʌnglɑːsɪz] Sonnenbrille
supermarket [ˈsuːpəmɑːkɪt] Supermarkt 3 (54)
sure [ʃʊə, ʃɔː] sicher 1 (28)
surprise [səˈpraɪz] Überraschung 2 (40)
°**swap** [swɒp] tauschen
sweatshirt [ˈswetʃɜːt] Sweatshirt 1 (24)
sweets *(pl)* [swiːts] Süßigkeiten 3 (54)
swim [swɪm] schwimmen (11)
swimming pool [ˈswɪmɪŋ puːl] Schwimmbad, Schwimmbecken 3 (52)
°**swimming trunks** *(pl)* [ˈswɪmɪŋ trʌŋks] Badehose
°**swimsuit** [ˈswɪmsuːt] Badeanzug

T

table [ˈteɪbl]:
1. Tisch 2 (39)
°**2.** Tabelle
tae kwon do [taɪ kwɒn ˈdəʊ] Taekwondo 1 (18)
take [teɪk]: **I'll take it.** Ich nehme es (ihn, sie). *(beim Einkaufen)* 3 (63) °**take away** [teɪk əˈweɪ] zum Mitnehmen °**take notes** (sich) Notizen machen
talk (to) [tɔːk] sprechen, reden (mit) 1 (28)
tea [tiː] Tee 5 (92)
teacher [ˈtiːtʃə] Lehrer/in 1 (16)
team [tiːm] Team, Mannschaft 4 (75)
°**teaspoon** [ˈtiːspuːn] Teelöffel
technology [tekˈnɒlədʒi] Technik, Technologie 1 (21)
teenager [ˈtiːneɪdʒə] Teenager 4 (75)
°**tell** [tel] erzählen; sagen
ten [ten] zehn (8)
tennis [ˈtenɪs] Tennis 5 (97)
terrible [ˈterəbl] schrecklich, fürchterlich 3 (55)
text [tekst]:
1. SMS; Text 2 (43)
2. text a friend einem Freund / einer Freundin eine SMS schicken 4 (74)
text message [ˈtekst mesɪdʒ] *(kurz auch:* **text***)* SMS 5 (101)
°**than** [ðæn, ðən]: **more than** mehr als
Thanks. [θæŋks] Danke 1 (17)

that [ðæt, ðət] das (dort) 1 (24)
that field das Feld (dort), jenes Feld 4 (81) **That's £ 159.** Das macht 159 Pfund. 3 (63)
°**there's one thing that I know** eins weiß ich
the [ðə, ði] der, die, das; die (8)
theatre ['θɪətə] Theater 1 (25)
their [ðeə] ihr/e *(Plural)* 3 (60)
them [ðem, ðəm] sie; ihnen 5 (97)
theme [θi:m] Thema (3)
°**theme park** ['θi:m pɑ:k] Themenpark *(Freizeitpark mit Attraktionen zu einem bestimmten Thema)*
then [ðen] dann, danach 3 (54)
there [ðeə] da, dort; dahin, dorthin 3 (54) **there's ...** es ist .../es gibt ... 2 (36) **there are ...** es sind .../es gibt ... 2 (36) °**over there** da drüben, dort drüben °**there's one thing that I know** eins weiß ich
°**these** [ði:z] die, diese (hier)
they [ðeɪ] sie *(Plural)* 1 (18)
they're ... [ðeə] **(= they are)** sie sind ... 1 (18)
thing [θɪŋ] Ding, Sache (13)
think [θɪŋk] denken, meinen, glauben 1 (25)
third [θɜ:d] dritte(r, s) 3 (57)
this [ðɪs] diese(r, s) 1 (18) **This is ...** Dies ist .../Das ist ... (14) °**like this** so
three [θri:] drei (8)
through [θru:] durch 4 (81)
°**throw** [θrəʊ] werfen
Thursday ['θɜ:zdeɪ, 'θɜ:zdi] Donnerstag 1 (21)
°**tick** [tɪk] ankreuzen, abhaken
ticket ['tɪkɪt] Eintrittskarte 4 (71)
tie [taɪ] Krawatte 1 (24)
tiger ['taɪgə] Tiger (12)
tights *(pl)* [taɪts] Strumpfhose 1 (24)
time [taɪm]:
1. Zeit; Uhrzeit 1 (21) **What's the time?** Wie spät ist es? 4 (73)
°2. Mal
timetable ['taɪmteɪbl] Stundenplan 1 (21)
tired ['taɪəd] müde 2 (40)
to [tu, tə]:
1. *(örtlich)* zu, nach (13) **to the cinema** ins Kino 3 (52)
2. **from Monday to Friday** von Montag bis Freitag 2 (43)
3. **He doesn't like to be lonely.** Er mag es nicht, allein zu sein. 4 (77)
toast [təʊst] Toast 5 (97)
today [tə'deɪ] heute 3 (55)
together [tə'geðə] zusammen 2 (37)
toilet ['tɔɪlət] Toilette 2 (35)
too [tu:]:
1. auch (11) **from Berlin too** auch aus Berlin (11) **Me too.** Ich auch. 1 (14)
2. **too old/big/...** zu alt/groß/... 2 (38)
tour [tʊə]: **a tour of the school** ein Rundgang durch die Schule 1 (20)
°**towel** ['taʊəl] Handtuch
town [taʊn] Stadt 2 (43) **in town** in der Stadt 2 (43)
°**tractor** ['træktə] Traktor
trainers *(pl)* ['treɪnəz] Turnschuhe 3 (55)
training ['treɪnɪŋ] Training, Ausbildung (3)
°**trampoline** ['træmpəli:n] Trampolin
tree [tri:] Baum 2 (37)
°**trip** [trɪp] Ausflug
trouble ['trʌbl]: **be in trouble** in Schwierigkeiten sein; Ärger kriegen 4 (81)
trousers *(pl)* ['traʊzəz] Hose 1 (24)
true [tru:] wahr 5 (99)
try [traɪ] probieren, ausprobieren 3 (63)
T-shirt ['ti:ʃɜ:t] T-Shirt 2 (38)
°**tube** [tju:b] Schwimmreifen
Tuesday ['tju:zdeɪ, 'tju:zdi] Dienstag 1 (21)
turn [tɜ:n]:
1. **It's your turn.** Du bist dran./Du bist an der Reihe. 2 (45)
°2. **Turn the page upside down.** Dreh die Seite auf den Kopf.
TV [ti:'vi:] Fernsehen, Fernsehgerät (11)
twelve [twelv] zwölf (8)
two [tu:] zwei (8)

U

°**umbrella** [ʌm'brelə] (Regen-)Schirm
uncle ['ʌŋkl] Onkel 2 (37)
under ['ʌndə] unter 5 (100)
understand [ʌndə'stænd] verstehen 4 (75)
unhappy [ʌn'hæpi] unglücklich 3 (60)
uniform ['ju:nɪfɔ:m] (Schul-)Uniform 1 (24)
unit ['ju:nɪt] Kapitel, Lektion (3)
°**upside down** [ʌpsaɪd 'daʊn]: **Turn the page upside down.** Dreh die Seite auf den Kopf.
upstairs [ʌp'steəz] oben; nach oben 2 (36)
us [ʌs, əs] uns 3 (58)
use [ju:z] benutzen, verwenden 4 (84)
°**useful** ['ju:sfl] nützlich, hilfreich
usually ['ju:ʒuəli] meistens, normalerweise 3 (54)

V

value ['vælju:]: **It's good value.** Es ist sein Geld wert. 3 (63)
vegetables *(pl)* ['vedʒtəblz] Gemüse 3 (54)
°**verb** [vɜ:b] Verb
°**verse** [vɜ:s] Strophe
very ['veri] sehr 1 (25) **very nice** sehr nett, sehr schön 1 (25)
village ['vɪlɪdʒ] Dorf 1 (18)
visit ['vɪzɪt] besuchen 3 (56)
visitor ['vɪzɪtə] Besucher/in; Gast 4 (70)
vocabulary ['vɪzɪtə] Wörterverzeichnis, Vokabelverzeichnis (3)

W

°**wait (for)** [weɪt] warten (auf)
wake [weɪk] wecken 4 (72)
walk [wɔ:k] (zu Fuß) gehen 3 (58)
°**wall** [wɔ:l] Wand
want [wɒnt]:
want sth. etwas (haben) wollen 3 (61) **want to do sth.** etwas tun wollen 3 (55)
wardrobe ['wɔ:drəʊb] Kleiderschrank 2 (39)
was [wɒz, wəz]: **it was Friday** es war Freitag 5 (98) **he wasn't ...** er war nicht ... 5 (99)
wash up [wɒʃ 'ʌp] abwaschen 5 (92)
watch sth. [wɒtʃ] sich etwas anschauen; etwas beobachten 2 (42)
watch TV fernsehen (11)
water ['wɔ:tə] Wasser 5 (92)
way [weɪ] Weg 5 (98) **on the way to ...** auf dem Weg zu/nach ... 5 (98)
we [wi:] wir 1 (18) **we're ...** [wɪə] **(= we are** [wi ɑ:]**)** wir sind ... 1 (18)
Wednesday ['wenzdeɪ, 'wenzdi] Mittwoch 1 (21)
week [wi:k] Woche 2 (43)

weekend [wi:k'end] Wochenende 1 (27) **at the weekend** am Wochenende 4 (73)
welcome ['welkəm]:
1. **Welcome to Plymouth.** Willkommen in Plymouth. (10)
2. **You're welcome.** Bitte, gern geschehen. / Nichts zu danken. 4 (73)
well [wel]: **work/speak/… well** gut funktionieren/sprechen/… 4 (75) **Well done.** [wel 'dʌn] Gut gemacht. 5 (99)
Well, … [wel] Nun, … / Also, … / Na ja, … 5 (96)
were [wɜ:, wə]: **they were on the bus** sie waren im Bus 5 (98)
wet [wet] nass 4 (80)
what [wɒt]:
1. was (8)
2. welche(r, s) 2 (45)
What about …? Wie wär's mit …? 3 (55) **What about you?** Und du? / Und was ist mit dir? (8) **What do you think?** Was meinst du? / Was denkst du? 1 (25) **What page is it?** Auf welcher Seite sind wir? / Auf welcher Seite steht das? 2 (45)
What's for homework? Was haben wir als Hausaufgabe auf? 2 (45) **What's it like?** Wie ist es? / Wie sieht es aus? 2 (44)
What's the time? Wie spät ist es? 4 (73) **What's your name?** Wie heißt du? (*wörtlich:* Was ist dein Name?) (8)
wheelchair ['wi:ltʃeə] Rollstuhl 4 (75)
when [wen]:
1. wann 3 (57)
2. wenn 4 (74)
When's your birthday? Wann hast du Geburtstag? 3 (57)
°**which** [wɪtʃ] welche(r, s)
where [weə] wo; wohin 1 (20)
white [waɪt] weiß (10)
who [hu:]:
1. wer 1 (18) **Who are you?** Wer bist du? / Wer seid ihr? 1 (18)
°2. **Who can you see?** Wen kannst du sehen?
3. **Find a person who …** Finde eine Person, die … 4 (79)
why [waɪ] warum 4 (78)
wild [waɪld] wild; wild lebend (12)
°**will: we will send …** [wɪl] wir werden … schicken
win [wɪn] gewinnen 4 (75)
window ['wɪndəʊ] Fenster 5 (97)
wishes ['wɪʃɪz]: **Best wishes** Viele Grüße, … (*Briefschluss*) 4 (83)
with [wɪð] mit 1 (22)
with Ellie mit Ellie 1 (22); bei Ellie 2 (34)
°**woman, *pl* women** ['wʊmən], ['wɪmɪn] Frau, Frauen
word [wɜ:d] Wort (3)
work [wɜ:k]:
1. arbeiten 2 (45); funktionieren 4 (74)
2. Arbeit 2 (42)
work hard hart arbeiten 5 (92)
workshop ['wɜ:kʃɒp] Workshop; Seminar 5 (95)
world [wɜ:ld] Welt 4 (70)
the best of both worlds das Beste von beidem 2 (42)
worried ['wʌrid]: **be worried (about)** beunruhigt sein, besorgt sein (wegen) 5 (93)
worry (about) ['wʌri] sich Sorgen machen (wegen, um) 4 (80)
would [wʊd]: **I'd love to come. (= I would love to come)** Ich komme sehr gern. / Ich würde sehr gern kommen. 4 (83)
write [raɪt] schreiben 1 (24)
wrong [rɒŋ] falsch 1 (21)
°**she is wrong** sie hat Unrecht

Y

year [jɪə] Jahr 4 (73)
yellow ['jeləʊ] gelb (10)
yes [jes] ja 1 (22)
you [ju, ju:]:
1. du; ihr; Sie (8)
2. dich; dir; euch; Sie; Ihnen (8)
you're … [jɔ:] **(= you are)** du bist …; ihr seid …; Sie sind … 1 (18) **you're lucky** du hast Glück 2 (36) **You're welcome.** Bitte, gern geschehen. / Nichts zu danken. 4 (73)
young [jʌŋ] jung 5 (95)
your [jɔ:, jə] dein/e; euer/eure; Ihr/e (8)
yours [jɔ:z] deiner, deine, deins 2 (38)
°**yourself** [jɔ:'self, jə'self]:
about yourself über dich selbst
°**Yummy!** ['jʌmi] Lecker!

Z

°**zip wire** ['zɪp waɪə] Seilrutsche
°**zone** [zəʊn] Zone
zoo [zu:] Zoo 3 (60)

Das **German – English dictionary** enthält den **Lernwortschatz** von *Lighthouse 1*.
Es kann dir eine erste Hilfe sein, wenn du vergessen hast, wie etwas auf Englisch heißt.

Wenn du wissen möchtest, wo das englische Wort zum ersten Mal in *Lighthouse 1* vorkommt, dann kannst du im **English – German dictionary** (S. 208–218) nachschlagen.

Es werden folgende **Abkürzungen** und **Symbole** verwendet:

sth. = something (etwas) *pl* = *plural* (Mehrzahl) *infml* = *informal* (umgangssprachlich)

A

Abend evening ['i:vnɪŋ] **am Abend** in the evening **zu Abend essen** have dinner
Abendbrot dinner ['dɪnə] **Abendbrot essen** have dinner
Abendessen dinner ['dɪnə]
abends in the evening ['i:vnɪŋ]
Abenteuer adventure [əd'ventʃə]
aber but [bʌt, bət]
abwaschen wash up [wɒʃ 'ʌp]
acht eight [eɪt]
Adresse address [ə'dres]
Affe monkey ['mʌŋki]
Afrika Africa ['æfrɪkə]
alle all (the) [ɔ:l]; *(jeder)* everybody ['evribɒdi] **Grüß alle.** Say hi to everybody.
Alphabet alphabet ['ælfəbet]
als Erstes first [fɜ:st]
Also, … Well, … [wel]
alt old [əʊld]
Alter age [eɪdʒ]
am: am 5. Mai on 5th May **am Abend** in the evening **am Freitagmorgen** on Friday morning **am Montag/Dienstag/…** on Monday/Tuesday/… **am Morgen** in the morning **am Nachmittag** in the afternoon **am Strand** on the beach **am Telefon** on the phone **am Wochenende** at the weekend
an: an dieser Schule at this school **an meinem Geburtstag** on my birthday
andere(r, s) other ['ʌðə]
anders *(verschieden)* different ['dɪfrənt]
anfangen start [stɑ:t]
anhören: sich etwas anhören listen to sth. ['lɪsn]
anrufen phone [fəʊn]
anschauen: sich etwas anschauen look at sth. [lʊk]; *(etwas beobachten)* watch sth. [wɒtʃ]
anschließen: sich einem Klub anschließen join a club [dʒɔɪn]
Anschrift address [ə'dres]
Antwort answer ['ɑ:nsə]
Anzeige *(Werbung)* advert ['ædvɜ:t]
Apfel apple ['æpl]
April April ['eɪprəl]
Aquarium aquarium [ə'kweəriəm]
Arbeit work [wɜ:k] **bei der Arbeit** at work **zur Arbeit gehen** go to work
arbeiten work [wɜ:k] **hart arbeiten** work hard
Ärger kriegen be in trouble ['trʌbl]
auch too [tu:] **Ich auch.** Me too.
auf on [ɒn] **auf dem Bild** in the picture **auf dem Feld** in the field **auf dem Foto** in the photo **auf dem Land** in the country **auf dem Markt** at the market **auf dem Weg zu/nach …** on the way to … **auf der linken Seite** on the left **auf der rechten Seite** on the right **auf dieser Schule** at this school **auf Englisch** in English **Auf welcher Seite steht das?** What page is it? **Auf Wiedersehen!** Goodbye.
Aufgabe exercise ['eksəsaɪz]
aufgeregt *(gespannt)* excited [ɪk'saɪtɪd]; *(nervös)* nervous ['nɜ:vəs]
aufpassen auf look after [lʊk 'ɑ:ftə]
aufstehen get up [get 'ʌp]
Augenblick moment ['məʊmənt]
August August ['ɔ:gəst]
aus from [frɒm, frəm] **Ich bin aus Plymouth. / Ich komme aus Plymouth.** I'm from Plymouth.
Ausbildung training ['treɪnɪŋ]
Ausdruck *(Wendung)* phrase [freɪz]
ausleihen: sich etwas ausleihen borrow sth. ['bɒrəʊ]
ausprobieren try [traɪ]
aussehen look [lʊk] **Es sieht schön aus.** It looks nice.
Auto car [kɑ:] **mit dem Auto** by car

B

Baby baby ['beɪbi]
Babysitter babysitter ['beɪbisɪtə]
Bad, Badezimmer bathroom ['bɑ:θru:m]
bald soon [su:n]
Ball ball [bɔ:l]
Band *(Musikgruppe)* band [bænd]
Bär bear [beə]
Basketball basketball ['bɑ:skɪtbɔ:l]
Bauernhof farm [fɑ:m]
Baum tree [tri:]
beginnen start [stɑ:t]
bei: bei der Arbeit *(am Arbeitsplatz)* at work **bei Ellie** with Ellie **bei Ellie daheim/zu Hause** at Ellie's house **bei MARTINS** at MARTINS
beide: das Beste von beidem the best of both worlds ['bəʊθ wɜ:ldz]
Bein leg [leg]
Beispiel example [ɪg'zɑ:mpl]
bekommen get [get]
benötigen need [ni:d]
benutzen use [ju:z]
beobachten watch [wɒtʃ]
beschäftigt sein *(viel zu tun haben)* be busy ['bɪzi]
beschreiben describe [dɪ'skraɪb]
besondere(r, s) special ['speʃl]
besorgt sein (wegen) be worried (about) ['wʌrid]
beste: meine besten Freunde/Freundinnen my best friends [best] **das Beste von beidem** the best of both worlds ['bəʊθ wɜ:ldz]
besuchen visit ['vɪzɪt]
Besucher/in visitor ['vɪzɪtə]
Bett bed [bed] **ins Bett gehen** go to bed
beunruhigt sein (wegen) be worried (about) ['wʌrid]
Beutel bag [bæg]

bevor du gehst before you go [bɪ'fɔː]
Bild picture ['pɪktʃə]
auf dem Bild in the picture
bis: von Montag bis Freitag from Monday to Friday **Bis dann. / Bis später.** See you. / See you later.
bisschen: ein bisschen a bit [ə 'bɪt]
bitte 1. *(in Fragen und Aufforderungen)* please [pliːz]
2. Bitte schön. / Hier, bitte. Here you are.
3. Bitte, gern geschehen. *(Nichts zu danken.)* You're welcome. ['welkəm]
blau blue [bluː]
Blazer blazer ['bleɪzə]
bleiben stay [steɪ]
Bleistift pencil ['pensl]
Bleistiftanspitzer pencil sharpener ['pensl ʃɑːpnə]
blöd stupid ['stjuːpɪd]
bloß *(nur)* only ['əʊnli]
BMX-Rad BMX (bike) [biː em 'eks]
borgen: sich etwas borgen borrow sth. ['bɒrəʊ]
Brathähnchen chicken ['tʃɪkɪn]
brauchen need [niːd]
braun brown [braʊn]
Brief letter ['letə]
bringen *(mitbringen)* bring [brɪŋ]
britisch British ['brɪtɪʃ]
Broschüre brochure ['brəʊʃə]
Bruder brother ['brʌðə]
Buch book [bʊk]
buchstabieren spell [spel]
Bus bus [bʌs] **im Bus** on the bus
mit dem Bus by bus
mit dem Bus fahren go by bus

C

Café cafe ['kæfeɪ]
CD CD [siː 'diː]
Center centre ['sentə]
Computer computer [kəm'pjuːtə]
cool cool [kuːl]
Cousin, Cousine cousin ['kʌzn]

D

da *(dort)* there [ðeə]
daheim at home
dahin *(dorthin)* there [ðeə]
danach then [ðen]
Danke. Thanks. [θæŋks]
Danke, (es geht mir) gut. I'm fine, thanks.
danken: Nichts zu danken. *(Gern geschehen.)* You're welcome. ['welkəm]
dann then [ðen]
das *(Artikel)* the [ðə, ði]
das (dort) that [ðæt, ðət]
das Feld (dort) that field
dasselbe the same [seɪm]
Datum date [deɪt]
decken: den Tisch decken set the table [set]
dein, deine *(vor Nomen)* your [jɔː, jə]
deiner, deine, deins yours [jɔːz]
denken think [θɪŋk] **daran denken** *(sich merken; nicht vergessen)* remember [rɪ'membə]
der *(Artikel)* the [ðə, ði]
derselbe the same [seɪm]
Deutsch; deutsch German ['dʒɜːmən]
Deutschland Germany ['dʒɜːməni]
Dezember December [dɪ'sembə]
Dialog dialogue ['daɪəlɒg]
dich you [juː, ju]
dieselbe(n) the same [seɪm]
die *(Artikel)* the [ðə, ði]
die *(Relativpronomen)*: **Finde eine Person, die ...** Find a person who ... [huː]
Diele hall [hɔːl]
Dienstag Tuesday ['tjuːzdeɪ, 'tjuːzdi]
Dies ist ... This is ... ['ðɪs ɪz]
diese(r, s) this [ðɪs]
Ding thing [θɪŋ]
dir you [juː, ju] **Und was ist mit dir?** What about you?
Diskussion discussion [dɪ'skʌʃn]
Donnerstag Thursday ['θɜːzdeɪ, 'θɜːzdi]
Dorf village ['vɪlɪdʒ]
dort there [ðeə]
dorthin there [ðeə]
dran: Du bist dran. *(an der Reihe)* It's your turn. [tɜːn]
draußen outside [aʊt'saɪd]
nach draußen outside
drei three [θriː]
drinnen inside [ɪn'saɪd]
nach drinnen inside
dritte(r, s) third [θɜːd]
du you [juː, ju] **Und du?** What about you?
dumm stupid ['stjuːpɪd]
durch through [θruː]
DVD DVD [diːviː'diː]

E

echt *(wirklich)* real [rɪəl]
ein, eine *(Artikel)* a/an [ə, ən]
ein paar some [sʌm, səm]
einfach *(nicht schwierig)* easy ['iːzi]
einhundert a hundred, one hundred ['hʌndrəd]
einige, ein paar some [sʌm, səm]
einkaufen gehen go shopping ['ʃɒpɪŋ]
Einkaufszentrum shopping centre ['sentə]
einladen (zu, nach) *(Gäste)* invite (to) [ɪn'vaɪt]
Einladung (zu, nach) invitation (to) [ɪnvɪ'teɪʃn]
einmal: noch einmal again [ə'gen]
eins one [wʌn]
einsam lonely ['ləʊnli]
eintreten: in einen Klub eintreten join a club [dʒɔɪn]
Eintrittskarte ticket ['tɪkɪt]
einzige(r, s): **der einzige Schüler / die einzige Schülerin** the only student ['əʊnli]
Elefant elephant ['elɪfənt]
elf eleven [ɪ'levn]
Eltern parents ['peərənts]
E-Mail email ['iːmeɪl]
Ende end [end] **zu Ende sein** be over ['əʊvə]
England England ['ɪŋglənd]
Englisch; englisch English ['ɪŋglɪʃ]
auf Englisch in English
Ente duck [dʌk]
Entschuldigung 1. *(Tut mir leid.)* Sorry. / I'm sorry. ['sɒri]
2. Entschuldigung, ... / Entschuldigen Sie, ... *(Darf ich mal stören?)* Excuse me, ... [ɪk'skjuːz miː]
er 1. *(männliche Person)* he [hiː]
2. *(Ding, Tier)* it [ɪt]
Erdkunde geography [dʒi'ɒgrəfi]
erinnern: sich an etwas erinnern remember sth. [rɪ'membə]
erraten guess [ges]
erste(r, s) first [fɜːst] **als Erstes** first **der erste Morgen** the first morning
Erzählung story ['stɔːri]
es it [ɪt] **es ist ... / es gibt ...** there's ... **es sind ... / es gibt ...** there are ...
Esel donkey ['dɒŋki]
essen eat [iːt] **(zu) Mittag essen** have lunch **Abendbrot**

essen, zu Abend essen have dinner
Essen *(Lebensmittel)* food [fu:d]
etwas something ['sʌmθɪŋ]; *(ein bisschen)* some [sʌm, səm]
Sonst noch etwas? Anything else? ['eniθɪŋ 'els]
euch you [ju:, ju]
euer, eure *(vor Nomen)* your [jɔ:, jə]

F

Fähre ferry ['feri]
fahren: mit dem Bus/Auto fahren go by bus/car **Rad fahren** ride a bike **Skateboard fahren** skateboard
Fahrrad bike [baɪk]
fallen fall [fɔ:l]
falsch wrong [rɒŋ]; *(unwahr)* false [fɔ:ls]
Familie family ['fæməli]
Familienname family name
Familienstammbaum family tree
Farbe colour ['kʌlə]
Farm farm [fɑ:m]
faul *(träge, arbeitsunwillig)* lazy ['leɪzi]
Februar February ['februəri]
Federmäppchen pencil case ['pensl keɪs]
feiern: eine Party feiern have a party
Feld field [fi:ld] **auf dem Feld** in the field
Fenster window ['wɪndəʊ]
Ferien holidays ['hɒlədeɪz]
fernsehen watch TV [wɒtʃ ti:'vi:]
Fernsehen, Fernsehgerät TV [ti:'vi:]
Fernsehsendung programme ['prəʊgræm]
fertig: sich fertig machen (für) *(vorbereiten)* get ready (for) ['redi]
Feuerwache fire station ['faɪə steɪʃn]
fies *(gemein)* mean [mi:n]
Film film [fɪlm]
finden find [faɪnd] **Finde eine Person, die ...** Find a person who ...
Fisch, Fische fish, *pl* fish [fɪʃ]
Flasche: eine Flasche ... a bottle of ... ['bɒtl]
flauschig *(pelzig)* furry ['fɜ:ri]
Flur *(Diele)* hall [hɔ:l]
Form form [fɔ:m]
fort away [ə'weɪ]
Foto photo ['fəʊtəʊ]
auf dem Foto in the photo
Frage question ['kwestʃn]
Fragen stellen ask questions
fragen ask [ɑ:sk] **sie fragte/hat gefragt** she asked
Französisch; französisch French [frentʃ]
Frau ... 1. *(allgemeine Anrede f. Frauen)* Ms ... [mɪz, məz]
2. *(Anrede f. verheiratete Frauen)* Mrs ... ['mɪsɪz]
3. *(Anrede f. unverheiratete Frauen)* Miss ... [mɪs]
frei free [fri:]
Freitag Friday ['fraɪdeɪ, 'fraɪdi]
freitagmorgens, am Freitagmorgen on Friday morning
fressen eat [i:t]
Freund/in friend [frend]; *(fester Freund)* boyfriend; *(feste Freundin)* girlfriend
freundlich friendly ['frendli]
Freut mich, dich/euch kennenzulernen. Nice to meet you!
froh happy ['hæpi]
früh early ['ɜ:li]
Frühstück breakfast ['brekfəst]
frühstücken have breakfast
fühlen; sich fühlen feel [fi:l]
Füller pen [pen]
fünf five [faɪv]
funktionieren work [wɜ:k]
für for [fɔ:, fə] **für mich selbst** for myself [maɪ'self]
fürchterlich terrible ['terəbl]
Fußball football ['fʊtbɔ:l]
Futter food [fu:d]
füttern feed [fi:d]

G

ganz: den ganzen Tag/Sommer/ ... (lang) all day/summer/...
Garage garage ['gærɑ:ʒ]
Garten garden ['gɑ:dn]
geben: es gibt ... there's ...; there are ... [ðeəz], ['ðeər ɑ:]
Geburtstag birthday ['bɜ:θdeɪ]
an meinem Geburtstag on my birthday **Herzlichen Glückwunsch zum Geburtstag!** Happy birthday! **Ich habe am 5. Mai Geburtstag.** My birthday is on 5th May. **Sie hat Geburtstag.** It's her birthday. **Wann hast du Geburtstag?** When's your birthday?
Gedicht poem ['pəʊɪm]
gefährlich dangerous ['deɪndʒərəs]
Gefühl feeling ['fi:lɪŋ]
gehen go [gəʊ] **zu Fuß gehen** walk [wɔ:k] **einkaufen gehen** go shopping ['ʃɒpɪŋ] **ins Bett gehen** go to bed **nach Hause gehen** go home **schwimmen gehen** go swimming **zur Arbeit gehen** go to work **zur Schule gehen** go to school **Wie geht's?** How are you? [haʊ 'ɑ: ju]; *(Wie läuft's?)* How's it going?
Wie geht es dir/euch? How are you?
gehören zu *(passen zu)* go with
gelb yellow ['jeləʊ]
Geld money ['mʌni] **Es ist sein Geld wert.** It's good value. ['vælju:]
gemein *(fies)* mean [mi:n]
Gemüse vegetables *(pl)* ['vedʒtəblz]
genervt sein feel fed up [fed 'ʌp]
Geografie geography [dʒi'ɒgrəfi]
gerade *(in diesem Moment)* at the moment ['məʊmənt]
Geräusch sound [saʊnd]; *(unangenehm, laut)* noise [nɔɪz]
gern: Ich sehe gern fern. I like watching TV. **Ich komme sehr gern. / Ich würde sehr gern kommen.** I'd love to come. (= I would love to come.
Bitte, gern geschehen. You're welcome.
gernhaben *(mögen)* like [laɪk]
Geschäft shop [ʃɒp]
geschehen happen ['hæpən]
Geschenk present ['preznt]
Geschichte 1. *(vergangene Zeiten)* history ['hɪstri]
2. *(Erzählung)* story ['stɔ:ri]
Gesicht face [feɪs]
gespannt *(aufgeregt)* excited [ɪk'saɪtɪd]
Getränk drink [drɪŋk]
gewinnen win [wɪn]
gewöhnlich *(normal)* normal ['nɔ:ml]
Gitarre guitar [gɪ'tɑ:]
Gitarre spielen play the guitar
glauben *(denken, meinen)* think [θɪŋk]
Glück: du hast Glück you're lucky ['lʌki]
glücklich happy ['hæpi]
Glückwunsch: Herzlichen Glückwunsch zum Geburtstag! Happy birthday! ['bɜ:θdeɪ]
grau grey [greɪ]

groß big [bɪg]
großartig great [greɪt]
Großeltern grandparents ['grænpeərənts]
Großmutter grandmother ['grænmʌðə]
Großvater grandfather ['grænfɑːðə]
grün green [griːn]
Gruppe group [gruːp]; *(Band)* band
Gruß: Viele Grüße, ... *(Briefschluss)* Best wishes ['wɪʃɪz]
grüßen: Grüß alle. Say hi to everybody.
gut good [gʊd]; *(in Ordnung)* fine [faɪn] **gut funktionieren/sprechen/...** work/speak/... well **Gut gemacht!** Well done. [wel 'dʌn] **Danke, (es geht mir) gut.** I'm OK, thanks./I'm fine, thanks. **Guten Morgen.** Good morning. **Guten Tag.** Hello. [hə'ləʊ]

H

haben have [hæv, həv] **die Nase voll haben** feel fed up [fed 'ʌp] **etwas haben wollen** want sth. [wɒnt] **Glück haben** be lucky ['lʌki] **Hunger haben** be hungry ['hʌŋgri] **Ich habe am 5. Mai Geburtstag.** My birthday is on 5th May. **viel zu tun haben** be busy ['bɪzi] **ich hatte/habe gehabt** I had [hæd], [həd]
Hafen harbour ['hɑːbə]
Hähnchen chicken ['tʃɪkɪn]
Hallo. Hi. [haɪ]; Hello. [hə'ləʊ]
halten: Halt den Mund! Shut up! *(infml)* [ʃʌt 'ʌp]
Hamster hamster ['hæmstə]
Handy mobile phone ['məʊbaɪl 'fəʊn]
hart hard [hɑːd] **hart arbeiten** work hard
hassen hate [heɪt]
hat: Er hat ... He has ... [hæz, həz]
hatte: ich hatte/habe gehabt I had [hæd], [həd]
Haus house [haʊs] **bei Ellie zu Hause** at Ellie's house **nach Hause gehen** go home **nach Hause kommen** come home **zu Hause** at home
Hausaufgabe(n) homework ['həʊmwɜːk] **Ich habe meine Hausaufgaben vergessen.** I forgot my homework. **Ich kann meine Hausaufgaben nicht machen.** I can't do my homework. **Was haben wir als Hausaufgabe auf?** What's for homework?
Haustier pet [pet]
Heim *(Zuhause)* home [həʊm]
heißen: Ich heiße Cyril. I'm Cyril. **Wie heißt du?** What's your name?
helfen help [help]
Helm helmet ['helmɪt]
Hemd shirt [ʃɜːt]
Herr Jahn Mr Jahn ['mɪstə]
herrisch bossy ['bɒsi]
herstellen make [meɪk]
Herzlichen Glückwunsch zum Geburtstag! Happy birthday!
heute today [tə'deɪ]
hier here [hɪə] **Hier, bitte.** Here you are.
hierher here [hɪə]
Hilfe! Help! [help]
hinfallen fall [fɔːl]
hinter behind [bɪ'haɪnd]
hinunter: diesen Hügel hinunter down this hill [daʊn]
Hobby hobby ['hɒbi]
hoffen hope [həʊp]
hören hear [hɪə]
Hose trousers *(pl)* ['traʊzəz]
Hügel hill [hɪl]
Huhn chicken ['tʃɪkɪn]
Hund dog [dɒg]
hundert a hundred, one hundred ['hʌndrəd]
Hunger haben be hungry ['hʌŋgri]
hungrig sein be hungry ['hʌŋgri]

I

ich I [aɪ] **Ich auch.** Me too. **Ich bin es, Sandy.** It's me, Sandy. **Ich nicht!** Not me!
Idee idea [aɪ'dɪə]
ihm him [hɪm]; *(bei Dingen und Tieren)* it
ihn him [hɪm]; *(bei Dingen und Tieren)* it
ihnen them [ðem], [ðəm]
Ihnen *(höfliche Anrede)* you [juː, ju]
ihr *(Mehrzahl von „du")* you
ihr: Hilf ihr. Help her. [hɜː]
ihr, ihre *(vor Nomen; besitzanzeigend)*
1. *(zu „she")* her [hɜː, hə]
2. *(zu „it")* its [ɪts]
3. *(zu „they")* their [ðeə]
Ihr, Ihre *(vor Nomen; besitzanzeigend) (zur höflichen Anrede „you")* your [jɔː, jə]
im: im Bus on the bus **im Kino** at the cinema **im Moment** at the moment ['məʊmənt]
immer always ['ɔːlweɪz]
in in [ɪn] **in das Wohnzimmer (hinein)** into the living room ['ɪntʊ] **in der Mitte** in the middle **in der Nacht** at night **in der Nähe von** near [nɪə] **in der Schule** at school **in der Stadt** in town **in Deutschland** in Germany **in einem Restaurant** at a restaurant **in England** in England **in Schwierigkeiten sein** be in trouble ['trʌbl]
Informations- und Kommunikationstechnologie ICT [aɪ siː 'tiː] *(information and communication technology)*
ins: ins Bett gehen go to bed **ins Kino** to the cinema
Instrument instrument ['ɪnstrəmənt]
interessant interesting ['ɪntrəstɪŋ]
Interview interview ['ɪntəvjuː]
Irgendwelche Ideen? Any ideas? ['eni]

J

ja yes [jes]
Jahr year [jɪə]
Januar January ['dʒænjuəri]
jede(r, s) *(vor Nomen)* every ['evri]
jeder *(alle)* everybody ['evribɒdi]
jenes Feld (dort) that field [ðæt, ðət]
jetzt now [naʊ]
Job job [dʒɒb]
Jugendliche(r) kid [kɪd]
Juli July [dʒu'laɪ]
jung young [jʌŋ]
Junge boy [bɔɪ]
Juni June [dʒuːn]

K

Kaffee coffee ['kɒfi]
Käfig cage [keɪdʒ]
Kalender diary ['daɪəri]
Kaninchen rabbit ['ræbɪt]
Kantine canteen [kæn'tiːn]
Kapuzenpullover, -jacke hoodie ['hʊdi]
Karte card [kɑːd]
Kästchen box [bɒks]
Kasten box [bɒks]
Katze cat [kæt]
kaufen buy [baɪ]

kein, keine no [nəʊ] **Ich bin kein Junge.** I'm not a boy. **Ich mag kein Blau.** I don't like blue. **sie hat kein/keine/keinen …** she doesn't have a … ['dʌznt] **sie sind keine …** they aren't … [ɑ:nt]
kennen know [nəʊ]
kennenlernen meet [mi:t] **Freut mich, dich/euch kennenzulernen.** Nice to meet you!
Kind, Kinder child, *pl* children [tʃaɪld], ['tʃɪldrən]; kid [kɪd]
Kino cinema ['sɪnəmə] **im Kino** at the cinema **ins Kino** to the cinema
Kissen cushion ['kʊʃn]
Kiste box [bɒks]
Klang sound [saʊnd]
Klasse class [klɑ:s]
Klassenlehrer/in class teacher ['klɒ:s ti:tʃə]
Klassenzimmer classroom ['klɑ:sru:m]
Klavier piano [pi'ænəʊ] **Klavier spielen** play the piano
Kleiderschrank wardrobe ['wɔ:drəʊb]
klein little ['lɪtl]; small [smɔ:l]
klingeln ring [rɪŋ]
Koch, Köchin cook [kʊk]
kochen cook [kʊk]
kommen come [kʌm] **Komm, Luca!** Come on, Luca! **nach Hause kommen** come home
können can [kæn, kən] **Ich kann meine Hausaufgaben nicht machen.** I can't do my homework. [kɑ:nt]
Konzert concert ['kɒnsət]
Kopfsprung: einen Kopfsprung machen dive [daɪv]
kosten: Der Taschenrechner kostet 1 Pfund. The calculator is £ 1. **Die Handys kosten 10 Pfund.** The mobiles are £ 10. **Was (Wie viel) kostet …?** How much is …? **Was (Wie viel) kosten …?** How much are …?
Krankenhaus hospital ['hɒspɪtl]
Krawatte tie [taɪ]
Krebs crab [kræb]
kriegen: Ärger kriegen be in trouble ['trʌbl]
Krokodil crocodile ['krɒkədaɪl]
Küche kitchen ['kɪtʃɪn]
Kugelschreiber pen [pen]
Kuh cow [kaʊ]
kümmern: sich kümmern um look after [lʊk 'ɑ:ftə]
Kunst art [ɑ:t]

L

Labor lab [læb]
lachen laugh [lɑ:f] **sie lachten/haben gelacht** they laughed
Laden shop [ʃɒp]
Lampe lamp [læmp]
Land country ['kʌntri] **auf dem Land** in the country
lang: den ganzen Tag/Sommer/… lang all day/summer/…
langweilig boring ['bɔ:rɪŋ]
Lärm noise [nɔɪz]
Lass uns … / Lasst uns … Let's … [lets]
laufen: Wie läuft's? How's it going?
Läufer *(Teppich)* rug [rʌg]
laut *(voller Lärm)* noisy ['nɔɪzi]
Laut sound [saʊnd]
läuten ring [rɪŋ]
Leben: (das) Leben, (die) Leben life, *pl* lives [laɪf], [laɪvz]
leben live [lɪv]
Lebensmittel food [fu:d]
Lehrer/in teacher ['ti:tʃə]
leicht *(einfach)* easy ['i:zi]
leidtun: Tut mir leid. Sorry. / I'm sorry. ['sɒri]
leihen *(sich borgen)* borrow ['bɒrəʊ]
leise quiet ['kwaɪət]
Lektion *(im Schulbuch)* unit ['ju:nɪt]
lernen learn [lɜ:n]
lesen read [ri:d]
letzte(r, s) last [lɑ:st] **der letzte Tag der Ferien** the last day of the holidays
Leute people ['pi:pl]; *(als Anrede verwendet)* guys [gaɪz]
Liebe … / Lieber … Dear … [dɪə]
lieben love [lʌv]
Lieblings- favourite ['feɪvərɪt] **Lieblingsfarbe** favourite colour
Lied song [sɒŋ]
lila purple ['pɜ:pl]
Lineal ruler ['ru:lə]
links left [left] **auf der linken Seite** on the left **nach links** left
Locher hole punch ['həʊl pʌntʃ]
los: In der Küche ist zu viel los. The kitchen is too busy. ['bɪzi]

M

machen *(tun)* do [du:]; *(herstellen)* make [meɪk] **Ich kann meine Hausaufgaben nicht machen.** I can't do my homework. [kɑ:nt] **Das macht 159 Pfund.** That's £ 159. **einen Kopfsprung machen** dive [daɪv] **sich fertig machen (für)** get ready (for) ['redi] **sauber machen** clean [kli:n] **sich Sorgen machen (wegen, um)** worry (about) ['wʌri] **Mach dir keine Sorgen.** Don't worry. [dəʊnt 'wʌri] **Gut gemacht!** Well done. [wel 'dʌn] **Ich muss Schluss machen.** *(am Telefon)* I must go.
Mädchen girl [gɜ:l]
Mai May [meɪ]
Mama mum [mʌm]
manchmal sometimes ['sʌmtaɪmz]
Mann, Männer man, *pl* men [mæn], [men]
Mannschaft team [ti:m]
Markt market ['mɑ:kɪt]
Marmelade jam [dʒæm]
März March [mɑ:tʃ]
Mathematik maths [mæθs]
Meer sea [si:]
mein, meine *(vor Nomen)* my [maɪ]
meinen *(denken, glauben)* think [θɪŋk] **Was meinst du?** What do you think?
meistens usually ['ju:ʒuəli]
Mensa canteen [kæn'ti:n]
Menschen people ['pi:pl]
merken: sich etwas merken remember sth. [rə'membə]
mich me [mi:] **für mich selbst** for myself [maɪ'self]
mir me [mi:]
mit with [wɪð] **mit dem Bus/Rad/Auto/…** by bus/bike/car/… **mit dem Bus/Rad/Auto fahren** go by bus/bike/car
mitbringen bring [brɪŋ]
Mittag: (zu) Mittag essen have lunch [lʌntʃ]
Mittagessen lunch [lʌntʃ]
Mitte middle ['mɪdl] **in der Mitte** in the middle
Mittwoch Wednesday ['wenzdeɪ, 'wenzdi]
Mobiltelefon mobile (phone) ['məʊbaɪl]
mögen like [laɪk] **Ich mag Rot.** I like red. **Ich mag Blau nicht. / Ich mag kein Blau.** I don't like blue. **Er mag es nicht, allein zu**

sein. He doesn't like to be lonely. **gar nicht mögen** *(hassen)* hate [heɪt]
Moment moment ['məʊmənt]
im Moment at the moment
Monat month [mʌnθ]
Montag Monday ['mʌndeɪ, 'mʌndi]
Morgen morning ['mɔːnɪŋ]
am Morgen in the morning(s)
morgens in the morning(s)
Möwe seagull ['siːgʌl]
müde tired ['taɪəd]
Mund mouth [maʊθ] **Halt den Mund!** Shut up! *(infml)* [ʃʌt 'ʌp]
Musik music ['mjuːzɪk]
Musiker/in musician [mju'zɪʃn]
müssen must [mʌst] **Ich muss Schluss machen.** *(am Telefon)* I must go.
Mutter mother ['mʌðə]
Mutti mum [mʌm]

N

Na ja, ... Well, ... [wel]
Na los, Luca! Come on, Luca!
nach 1. *(zeitlich)* after ['ɑːftə]
nach dem Abendessen after dinner
2. *(örtlich)* **to** [tu, tə]
nach draußen outside [aʊt'saɪd]
nach drinnen inside [ɪn'saɪd]
nach Hause gehen go home
nach Hause kommen come home **nach links** left [left]
nach oben upstairs [ʌp'steəz]
nach rechts right [raɪt]
nach unten downstairs [daʊn'steəz]
Nachmittag afternoon [ɑːftə'nuːn]
am Nachmittag in the afternoon
nachmittags in the afternoon
Nachname family name
Nachrichten news [njuːz]
nächste(r, s) next [nekst]
Nacht night [naɪt] **in der Nacht** at night
nachts at night [ət 'naɪt]
nahe (bei) near [nɪə]
Nähe: in der Nähe von near [nɪə]
Name name [neɪm]
Nase: die Nase voll haben feel fed up [fed 'ʌp]
nass wet [wet]
Naturwissenschaft science ['saɪəns]
neben next to ['nekst tʊ]
nehmen: Ich nehme es (ihn, sie). *(beim Einkaufen)* I'll take it. [aɪl 'teɪk ɪt]
nein no [nəʊ]
nervös nervous ['nɜːvəs]
nett nice [naɪs]
Netz network ['netwɜːk]
neu new [njuː]
neun nine [naɪn]
nicht: ich bin nicht ... I'm not ... [nɒt] **Ich nicht!** Not me!
nichts nothing ['nʌθɪŋ] **Nichts zu danken.** You're welcome.
nie never ['nevə]
niedlich cute [kjuːt]
niemals never ['nevə]
noch: noch einmal again [ə'gen]
Sonst noch etwas? Anything else? ['eniθɪŋ 'els]
normal normal ['nɔːml]
normalerweise usually ['juːʒuəli]
November November [nəʊ'vembə]
Nummer number ['nʌmbə]
nun now [naʊ] **Nun, ...** Well, ... [wel]
nur only ['əʊnli]
Nuss nut [nʌt]

O

oben upstairs [ʌp'steəz]
nach oben upstairs
Obst fruit [fruːt]
oder or [ɔː]
oft often ['ɒfn, 'ɒftən]
okay OK [əʊ'keɪ]
Oktober October [ɒk'təʊbə]
Omelett omelette ['ɒmlət]
Onkel uncle ['ʌŋkl]
orange orange ['ɒrɪndʒ]
Ordnung: in Ordnung fine [faɪn]
Ort place [pleɪs]

P

Paar pair [peə]
paar: ein paar some [sʌm], [səm]
Papa dad [dæd]
Papier paper ['peɪpə]
Park park [pɑːk]
Partner/in partner ['pɑːtnə]
Party party ['pɑːti] **eine Party feiern** have a party
passen zu *(gehören zu)* go with
passieren happen ['hæpən]
Pause break [breɪk]
pelzig *(flauschig)* furry ['fɜːri]
Pence: 50 Pence 50p [fɪfti 'piː]
Pfund *(britische Währung)* pound (£) [paʊnd] **Das macht 159 Pfund.** That's £ 159.
Der Taschenrechner kostet 1 Pfund. The calculator is £ 1.
Die Handys kosten 10 Pfund. The mobiles are £ 10.
Piano piano [pi'ænəʊ]
Picknick picnic ['pɪknɪk]
pink pink [pɪŋk]
planen plan [plæn]
Platz 1. *(Stelle, Ort)* place [pleɪs]
2. *(freier Raum)* space [speɪs]
3. *(Sitzplatz)* seat [siːt]
Pommes frites chips *(pl)* [tʃɪps]
Pony pony ['pəʊni] **auf einem Pony reiten** ride a pony
Poster poster ['pəʊstə]
Preis *(Kaufpreis)* price [praɪs]
prima great [greɪt]
probieren *(ausprobieren)* try [traɪ]
Problem problem ['prɒbləm]
Prospekt brochure ['brəʊʃə]
Pullover pullover ['pʊləʊvə]
putzen clean [kliːn]

Q

Quiz quiz [kwɪz]

R

Rad *(Fahrrad)* bike [baɪk]
Rad fahren ride a bike [raɪd]
mit dem Rad by bike
mit dem Rad fahren go by bike
Radiergummi rubber ['rʌbə]
Rap *(rhythmischer Sprechgesang)* rap [ræp]
rappen rap [ræp]
Rapper/in rapper ['ræpə]
raten guess [ges]
Ratespiel quiz [kwɪz]
Ratte rat [ræt]
Raum *(Zimmer)* room [ruːm, rʊm]
rechthaberisch bossy ['bɒsi]
rechts right [raɪt]
auf der rechten Seite on the right **nach rechts** right
reden (mit) talk (to) [tɔːk]
Regal, Regale shelf, *pl* shelves [ʃelf], [ʃelvz]
Reihe: Du bist an der Reihe. It's your turn. [tɜːn]
reiten ride [raɪd] **auf einem Pony reiten** ride a pony
Rektor/in *(Schulleiter/in)* principal ['prɪnsəpl]
Restaurant restaurant ['restrɒnt]
in einem Restaurant at a restaurant
Rezept *(Kochrezept)* recipe ['resəpi]
richtig right [raɪt]

Rock skirt [skɜːt]
Rollstuhl wheelchair ['wiːltʃeə]
rosa pink [pɪŋk]
rot red [red]
ruhig quiet ['kwaɪət]
Rundgang: ein Rundgang durch die Schule a tour of the school [tʊə]

S

Sache *(Ding)* thing [θɪŋ]
Saft juice [dʒuːs]
sagen say [seɪ] **er sagte/hat gesagt** he said [sed]
Sahne cream [kriːm]
Salat *(als Gericht oder Beilage)* salad ['sæləd]
Samstag Saturday ['sætədeɪ, 'sætədi]
Sandwich sandwich ['sænwɪtʃ, 'sændwɪdʒ]
Sänger/in singer ['sɪŋə]
sauber machen clean [kliːn]
sauer sein *(genervt sein)* feel fed up [fed 'ʌp]
Schaf, Schafe sheep, *pl* sheep [ʃiːp]
Schauspiel *(darstellende Kunst)* drama ['drɑːmə]
Schere scissors *(pl)* ['sɪzəz]
Scheune barn [bɑːn]
schicken send [send] **einem Freund / einer Freundin eine SMS schicken** text a friend [tekst]
Schild sign [saɪn]
schlafen sleep [sliːp] **Schlaf jetzt!** Go to sleep!
Schlafparty sleepover ['sliːpəʊvə]
Schlafsack sleeping bag ['sliːpɪŋ bæg]
Schlafzimmer bedroom ['bedruːm]
Schlagzeug drums [drʌmz] **Schlagzeug spielen** play the drums
Schlange snake [sneɪk]
schlecht bad [bæd]
schließen *(zumachen)* close [kləʊz]
schlimm bad [bæd]
Schluss end [end] **Ich muss Schluss machen.** *(am Telefon)* I must go.
Schlussverkauf sale [seɪl]
schnell fast [fɑːst]
schön *(nett)* nice [naɪs] **Ich wünsche dir einen schönen Tag. / Schönen Tag noch.** Have a good day.
schrecklich terrible ['terəbl]
schreiben write [raɪt]
Schreibtisch desk [desk]
Schuh shoe [ʃuː]
Schule school [skuːl] **auf/an dieser Schule** at this school **in der Schule** at school **zur Schule gehen** go to school
Schüler/in student ['stjuːdənt]
Schulheft exercise book ['eksəsaɪz bʊk]
Schulklasse class [klɑːs]
Schulleiter/in principal ['prɪnsəpl]
Schulsport PE [piː 'iː] *(physical education)*
Schultasche school bag ['skuːl bæg]
Schulter shoulder ['ʃəʊldə]
Schulversammlung assembly [ə'sembli]
schwarz black [blæk]
Schwein pig [pɪg]
schwer *(schwierig)* difficult ['dɪfɪkəlt]; hard [hɑːd]
Schwester sister ['sɪstə]
schwierig difficult ['dɪfɪkəlt]; hard [hɑːd]
Schwierigkeit: in Schwierigkeiten sein be in trouble ['trʌbl]
Schwimmbad swimming pool ['swɪmɪŋ puːl]
Schwimmbecken swimming pool ['swɪmɪŋ puːl]
schwimmen swim [swɪm] **schwimmen gehen** go swimming
sechs six [sɪks]
sehen see [siː] **Sieh mal, Adam.** Look, Adam.
sehr very ['veri] **sehr nett, sehr schön** very nice
sein be [biː] **Sei still/leise.** Be quiet. ['kwaɪət]
sein, seine *(vor Nomen; besitzanzeigend)*
1. *(zu „he")* his [hɪz]
2. *(zu „it")* its [ɪts]
Seite 1. page [peɪdʒ] **Auf welcher Seite sind wir? / Auf welcher Seite steht das?** What page is it?
2. **auf der linken Seite** on the left **auf der rechten Seite** on the right
selbst: für mich selbst for myself [maɪ'self]
senden send [send]
Sendung *(Radio, Fernsehen)* programme ['prəʊgræm]
September September [sep'tembə]
setzen: sich setzen sit [sɪt]
sicher sure [ʃʊə, ʃɔː]
sie 1. *(Einzahl; weibliche Person)* she [ʃiː] **Frag sie.** Ask her. [hɜː]
2. *(Einzahl; Ding, Tier)* it [ɪt]
3. *(Mehrzahl)* they [ðeɪ] **Frag sie.** Ask them. [ðem, ðəm]
Sie *(höfliche Anrede)* you [juː, ju]
sieben seven ['sevn]
singen sing [sɪŋ]
sitzen sit [sɪt]
Skateboard fahren skateboard ['skeɪtbɔːd]
SMS text message ['tekst mesɪdʒ]; text **eine SMS von Mama** a text from mum **einem Freund / einer Freundin eine SMS schicken** text a friend [tekst]
so langweilig/müde/... so boring/tired/... [səʊ]
Socke sock [sɒk]
Sommer summer ['sʌmə]
Sonderangebot special offer [speʃl 'ɒfə]
Sonnabend Saturday ['sætədeɪ, 'sætədi]
Sonntag Sunday ['sʌndeɪ, 'sʌndi]
Sonst noch etwas? Anything else? ['eniθɪŋ 'els]
Sorge: sich Sorgen machen (wegen, um) worry (about) ['wʌri] **Mach dir keine Sorgen.** Don't worry. [dəʊnt 'wʌri]
Spaß: es macht Spaß it's fun [fʌn]
spät late [leɪt] **Wie spät ist es?** What's the time?
später later ['leɪtə] **Bis später.** See you. / See you later. ['leɪtə]
Spiegel mirror ['mɪrə]
Spiel game [geɪm]
spielen play [pleɪ] **Gitarre/Klavier/Schlagzeug spielen** play the guitar/the piano/the drums
Sport sport [spɔːt]; *(in der Schule)* PE [piː 'iː] *(physical education)* **Sport treiben** do sport
Sporthalle sports hall ['spɔːts hɔːl]
Sprache language ['læŋgwɪdʒ]
sprechen (mit) speak (to) [spiːk]; talk (to) [tɔːk]
Sprechgesang chant [tʃɑːnt]
Stadt *(Großstadt)* city ['sɪti]; *(Kleinstadt)* town [taʊn] **in der Stadt** in town
Stammbaum *(der Familie)* family tree
Stelle place [pleɪs]
stellen: Fragen stellen ask questions ['kwestʃnz]

Stiefbruder stepbrother ['stepbrʌðə]
Stiefmutter stepmother ['stepmʌðə]; stepmum ['stepmʌm]
Stiefschwester stepsister ['stepsɪstə]
Stiefvater stepdad ['stepdæd]; stepfather ['stepfɑːðə]
Stift *(zum Schreiben)* pen [pen]
still quiet ['kwaɪət]
stolz (auf) proud (of) [praʊd]
Strand beach [biːtʃ] **am Strand** on the beach
Straße *(in Orten)* street [striːt]; *(Landstraße zwischen Orten, aber auch Straße in Orten)* road [rəʊd]
streicheln stroke [strəʊk]
streng strict [strɪkt]
Strumpf *(Socke)* sock [sɒk]
Strumpfhose tights *(pl)* [taɪts]
Student/in student ['stjuːdənt]
Studio studio ['stjuːdiəʊ]
Stuhl chair [tʃeə]
Stunde *(Schulstunde)* lesson ['lesn]
Stundenplan timetable ['taɪmteɪbl]
Supermarkt supermarket ['suːpəmɑːkɪt]
Suppe soup [suːp]
süß *(niedlich)* cute [kjuːt]
Süßigkeiten sweets *(pl)* [swiːts]
Sweatshirt sweatshirt ['swetʃɜːt]
Szene scene [siːn]

T

Taekwondo tae kwon do [taɪ kwɒn 'dəʊ]
Tag day [deɪ] **Ich wünsche dir einen schönen Tag. / Schönen Tag noch.** Have a good day.
Tagebuch diary ['daɪəri]
Tante aunt [ɑːnt]
tanzen dance [dɑːns]
Tasche *(Tragetasche, Beutel)* bag [bæg]
Taschenrechner calculator ['kælkjuleɪtə]
Tasse: eine Tasse ... a cup of ... [kʌp]
Team team [tiːm]
Technik *(Technologie)* technology [tek'nɒlədʒi]
Technologie technology [tek'nɒlədʒi]
Tee tea [tiː]
Teenager teenager ['tiːneɪdʒə]
Teich pond [pɒnd]
teilen: sich ein Zimmer mit ... teilen share a room with ... [ʃeə]
Telefon phone [fəʊn]
am Telefon on the phone
Telefonnummer phone number ['fəʊn nʌmbə]
Tennis tennis [tenɪs]
Teppich *(Läufer)* rug [rʌg]
teuer expensive [ɪk'spensɪv]
Text text [tekst]
Theater theatre ['θɪətə]
Thema theme [θiːm]
Tier animal ['ænɪml]
Tiger tiger ['taɪgə]
Tisch table ['teɪbl] **den Tisch decken** set the table [set]
Toast toast [təʊst]
Toilette toilet ['tɔɪlət]
Training training ['treɪnɪŋ]
Traum dream [driːm]
treffen; sich treffen meet [miːt]
treiben: Sport treiben do sport
trinken drink [drɪŋk]
Trommel drum [drʌm]
Tschüs. Bye. [baɪ]
T-Shirt T-shirt ['tiːʃɜːt]
tun do [duː] **etwas tun wollen** want to do sth. [wɒnt] **viel zu tun haben** be busy ['bɪzi]
Tür door [dɔː]
Turnschuhe trainers *(pl)* ['treɪnəz]

U

über about [ə'baʊt] **über mich/dich/...** about me/you/...
Überraschung surprise [sə'praɪz]
Übung *(im Schulbuch)* exercise ['eksəsaɪz]
Übungsheft exercise book
Uhr: 9 Uhr morgens/vormittags 9 am [eɪ'em] **5 Uhr nachmittags/abends / 17 Uhr** 5 pm [piː'em] **um 1 Uhr / 13 Uhr** at 1 o'clock [ə'klɒk]
Uhrzeit time [taɪm]
um 1 Uhr / 13 Uhr at 1 o'clock [ə'klɒk]
und and [ænd, ənd] **Und du? / Und was ist mit dir?** What about you?
ungefähr about [ə'baʊt]
unglücklich unhappy [ʌn'hæpi]
Uniform uniform ['juːnɪfɔːm]
unordentlich messy ['mesi]
uns us [ʌs, əs]
unser, unsere *(vor Nomen)* our ['aʊə]
unten downstairs [daʊn'steəz]
nach unten downstairs [daʊn'steəz]
unter under ['ʌndə]
Unterrichtsstunde lesson ['lesn]
Unterschied difference ['dɪfrəns]

V

Vater father ['fɑːðə]
Vati dad [dæd]
vergessen: Ich habe meine Hausaufgaben vergessen. I forgot my homework. [fə'gɒt]
verirrt: Ich habe mich nicht verirrt. I'm not lost. [lɒst]
Verkauf sale [seɪl]
verlaufen: Ich habe mich nicht verlaufen. I'm not lost. [lɒst]
vermissen miss [mɪs]
verschieden different ['dɪfrənt]
verstecken; sich verstecken hide [haɪd]
verstehen understand [ʌndə'stænd]
verwenden use [juːz]
viel ..., viele ... *(vor Nomen)* lots of ... ['lɒts əv] **Wie viel kostet ...?** How much is ...? **Wie viel kosten ...?** How much are ...? **Viele Grüße, ...** *(Briefschluss)* Best wishes ['wɪʃɪz]
vielleicht maybe ['meɪbi]
vier four [fɔː]
violett purple ['pɜːpl]
Vogel bird [bɜːd]
von: eine SMS von Mama a text from mum **von Montag bis Freitag** from Monday to Friday
vor 1. *(zeitlich)* before [bɪ'fɔː] **vor dem Frühstück** before breakfast
2. *(örtlich)* **in front of** [ɪn 'frʌnt əv]
vorbei sein be over ['əʊvə]
vorbereiten: sich vorbereiten (auf) get ready (for) ['redi]

W

wahr true [truː]
wann? when? [wen] **Wann hast du Geburtstag?** When's your birthday?
war: es war Freitag it was Friday [wɒz], [wəz]
waren: sie waren im Bus they were on the bus [wɜː], [wə]
warum? why? [waɪ]
was? what? [wɒt] **Was haben wir als Hausaufgabe auf?** What's for homework? **Was kostet ...?** How much is ...? **Was kosten ...?** How much are ...? **Was meinst du? / Was denkst du?** What do you think?

Wasser water ['wɔːtə]
wecken wake [weɪk]
Wecker alarm clock [ə'lɑːm klɒk]
weg away [ə'weɪ]
Weg way [weɪ] **auf dem Weg zu/nach ...** on the way to ...
wehtun: Mein Bein tut weh. I have a sore leg. [sɔː]
Weide field [fiːld] **auf der Weide** in the field
weil because [bɪ'kɒz]
weiß white [waɪt]
welche(r, s) ...? what ...? [wɒt] **Auf welcher Seite sind wir? / Auf welcher Seite steht das?** What page is it?
Welt world [wɜːld]
Wendung *(Ausdruck, Redewendung)* phrase [freɪz]
wenn when [wen]
wer? who? [huː] **Wer bist du? / Wer seid ihr?** Who are you?
Werbung *(Anzeige)* advert ['ædvɜːt]
wert: Es ist sein Geld wert. It's good value. ['væljuː]
wichtig important [ɪm'pɔːtnt]
wie *(ähnlich wie; so wie)* like [laɪk]
wie? how? [haʊ] **Wie geht's?** How are you? [haʊ 'ɑː ju]; *(Wie läuft's?)* How's it going? **Wie geht es dir/euch?** How are you? **Wie heißt du?** What's your name? **Wie ist es? / Wie sieht es aus?** What's it like? **Wie spät ist es?** What's the time? **Wie wär's mit ...?** What about ...? **Wie viel kostet ...?** How much is ...? **Wie viel kosten ...?** How much are ...?
wieder again [ə'gen]
Wiedersehen: Auf Wiedersehen! Goodbye. [gʊd'baɪ]
wild wild [waɪld]
Willkommen in Plymouth. Welcome to Plymouth. ['welkəm]
wir we [wiː]
wirklich **1.** *(tatsächlich)* really ['rɪəli] **2.** *(echt)* real [rɪəl]
wissen know [nəʊ]
wo? where? [weə]
Woche week [wiːk]
Wochenende weekend [wiːk'end] **am Wochenende** at the weekend
wohin? where? [weə]
wohnen live [lɪv]
Wohnung flat [flæt]
Wohnzimmer living room ['lɪvɪŋ ruːm]
wollen: etwas (haben) wollen want sth. [wɒnt] **etwas tun wollen** want to do sth.
Workshop workshop ['wɜːkʃɒp]
Wort word [wɜːd]
Wörterbuch dictionary ['dɪkʃənri]
Wörterverzeichnis *(alphabetisch)* dictionary ['dɪkʃənri]
wünschen: Ich wünsche dir einen schönen Tag. Have a good day.
würde: Ich würde sehr gern kommen. I'd love to come. (= I would love to ...) [wʊd]

Z

zehn ten [ten]
Zeichen sign [saɪn]
Zeit time [taɪm]
Zentrum centre ['sentə]
Zimmer room [ruːm, rʊm]
Zoo zoo [zuː]
zu **1.** *(örtlich)* to [tu, tə] **zur Arbeit/Schule gehen** go to work/school **2. zu alt/groß/...** too old/big/... [tuː] **3. Er mag es nicht, allein zu sein.** He doesn't like to be lonely.
zubereiten *(Essen)* cook [kʊk]
zuerst first [fɜːst]
Zuhause home [həʊm]
zuhören listen ['lɪsn] **jemandem zuhören** listen to somebody
zumachen *(schließen)* close [kləʊz]
zurück back [bæk]
zusammen together [tə'geðə]
zwei two [tuː]
zweite(r, s) second ['sekənd]
zwischen between [bɪ'twiːn]
zwölf twelve [twelv]

First names (Vornamen)

Adam ['ædəm]
Alan ['ælən]
Alisha [ə'lɪʃə]
Amanda [ə'mændə]
Anna ['ænə]
Ava ['eɪvə]
Babe [beɪb]
Ben [ben]
Benny ['beni]
Berry ['beri]
Bob [bɒb]
Bunny ['bʌni]
Casper ['kæspə]
Charles [tʃɑ:lz]
Charlie ['tʃɑ:li]
Chloe ['kləʊi]
Connie ['kɒni]
Conor ['kɒnə]
Cyril ['sɪrɪl]
Darek ['dærɪk]
David ['deɪvɪd]
Debbie ['debi]
Ellie ['eli]
Emily ['eməli]
Emma ['emə]
Finn [fɪn]
Frisky ['frɪski]
Gemma ['dʒemə]
Grace [greɪs]
Harry ['hæri]
Jack [dʒæk]
Jackie ['dʒæki]
Jimmy ['dʒɪmi]
Joe [dʒəʊ]
John [dʒɒn]
Josie ['dʒəʊsi]
Katie ['keɪti]
Laura ['lɔ:rə]
Lily ['lɪli]
Linda ['lɪndə]
Liz [lɪz]
Luca ['lu:kə]
Lulu ['lu:lu:]
Lynn [lɪn]
Maria [mə'ri:ə]
Martin ['mɑ:tɪn]
Olivia [ə'lɪviə]
Paul [pɔ:l]
Pete [pi:t]
Peter ['pi:tə]
Pip [pɪp]
Rick [rɪk]
Ruby ['ru:bi]
Sally ['sæli]
Sam [sæm]
Sandy ['sændi]
Sarah ['seərə]
Shanaze [ʃə'neɪz]
Simon ['saɪmən]
Sophie ['səʊfi]
Steve [sti:v]
Susan ['su:zən]
Tamara [tə'mɑ:rə]
Tim [tɪm]
Timothy ['tɪməθi]
Toby ['təʊbi]
Tom [tɒm]
Uma ['u:mə]
Vanessa [və'nesə]
William ['wɪljəm]
Zack [zæk]
Zoe ['zəʊi]

Family names / Surnames (Familiennamen)

Boateng ['bwɑ:teŋ]
Borowski [bə'rɒvski]
Brown [braʊn]
Cole [kəʊl]
Donovan ['dɒnəvən]
Finden ['fɪndən]
Ford [fɔ:d]
Johnson ['dʒɒnsn]
Lee [li:]
Osmanovic [ɒz'mænəvɪtʃ]
Potter ['pɒtə]
Reade [ri:d]
Victor ['vɪktə]
Windsor ['wɪnzə]

Place names (Ortsnamen)

Africa ['æfrɪkə]
America [ə'merɪkə]
The **Aquarium** [ə'kweəriəm]
Berlin [bɜ:'lɪn]
Cawsand ['kɔ:sænd]
Central Park [sentrəl 'pɑ:k]
Charles Street ['tʃɑ:lz stri:t]
Chile ['tʃɪli]
Coburg Street ['kəʊbɜ:g stri:t]
Dartmoor ['dɑ:tmɔ:]
Drake Circus [dreɪk 'sɜ:kəs]
Eggbuckland Community College [eg'bʌklənd kə'mju:nəti kɒlɪdʒ]
England ['ɪŋglənd]
Exeter ['eksɪtə]
Fore Street ['fɔ: stri:t]
France [frɑ:ns]
George Street ['dʒɔ:dʒ stri:t]
Germany ['dʒɜ:məni]
Ghana ['gɑ:nə]
Gratefeld Street ['greɪtfeld stri:t]
Great Field Road [greɪt fi:ld 'rəʊd]
Greatfield Street ['greɪtfi:ld stri:t]
Greenbank Road [gri:nbæŋk 'rəʊd]
Harbour Road [hɑ:bə 'rəʊd]
The **Hoe** [həʊ]
Ireland ['aɪələnd]
Jamaica [dʒə'meɪkə]
Kingsand ['kɪŋsænd]
London ['lʌndən]
Malaga ['mæləgə]
Martins ['mɑ:tɪnz]
Merryweather Farm [meriweðə 'fɑ:m]
National Marine Aquarium [næʃnəl mə'ri:n əkweəriəm]
New York [nju: 'jɔ:k]
Plymouth ['plɪməθ]
Plymouth High School [plɪməθ 'haɪ sku:l]
Plymouth Pavilions [plɪməθ pə'vɪliənz]
Poland ['pəʊlənd]
Reel Cinema [ri:l 'sɪnəmə]
Saltash ['sɔ:ltæʃ]
The **Smuggler's Rest** [smʌgləz 'rest]
Spain [speɪn]
Theatre Royal Plymouth [θɪətə rɔɪəl 'plɪməθ]
Tinside Lido [tɪnsaɪd 'laɪdəʊ]
Turkey ['tɜ:ki]
USA [ju: es 'eɪ]
Wembley ['wembli]
Windsor Road [wɪnzə 'rəʊd]
Windsor Street ['wɪnzə stri:t]
Winsbury Road [wɪnzbəri 'rəʊd]
Woodlands ['wʊdləndz]
Woolwell ['wʊlwel]

Other names (Andere Namen)

British Fireworks Championships [brɪtɪʃ 'faɪəwɜ:ks tʃæmpjənʃɪps]
Canoe Tamar [kə'nu: 'teɪmɑ:]
Christmas Day [krɪsməs 'deɪ]
Christmas Eve [krɪsməs 'i:v]
Francis and the Drakes ['frɑ:nsɪs ənd ðə 'dreɪks]
Manchester United ['mæntʃɪstə ju'naɪtɪd]
The **Roof Raisers** ['ru:f reɪzəz]
Russell's Circus [rʌslz 'sɜ:kəs]
Whoopee [wʊ'pi:]
Young Spirit Adventures [jʌŋ spɪrɪt əd'ventʃəz]

English numbers

0 oh, zero, nil [əʊ, 'zɪərəʊ, nɪl]
1 one [wʌn]
2 two [tu:]
3 three [θri:]
4 four [fɔ:]
5 five [faɪv]
6 six [sɪks]
7 seven ['sevn]
8 eight [eɪt]
9 nine [naɪn]
10 ten [ten]

11 eleven [ɪ'levn]
12 twelve [twelv]
13 thirteen [θɜ:'ti:n]
14 fourteen [fɔ:'ti:n]
15 fifteen [fɪf'ti:n]
16 sixteen [sɪks'ti:n]
17 seventeen [sevn'ti:n]
18 eighteen [eɪ'ti:n]
19 nineteen [naɪn'ti:n]
20 twenty ['twenti]

21 twenty-one [twenti'wʌn]
22 twenty-two [twenti'tu:]
23 twenty-three [twenti'θri:]
...

30 thirty ['θɜ:ti]
40 forty ['fɔ:ti]
50 fifty ['fɪfti]
60 sixty ['sɪksti]
70 seventy ['sevnti]
80 eighty ['eɪti]
90 ninety ['naɪnti]
100 a/one hundred [ə/wʌn 'hʌndrəd]

101 one hundred and one
102 one hundred and two
...

1st first [fɜ:st]
2nd second ['sekənd]
3rd third [θɜ:d]
4th fourth [fɔ:θ]
5th fifth [fɪfθ]
6th sixth [sɪksθ]
7th seventh ['sevnθ]
8th eighth [eɪtθ]
9th ninth [naɪnθ]
10th tenth [tenθ]

11th eleventh [ɪ'levnθ]
12th twelfth [twelfθ]
13th thirteenth [θɜ:'ti:nθ]
14th fourteenth [fɔ:'ti:nθ]
15th fifteenth [fɪf'ti:nθ]
16th sixteenth [sɪks'ti:nθ]
17th seventeenth [sevn'ti:nθ]
18th eighteenth [eɪ'ti:nθ]
19th nineteenth [naɪn'ti:nθ]
20th twentieth ['twentiəθ]

21st twenty-first [twenti'fɜ:st]
22nd twenty-second [twenti'sekənd]
23rd twenty-third [twenti'θɜ:d]
...

30th thirtieth ['θɜ:tiəθ]
40th fortieth ['fɔ:tiəθ]
50th fiftieth ['fɪftiəθ]
60th sixtieth ['sɪkstiəθ]
70th seventieth ['sevntiəθ]
80th eightieth ['eɪtiəθ]
90th ninetieth ['naɪntiəθ]
100th hundredth ['hʌndrədθ]

101st hundred and first
102nd hundred and second
...

Du und dein Lehrer/deine Lehrerin	You and your teacher
Guten Morgen, Herr/Frau …	Good morning, Mr/Mrs/Miss … (bis 12 Uhr)
Guten Tag, Herr …	Good afternoon, Mr … (ab 12 Uhr)
Entschuldigung, dass ich zu spät komme.	Sorry, I'm late.
Kann ich bitte das Fenster öffnen/zumachen?	Can I open/close the window, please?
Kann ich bitte zur Toilette gehen?	Can I go to the toilet, please?
Auf Wiedersehen!/Bis morgen.	Goodbye./See you tomorrow.

Hausaufgaben und Übungen	Homework and exercises
Es tut mir leid, ich habe mein Schulheft nicht dabei.	Sorry, I have no exercise book.
Ich verstehe die Übung nicht.	I don't understand this exercise.
Ich kann Nummer 3 nicht lösen.	I can't do number 3.
Entschuldigung, ich bin noch nicht fertig.	Sorry, I haven't finished.
Ich habe … Ist das auch richtig?	I have … Is that right?
Es tut mir leid, das weiß ich nicht.	Sorry, I don't know.
Was haben wir (als Hausaufgabe) auf?	What's for homework?

Du brauchst Hilfe	You need help
Können Sie mir bitte helfen?	Can you help me, please?
Auf welcher Seite sind wir/steht das?	What page is it, please?
Was heißt … auf Englisch/Deutsch?	What's … in English/German?
Können Sie das bitte an die Tafel schreiben?	Can you write it on the board, please?
Kann ich das auf Deutsch sagen?	Can I say it in German?
Können Sie/Kannst du bitte lauter sprechen?	Can you speak louder, please?
Können Sie das bitte noch einmal sagen/abspielen?	Can you say/play that again, please?

Partnerarbeit	Work with a partner
Kann ich mit Julian arbeiten?	Can I work with Julian?
Du bist dran.	It's your turn.
Lass uns ein … machen/zeichnen.	Let's make/draw a …
Lass uns die Geschichte/den Dialog spielen.	Let's act the story/dialogue.

What your teacher says	Was dein Lehrer/deine Lehrerin sagt
Listen, please./Quiet, please.	Hört bitte zu./Ruhe bitte.
Open your books at page 24.	Schlagt bitte Seite 24 auf.
Do exercise 5 for homework, please.	Macht bitte Übung 5 als Hausaufgabe.
Where's your book, David?	Wo ist dein Buch, David?
Try again!	Versuche es noch einmal.
That's really good!	Das ist wirklich gut!
That's all for today. You can go.	Das ist alles für heute. Ihr könnt gehen.

Diese Arbeitsanweisungen findest du häufig im Schülerbuch

Act the dialogue / the scenes for the class.	Spiel(t) den Dialog / die Szenen vor der Klasse.
Ask questions. / Ask different partners.	Stelle Fragen. / Frage verschiedene Partner/innen.
Answer the questions (about the story).	Beantworte die Fragen (über die Geschichte).
… as many as you can.	… so viele wie du kannst.
Before you listen /read /…	Bevor du hörst / liest …
Choose a picture / the right answer.	Wähle ein Bild / die richtige Antwort aus.
Compare with a partner.	Vergleiche mit einem Partner / einer Partnerin.
Complete the questions / the rules / the sentences.	Vervollständige die Fragen / die Regeln / die Sätze.
Copy and complete the table / your learner log.	Schreibe die Tabelle / dein Lerntagebuch ab und vervollständige sie / es.
Correct the sentences.	Berichtige die Sätze.
Fill in the table.	Fülle die Tabelle aus.
Find the right answers.	Finde die richtigen Antworten.
Find a heading for each photo.	Finde eine Überschrift für jedes Foto.
Finish the sentences.	Vervollständige die Sätze.
Go to page 25.	Gehe zu Seite 25.
Listen and check / repeat / write.	Hör zu und überprüfe / wiederhole / schreibe auf.
Look at the brochure / photos / pictures.	Sieh die Broschüre / Fotos / Bilder an.
Make a dialogue / a mind map / a table.	Fertige einen Dialog / eine Mindmap / eine Tabelle an.
Match the sentences / headings with the pictures.	Ordne die Sätze / Überschriften den Bildern zu.
Pick a card / words from the box.	Nimm eine Karte / Wörter aus dem Kasten.
Point at the right picture	Zeige auf des richtige Bild.
Practise with a partner.	Übe mit einem Partner / einer Partnerin.
Put the answers in the right order.	Bringe die Antworten in die richtige Reihenfolge.
Read the text / story.	Lies den Text / die Geschichte.
Right or wrong?	Richtig oder falsch?
Swap partners.	Tausche den Partner / die Partnerin.
Talk about …	Sprich über …
Talk to different partners.	Sprich mit verschiedenen Partnern / Partnerinnen.
Tell the class.	Erzähle das der Klasse.
Use your notes / table.	Benutze deine Notizen / Tabelle.
Walk around.	Gehe herum.
Write a dialogue / sentences about you.	Schreibe einen Dialog / Sätze über dich.
You can put it in your DOSSIER.	Du kannst es in deinem Dossier abheften.

QUELLENVERZEICHNIS

Illustrationen

Roland Beier, Berlin (Umschlaginnenseite Karte Ireland castle icon (M)); **Carlos Borrell**, Berlin (Umschlaginnenseite Karte (M)); **Cornelsen Verlag**, Berlin (S. 44 oben: Arnold; S. 52 Arnold; S. 89: Arnold; S. 125: Bensmann; S. 131: Arnold; S. 140: Arnold; S. 145: Bensmann; S. 162 mindmaps); **Christian Görke**, Berlin (S. 52/53 Hintergrund Karte); **Jeongsook Lee**, Heidelberg (Umschlaginnenseite icons (M); S. 100; S. 105; S. 120; S. 147; S. 159; S. 160; S. 161; S. 162 oben; S. 165; S. 166; S. 168 oben re.; S. 169 Mitte u. unten; S. 175; S. 179–207; S. 230; S. 231); **David Norman**, Meerbusch (S. 70; S. 72; S. 86; S. 93; S. 152–154; S. 156–158); **Elwood H. Smith**, Rhinebeck NY (S. 9 unten; S. 17; S. 21; S. 22; S. 26; S. 30 unten Bild A–D; S. 31; S. 44 unten; S. 46; S. 48 unten; S. 49; S. 59 Cyril's eyes, Bild 1–6 (u. 5); S. 67; S. 76; S. 87 (u. 139); S. 104; S. 109; S. 129; Cyril's and Sandy's day Bild 1–6; S. 150–151; S. 167; S. 168 oben li. u. unten; S. 169 oben; S. 170) **Steffen Wolff**, Brohl-Lützing (S. 8/9; S. 14–15; S. 16; S. 18; S. 23; S. 24; S. 30 oben Bild A u. B; S. 32; S. 36; S. 38; S. 39; S. 41; S. 42; S. 43; S. 45; S. 48 oben; S. 50 (u. 119); S. 51; S. 54; S. 55; S. 56; S. 58; S. 59 oben; S. 62; S. 63; S. 77 (u. 136); S. 80; S. 81; S. 88; S. 94; S. 98; S. 99 (u. 6); S. 112–115 (u. 7); S. 118; S. 119; S. 121; S. 123; S. 126; 127; S. 130 A birthday calendar Bild 1–4; S. 132)

Bildquellen

Susan Abbey/Frank Donoghue, Nenagh (S. 82 Bild A-D); **Alamy**, Abingdon (S. 8: Picture Partners; S. 11 Bild 5: image100 (RF); S. 12 crocodile: moodboard (RF), fish: blickwinkel, hamster: Wildlife GmbH (RF); S. 13 games console (u. 174): mediablitzimages (uk) Limited/Martin Lee, toy car (u. 174): Oleksiy Maksymenko Photography; S. 19 unten re.: kris Mercer; S. 34 Bild 5: Elizabeth Whiting & Associates/ ewastock kitchens; S. 35 Bild 3 kitchen (M): Andrew Butterton, Bild 4: Brian Hoffman, Bild 8: Ivan Barta; S. 39 Bild 1: Elizabeth Whiting & Associates/ewastock DIY, Bild 11 re.: Big Cheese Photo LLC/Big Cheese Special; S. 52 Bild 1 dad, Grace (M) (u. 5): Golden Pixels LLC/ Kablonk! RF; S. 53 Bild 5: Benjamin Volant; S. 60 Bild 1 u. 2 (M): Golden Pixels LLC/ Kablonk! RF; S. 65 market: Marc Hill; S. 66 Bild 4: VIEW Pictures Ltd/ Fisher Hart/VIEW; S. 70 unten li.: The Photolibrary Wales/ Rex Moreton; S. 73 Bild A: Kuttig – People, Bild B: Stephen Bardens, Bild D: isifa Image Service s.r.o./ Kysa Rostislav; S. 77 (u. 136): Juniors Bildarchiv/F314; S. 90/91 Hintergrund: Marc Hill, Bild A ferry (M): Marc Hill; S. 108 Bild A oben: Brian Mitchell (u. 7), Bild A unten li.: snappdragon, Bild A unten re.: Iain Davidson Photographic; Bild B oben: Corbis Bridge/Ariel Skelley; S. 109 Bild D oben li.: Carpe Diem-France; S. 114 oben: Ian Woolcock; S. 121 Bild 1: Gareth Byrne (RF); S. 155 helmet: Photodisc (RF); S. 173 making models: Corbis Super RF/Steve Prezant (RF); S. 174 biology: Adam Burn (RF), chemistry: Juice Images/Juice Images242 (RF); ethics: Eyebyte (RF), home economics li. u. re.: MBI/Stockbroker (RF), physics: Image Source/IE371 (RF), woodwork: MBI/Stockbroker (RF); S. 175 Wordbank 4 dad (M): F1online digitale Bildagentur GmbH, Wordbank 4 family (M): Big Cheese Photo LLC (RF); S. 176 police station: Justin Kase zsixz, video shop: mambo, youth centre: Wildscape/ Jason Smalley; S. 177 sleep: Maximilian Weinzierl); **AP Images**, Frankfurt/Main (S. 69 oben: Plymouth Herald/Amy Standford); **Trevor Burrows Photography** Ltd, Plymouth (S. 4–5 schoolbook kids; S. 10 Bild 1–4; S. 11 Bild 1; S. 12 oben li.; S. 13 oben; S. 16–17 Bild A-D; S. 18; S. 20; S. 23; S. 24–25 Bild 5 u. 6; S. 28; S. 31 (M) (u. 124); S. 32; S. 34 Bild 1, 2 u. unten; S. 37 (u. 126) Zoe, Conor, Ellie; S. 40 unten; S. 46; S. 52 Bild 1 Luca, mom, Jack (M), 4, 6; S. 53 Bild 2, 3; S. 55 Bild B, C; S. 60 Bild 1 (M) Luca, Jack, mum, Bild 2 (M) Luca, Jack mum, Bild 3; S. 61 Bild 4 Jack, Luca (M), Bild 5–7; S. 63 (u. 133); S. 70 oben li.; (u. 6), unten re.; S. 71 Mitte li., unten li.; S. 74 oben u. unten; S. 75 (u. 6); S. 76; S. 79 (u. 4); S. 82 Bild E; S. 85; S. 87; S. 88 (u. 139); S. 90 Bild A dad (M), Bild B, S. 91 Bild D; S. 92 Mitte, unten; S. 93 oben re.; S. 96 Bild A-D; S. 97 Ellie, Adam; S. 105; S. 107; S. 110 oben; S. 121 Bild 2, 4, 5, 6; S. 124; S. 131; S. 143; S. 166 LF1 u. LF2 schoolbook kids; S. 169; S. 170 oben re. u. unten; S. 171 oben u. Mitte); **Clipdealer**, München (S. 180: Feverpitch); **Corbis**, Düsseldorf (S. 66 Bild 8: Corbis Sports/Matthew Ashton/ AMA; S. 111 bodyboard: Corbis Yellow/Laurence Manning (RF); S. 155 Mitte li.: Corbis Sports/Tim de Waele); **Cornelsen Verlag**, Berlin (S. 10 hand: Griebel; S. 11 cycling; S. 17 Hintergrund: Zieschang; S. 25 Mitte: Bensmann; S. 29; S. 47; S. 65 oben, Bild 1–4, unten Hoe, Lido, shopping centre, aquarium, S. 65 cinema: Bensmann; S. 62 (u. 133): Catania; S. 85; S. 90 Bild C: Bensmann; S. 96 Bild E: Bensmann; S. 102 Bild A–H: Bensmann; S. 103 oben kids, Mitte, u. unten; S. 114 li.: Bensmann; S. 117 oben, Mitte Bild A-D u. unten; S. 121 Bild 7: Zieschang; S. 147 (u. 149): Griebel; S. 148: Bensmann; S. 149 oben, Mitte u. unten li.: Bensmann); **Cornwall365.co.uk** (S. 113); **Eggbuckland Community College**, Plymouth (S. 93 oben li logo.); **Fotolia**, Berlin (S. 173 in-line skating: Kathrin39; S. 181 oben: Monkey Business; S. 191 oben: Tamas Vargyasi, S. 194 oben: Michelle Robek); **Getty Images**, München (S. 11 Bild 4: Image Source (RF), Bild 7: Sean Justice, Bild 8: Chris Ryan (RF), drawing: Fuse (RF); S. 35 Bild 7 (und S. 5 oben): Bob Stevens (RF); S. 155 unten: Getty Images Sport/Bryn Lennon; S. 173 canoeing: Flickr/An Lumatic image (RF), collecting stamps: Photodisc/Vasiliki Varvaki (RF)); **iStockphoto**, Calgary (S. 11 Bild 2: Michael Braun, Bild 6: Hedda Gjerpen; S. 12 monkey: Mr_Jamsey, bird: Mr_Jamsey, elephant: Peter Malsbury, snake: VMJones, rabbit: Nikola Spasenoski; S. 13 DVD player (u. 174): mbbirdy, scooter (u. 174): nyul, mobile phone (u. 174): Baris Simsek; S. 19 sisters: knape; S. 26 pencils: mahesh14, exercise book: Nikolaas Boden; S. 33 oben (u. 118; 181): Cliff Parnell; S. 37 Alisha (u. 126): Kelly Cline, Finn (u. 126): manley099; S. 39 Bild 3: Floortje, Bild 12 (2x): paul kline, Bild 5: David Morgan, Bild 6: Oleg Prikhodko; S. 50 tae kwon do outfit: tarras79, football, tennis, golf: Jamie Parker; S. 55 Bild D: Jitalia17, red hoodie: Fabio Cecconello; S. 66 Bild 2: Barbara Helgason, Bild 3: Vasiliki Varvaki, Bild 7: Mikkel William Nielsen; S. 89 budgie: jeridu, S. 92 Bild I: Gary Radler; S. 95 guitar player (M): Jamie Carroll; S. 101 Bild B (u. 144) u. Mediation phone: Tatiana Popova, Bild D (u. 154): Amanda Rohde, unten: 77 studio; S. 102 oben: Nikki Bidgood; S. 108 Bild B canoes: Marco Maccarini, S. 109 Bild D oben re.: Carmen Martí nez Banús, S. 111 suncream: onur kocamaz, S. 121 Bild 8 u. 9: vofpalabra, Bild 10: Gabor Izso; S. 122 li.: Aivolie, re.: Raisa Kanareva; S. 129 school bag: Graça Victoria, homework: Photo_Concepts, village: fotoVoyager; S. 152 oben: Richard Hobson; S. 153 unten re.: Edward Shaw; S. 155 Mitte: Jorg Hackemann, Mitte re.: Snezana Kundric; S. 163 oben re.: LowfatImages; S. 166 flags (u. 168, 171): Christopher Poliquin; S. 170 oben li.: Steven van Soldt; S. 173 boxing.: Chris Schmidt, ice skating: Yin Yang; S. 176 bus station: Adrian beesley, museum: Jello5700, mosque: Edward Shaw, sports club: Chris Schmidt, S. 177 clarinet: Christopher Futcher; S. 182 girls: Silvia Boratti); **Jason Marker Photography**, Chelmsford (S. 108 Bild A Mitte); **Okapia**, Frankfurt/Main (S. 12 rat: J-L Klein & M-L Hubert/OKAPIA); **Photolibrary**, London (S. 11 Bild 3: pixtal Images (RF), chess: Fotosearch Premium (RF); S. 19 oben: Imagesource (RF); S. 153 unten li.: Fresh Food Images/Heather Brown; S. 154 unten (M): Fresh Food Images/Tony Robbins); **Picture Alliance**, Frankfurt/Main (S. 174 RE:dpa); **Plymouth Music Zone**, Plymouth (S. 95 PMZ logo); **Thomas Schulz**, Teupitz (S. 57; S. 73 unten); **Shutterstock**, New York (S. 9: wow; S. 12 cat: Irina Bondareva, bear: red-feniks, monkey: Simone van den Berg, dog: Eastimages, tiger: Tiago Jorge da Silva Estima, unten: Eric Isselee; S. 13 bag (u. 174): Nokolay Postnikov, guitar (u. 174): Lebedinski Vladislav, book (u. 174): Vakhrushev Pavel, notebook (u. 174): Elnur, watch (u. 174): Ronen, TV (u. 174): gordana, football (u. 174): Luis Luoro; S. 19 unten li.: Monkey Business Images, unten Mitte: Eric Isselée, Tim: Andrea Slatter; unhappy emoticon (u. 33; 69; 74; 75; 89; 107; 128; 135; 136; 160): Dawn Hudson, happy emoticon (u. 33; 69; 74; 75; 89; 107; 128; 135; 136; 160):